Population Management

Introduction

I waited a while to write and publish this book. I had to make sure I wasn't overly biased based on my personal life experience. I had to be reasonably sure that we are suffering deliberately from obvious attacks on our lives. It appears to me that forms of population management are against us all shortening life-spans, decreasing birth rates and increasing death rates. Over ten years of research went into this effort and I present it to the public for your serious consideration.

The first time I heard that phrase, "population management", was after many attempts at contacting authorities in an effort to get doctors and nurses that tried to murder me properly arrested for public safety. I had contacted local authorities, state and federal authorities in all branches of our government and after contacting the White House and US Prosecutors, even the Attorney General's Office, I had a message left on my answering machine that said, "It's a form of population management. It works out perfect." I have that recorded message on my website at the bottom of the first page, you can listen to it now on https://www.blastthetrumpet.org/ .

It was the only explanation I had been given for why authorities refused to investigate homicide attempts on my life, attempts that had left me so injured I was unable to continue working and medically speaking was left terminally ill. Every day of my existence since the attacks on my life has been one of intense struggle, agonizing pain and suffering. I realized I was a rare survivor of something that is in place that is diabolically evil. If you're wondering what took me so long to write this book, it was due to the fact that I had to be sure about it, it looks to me that innocent citizens have been getting killed in hospitals worldwide, while we all go about our business. It's does indeed seem like MILLIONS have been murdered this way ever since it began, I think in the 1960s. WE MUST HAVE ROUTINE INVESTIGATIONS DONE ON ALL

HOSPITALS CAUSED DEATHS AND WE MUST HOLD ALL PRACTITIONERS RESPONSIBLE. We have cameras supervising even teenagers with cash registers, but none when our lives are on the line!

When I saw just how far back these crimes reached, I filed a Ten Trillion Dollar Class Action Lawsuit in an effort to get these HOPITAL HOMICIDES to cease. It was illegally dismissed, as all of the parties were served. MASSIVE CORRUPTION BY THE US GOVERNMENT! You can read about it here:

http://www.blastthetrumpet.org/iTestifytheTRUTH/USGov EuthanizingUSCitizens.pdf

My personal suffering motivated me to research this topic until I am convinced that the lives of the general population are indeed under attack in various ways. Forms of population management include not just controlling the population, but include attempts to control the numbers of people by increasing death rates and lowering birth rates by various deliberate methods. Those methods of depopulation are crimes against humanity. The evidence is before our eyes worldwide.

It is not my intention to be exhaustive about this topic but only to mention some of the methods, and trust that honorable people will spread the word and do what's necessary to put an end to this evil upon us. I write with the hope that people will become informed, unite and implement measures to protect themselves from further attacks upon the general population.

Anytime you come across important information online, be sure to take screen shots, download, record or otherwise document that information. (There are keyboard short cuts like Alt-Print Screen, or even free software that allows you to capture anything you have on your screen, even videos.) Over the years I have found important information disappearing from the Internet or being buried so low in search engines that it can no longer be found under mountainous piles of disinformation. I have also experienced censorship and other attempts on myself and others for merely posting facts or making truthful statements.

Some topics worth researching:

- Coerced Indoctrination as relates to nation of workers; not thinkers and the "dumbing down" of Americans

- To Pray or Not to Pray Graphs by David Barton, Wallbuilders.

-transhumanism

- Fluoride neurotoxins

- Use of High Fructose Corn Syrup and Refined Sugars by manufacturers despite proven link to causing type 2 diabetes. Type 2 diabetes is the largest epidemic in the history of the world.

- Carcinogens in Processed Food, Beverages, Hygiene Products and Cosmetics

- Medical Malpractice One of the Leading Causes of Premature Death BUT NO INVESTIGATIONS INTO THEM!

- Illegal Organ Harvesting

- Iatrogenic Deaths Worldwide

- Missing Persons Statistics

- Underground Networks and Bunkers

- Experiments done on Military Servicemen and women

- Human Experimentation

- Plum Island

- "Darwin's Deadly Legacy" from the archives of Dr. James Kennedy

- Enemy Infiltration with regards to Hollywood, Demoralization, Ideological Subversion, in order to corrupt Americans and cause our nation to fall

- Psychiatric Industry of Death - link to big pharma injuries and deaths

- "Making a Killing" - big pharma death statistics, psychologists and psychiatrists have invented harmful diagnoses to not only slander and libel innocent people but to drug the masses including innocent children with extremely toxic, harmful substances

- Satanic Bloodlines, Link Between Governments and Corporations, Nepotism

- Organized Crime in Governments

- Abortion Statistics: numbers worldwide, reasons given

- Demoralization

- Ideological Subversion

- Franklin Scandal

- Red Hollywood

- SRAs, Satanic Underground

- Ted Gunderson

- Bilderberg Group

- Trilateral Commission

- Television Frequencies relating to Mind Control "Programming"

- UN Sustainable Future, Depopulation, Agenda 21, Vaccines, Population Control, Population Management

- False Flags

- Private Mercenaries for hire

- Mass Psyops

- Zoonotic Pandemics versus the dates Patents of Record show research began on those respective viruses. With the advent of GMOs, it's ASTONISHING how these zoonotic pandemics CAME ABOUT AFTER they began researching them. It makes people wonder if they are engineered bio-weapons as opposed to just naturally occurring "zoonotic pandemics".

- Patents for: Geoengineering, Biological Weapons, Chemical Weapons, Mind Control, Genetically Modified Viruses, Genetically Modified Organisms, Zoonotic Viruses

- Barcodes 666

- Biometric Scanning and Tracking Devices (i.e. "fitness trackers, GPS locators, any device or technology that tracks you and your personal information and location) and Bio-chip Implants. These devices are precursors to the total enslavement and oppression of humanity by wicked people who desire to rule you all on pain of death

- Food Babe - pointing out that processed foods and beverages have many harmful substances in them and yet no one manufacturing them are being held accountable.

- Big Pharma and the FDA link (people working for both manufacturing and the governing agency that regulate them - CORRUPTION and PROFITING at the suffering and deaths of the general population!) Big Pharma has injured and killed more people in recent history than genocides in the past! And yet no one in either the toxic pill-pushing system or those that supposedly regulate them have been arrested.

And wealth inequality nationally and globally

Toxic chemicals are not healthcare instead it's a scheme to get rich by making you sicker; even killing you prematurely. (i.e. chemotherapy and radiation administered to cancer victims who got the cancer due to all the toxins in our food, beverages, hygiene products and cosmetics, known carcinogens still being used by manufacturers without criminal or civil consequences.) The wealthiest on earth MAKE THE MONEY everyone else works for! so, fining them does NOTHING to stop the evil! They need to be arrested for crimes against humanity!

Proper healthcare in the 21st century is to study immune systems and create DNA compatible synthesized leukocytes that are modified stem cells that are exposed to diseases of all kinds and are proven to attack those diseases like a healthy immune system. Exposed also to cancers and so on, and then the DNA compatible synthesized blood is given to the suffering patient via transfusion until the disease is eradicated or the cancerous cells eliminated with no harm to the patient because they have only received totally compatible blood, a ramped-up version of what a healthy immune system does to maintain our health! PROPER HEALTHCARE HEALS YOU WITHOUT ANY HARMFUL SIDE EFFECTS! And definitely is not drugs so toxic they carry LETHAL warnings! (like some psychotropics and other drugs APPROVED for us today!)

This kind of healthcare is currently claimed to be still under Research and Development but such "bio-nanotech" is available to the wealthiest on earth, just not to the general population. "Lab grown" organs even hearts have already been done. So healthy immune systems that are DNA compatible are a present-day reality that unfortunately is not in use worldwide. (Because the paradigm on earth sadly and truly is under "population management" by the wealthiest on earth AGAINST the masses.)

- Social Engineering - our so-called civilization has been designed by the wealthiest to rule over, oppress and control the poor masses

- military robots and drones - ANY weapon can be used against ANYONE so THINK before helping people sow death and destruction! FOCUS ON LIFE AND QUALITY OF LIFE for EVERYONE or widespread death and destruction follows those who sow it! That is to say, IF YOU ARE ALWAYS HATING AND KILLING EACH OTHER, THEN YOU CREATE A HELL ON EARTH OF DEATH AND DESTRUCTION THAT WILL EVENTUALLY CONSUME YOU ALL! Which is why Jesus Christ, the One True God, told us His Greatest Commandments are to LOVE HIM (because Love and every Good thing comes from Him) and to LOVE each other! Then instead of hellish conditions on earth, you will by His Grace, Power and Knowledge and Virtues create Heavenly ones instead.

- GMO monocultures - Instead of harmfully producing food, mankind must focus on PRESERVING DIVINE DESIGNS, organic biodiversity, or one blight can wipe out an entire food source, like the kind of banana trees that went extinct not long ago.

Even if people genetically modify our crops to withstand use of herbicides and pesticides, WE ARE NOT! The pollinating insects are not, the birds that eat the poisoned insects and plants are not and so on up the food chain all the way to us. So, GMO corporate monocultures and the practice of using tons of toxic chemicals on them is HARMFUL TO US AND LIFE ON EARTH! Instead, MANY MORE PEOPLE need to be involved in agriculture and aquaculture and in keeping our planet clean and green. CEASE USING POISONS ON/IN OUR FOOD! POISONING THE EARTH IS LEADING TO EXTINCTION EVENTS, INCLUDING OUR OWN. FOCUS ON LIFE AND QUALITY OF LIFE, INSTEAD OF DEATH!

Dummying Down the General Populace So They Can Continue to Get Away with These Crimes Against Humanity

The powers that be ripped public education away from the hands of the people and put it entirely on our government. Prior to that time American education was centered on Biblical Orthodoxy. It is from the Divine Commandments that public education arose as to the education of each and every generation with the Commands of God.

Now that it has been ripped away, education has become public indoctrination with nothing of educating the public with the Commands of God as public education was founded to be. Brainwashing has replaced education and our nation shows that in its culture and test scores, because of that "dummying down" process.

Rockefeller and others wanted a nation of slaves to do their evil bidding ("workers" instead of "thinkers"), he should have NEVER been allowed to take over the board of education. We have to return to our nations Godly Heritage as quickly as possible by putting the Holy Bible back in our public schools.

It's no wonder that schools have begun over-sexualizing children and promoting abortions instead of teaching them our God-given Divine Commandments in the Holy Bible. Whenever mankind concentrates on lusts of the flesh, gratification of their own selfish desires, instead of the pure and undefiled Commandments of God to Love Him and each other, we are headed toward suffering, death and destruction. These bodies are bodies of death, if we concentrate on gratifying those selfish lusts, we increase death and destruction. Our spirits, once enlightened by God, concentrate on Eternal Things, like Loving God and one another, and so we increase life and quality of life for us all. More and more our institutions are practicing brainwashing upon our children and even as adults, instead of just being concerned with teaching TRUTH!

But right now, our leaders, people like Rockefeller, concentrate on greed, on his will be done, instead of God's, and so right now our nation is falling behind in global economics, in global industry, and in overall test scores for those graduating. About the only thing that we show merit in, is in our multi-trillion-dollar military industrial complex. If you want to consider sewing death and destruction, merit worthy.

https://whatyouknowmightnotbeso.com/graphs.html

RIGHT NOW, EVERYONE EVERYWHERE NEEDS TO BE HEARING THAT THEY CAN KNOW GOD! HE IS THE ONLY ONE WHO CAN RIGHT ALL THESE WRONGS! PREACH IN SEASON AND OUT! TELL EVERYONE ABOUT OUR LORD JESUS CHRIST.

Hospital Homicides and Medical Malpractice Resulting in Premature Death

I suppose what I want to shed light on is my own harrowing tale of coming into context with just one of the many forms of population management; a thing called iatrogenic deaths. Iatrogenic deaths are not death due to something someone went into the hospital for, but are due to medical malpractice and intentional homicides. Many people have been killed this way and not even realizing it was possible.

I had corroborating evidence but could not find any investigators for hospital homicides. It seems doctors and nurses can get away with intentionally murdering their own patients. The reasons why this particular form of homicide is so insidious is there are multiple ways doctors and nurses can kill you instantly or otherwise send you home to suffer and die based on what they did to you. The kind I'm particularly keen on is where they kill one of their patients in order to harvest their organs for others. Illegal organ harvesting for millions of dollars in revenue.

I didn't realize how many people have been murdered this way because NO ONE SUSPECTS DOCTORS AND NURSES of medical malpractice especially

DELIBERATE medical malpractice, HOMICIDES. Most are highly commendable citizens, so when I went to authorities I didn't realize I was someone like one in a hundred million who had survived hospital homicides and that they wouldn't even listen to me. They told me I'd get arrested for troubling them about it! I went to the FBI and an agent threatened me that if I ever came into their office reporting hospital homicides again, he would be arresting me. I went on, at my own expense, of trying to report these crimes I witnessed and personally survived, to the state attorney general and when he grew tired of snickering at me, he just dismissed me out of hand. I said, look these people are well practiced, they have killed people before and as far as I can tell, NO ONE INVESTIGATES THEM FOR IT! He asked me if I had hired a civilian attorney for a malpractice suit and when I said, no, He didn't seem to think it was worth his time to investigate. I HADN'T BEEN CONCERNED ABOUT MY OWN WELFARE! I DIDN'T WANT MASS MURDERING DOCTORS AND NURSES LOOSE! I was trying to get them arrested! So, I hadn't even thought of a civil case in my own behalf at that time. So then after that dialog with the Attorney General of Idaho, I did go to see private attorneys and THEY TOLD ME, "WHY DIDN'T I GO TO FILE POLICE REPORTS!" Everywhere I turned people were making excuses as to why someone else didn't do their job as a way of avoiding doing theirs! When I told some of the attorneys, the length I had gone through trying to get the authorities to take my complaint seriously, they said if the police won't investigate neither would they file in my behalf for medical malpractice even though I had incriminating evidence!

LAZINESS, APATHY, AND PEOPLE JUST WANTING TO DRAW A PAYCHECK WITH NO WORK INVOLVED IS WHAT I MET WITH UNIVERSALLY! It appeared to me that our entire civilization is suffering from a lack of moral values and a proper work ethic. And that is due to a departure from our Eternal Creator the God of the Holy Bible, Jesus Christ. It's why I'm so zealous to have the Holy Bible put back in our schools!

If people had gone through what I had went through, they would have thought they entered the twilight zone! I sent faxes and affidavits to what seemed like over a thousand attorney firms with any medical malpractice across these United States. I filed reports all the way up to the president of the United States; any and all persons with jurisdiction, and it was just a taboo, NO ONE WANTED TO TALK ABOUT MEDICAL MALPRACTICE THAT RELATED TO HOSPITAL HOMICIDES! In all my research since, it looks to me that it's been going on FOR DECADES probably about the same time all the Nazis came over here through project paperclip. It looks to me that perhaps MILLIONS have been killed this way. And all the time the doctors and nurses tell you that your loved one died despite all their efforts. As far as I can tell there are doctors and nurses involved across the USA and they routinely lie for each other. It would be a small group in every major hospital of large cities, but that they routinely lie for one another; if anyone even investigates.

You just don't understand. MILLIONS of Americans go missing every year. Millions! And so, if you don't have friends or family that cares, you could be slated for DEATH and no one would even investigate. As far as I'm concerned after researching this topic as long as I have, the death records of EVERYONE must be gone through with a fine tooth come by medical experts for every hospital!

Police MUST take ALL HOMICIDE REPORTING SERIOUSLY, NO ONE SHOULD GO THROUGH WHAT I WENT THROUGH, in their disbelief! There needs to be police specialists that take all reports seriously in every precinct. They need to have victims' awareness at heart and should as graciously as possible enter all reports as seriously as they can.

The reason I'm fighting just as hard as I can for OUR CHRISTIAN HERITAGE, it's the only one worth defending! Murder is not acceptable! And these other worldviews like islam allows for it! Evolutionists constantly believe anyone they deem less worthy, should be removed, (survival of the fittest) and so they looked at me like a greedy real estate agent, and that no one would miss me! Instead, I was looking at development communities that placed Codes Covenants and Restrictions and made it perpetually affordable to the people working in the area there, so they couldn't be replaced by immigration. I was trying to work out a way to make everyone a home owner by law, because I saw it as essential to creating equal rights among citizens. Resort communities need to build working homes that are not subject to the free market or working people won't be able to afford to live there! Frankly, EVERYONE should be a homeowner as a RIGHT BY LAW, or we do not live in anything that is equality in our Constitutionally protected civilization. You can subject SECONDARY housing to the free-market but not PRIMARY! When lawmakers are resistant to passing laws such as these, THEY WANT LANDLORDS TO DEPOPULATE THE WORLD THROUGH THEIR GREED AS THEY ARE CONTRIBUTING TO THE HOMELESS POPULATION! They want citizens to extort others citizens and are perpetuating ONGOING CRIMES AGAINST HUMANITY this way! There is no reason for people who get old or injured and disabled to lose their life's earnings and savings, making them homeless, because they ARE UNABLE to pay their mortgage or rent. It's CRUEL what our society does to the elderly and disabled and a punishment to them, even though the fault is not theirs! Everyone MUST become a primary homeowner or the evidence is in that landlords will charge so much that it amounts to

EXTORTION and OTHER CRIMES against the less fortunate! The hardworking poor, have the cost of living raised on them every time a new landlord take possession, and the tenants cannot keep up with their GREEDY DEMANDS! NO MORE LANDLORDS FOR PRIMARY RESIDENCES is the only solution! Everyone MUST become a homeowner to prevent deaths by homelessness! The evidence is in that landlords and bankers don't care that they drive the elderly and disabled to their DEATHS!

So, I was one of those involved in real estate looking out for the hardworking masses that was trying to get the so called "little guys", first time homeowners, into houses and made advertising circulation at my costs to do so. I didn't want to see such people pushed further and further out due to rising costs of home ownership that are outstripping so many of the working populace to be able to afford them! (About half of Americans now are reduced to renting and are in danger by the greed of treating real estate merely as an investment for the rich.)

Try not to put everyone into your imaginary boxes of how you disdain them. Not all lawyers, doctors and the most successful people are in it for the money. We have to take each person as a valuable member of society. I'm just pointing out what happened to me and the reason it happened to me is due to how many DO NOT HAVE THE

BIBLICAL WORLDVIEW, that tells us that each and every one of you are accountable to GOD ALMIGHTY for everything you think, say and do!

There is NO WAY I contacted Christians in all my dealing with law enforcement, lawyers, and our government, THESE PEOPLE WERE WAY TOO LAZY! NONE OF THEM WANTED TO DO THE JOBS THEY WERE SUPPOSED TO DO! To think that so many people in influence and public trust are no longer Christians, was disheartening to me, because Christians should be in all offices of public trust in our nation. America was founded as a Christian nation, but antichrists are quickly turning our nation into an unethical, immoral one, one that lacks integrity at all levels. They were all godless, hoping to draw a paycheck without much work!

He tells us that extreme violations of His Law are met with extreme consequences:

8But to the
cowardly and unbelieving and abominable and murderers and sexually
immoral and sorcerers and idolaters and all liars, their plac
e will be in the lake that burns with

fire and sulfur. This is the second death." -
https://biblehub.com/revelation/21-8.htm

So, NO ONE should be contemplating MURDERING others for any reason! If everyone had seen what I saw in the final judgment, they would immediately bow before the living God and plead with Him to forgive all their sins and ask Him to do whatever is necessary in their lives to never sin again! God says what He means and means what He says. Make sure you commit yourself to the care of our Lord Jesus Christ, who is faithful in life and in death; make sure you ask Him to take you to Heaven with Him, because the lake of fire is TERRIBLE beyond words, you don't want to end up there!

People say, how could they have gotten away with murdering MILLIONS over the past 60+ years in hospitals. Millions of citizens disappear every year. They don't even have to report iatrogenic deaths except in the most extreme circumstances. Just in America https://pubmed.ncbi.nlm.nih.gov/28186008/ 250,000 deaths annually and it isn't closely monitored.

https://www.google.com/search?client=opera&q=how+many+people+die+in+hospitals+every+year&sourceid=opera&ie=UTF-8&oe=UTF-8 - About (700,000) seven hundred thousand die in hospitals every year officially, many NOT from what they went into one for. As we can see, THERE ISN'T LAW ENFORCEMENT AVAILABLE FOR ALL HOSPITAL CAUSED DEATHS. In my case, it was intentional. I was given an incompatible blood transfusion that caused me to have an acute hemolytic reaction; causing my lungs to fill with bodily fluids, suffocating and ending with a cardiac arrest and death. Then those who tried to murder me were forced to resuscitate me because other doctors and nurses not in on the homicide attempt responded to the code alarm given off by my monitor. Then the same ones that tried to kill me the first time, put me to sleep and fastened me down on a gurney when the other doctors and nurses had left, with my hands and feet tied down, and forced an intubator tube down my throat so I couldn't scream for help, and then shut it off so that I suffocated to death a second time. Afterward, they were again forced to resuscitate me, they nevertheless sent me home without any treatment. It's considered terminal to do that; I should have been given compatible transfusion therapy after that acute hemolytic reaction and cardiac arrest and THE DOCTORS SHOULD HAVE BEEN ARRESTED for their two homicide attempts on my life. I NOTIFIED THEM IN WRITING NOT TO GIVE ME A O-NEGATIVE BLOOD TRANSFUSION! because I knew it could kill me. But they gave it to me anyway, while I was sedated from the surgery. I REPEAT, it wasn't just that the acute hemolytic response causing my lungs to fill with fluid and caused me to suffocate, it was AFTERWARD they resuscitated me and then again sedated me, so they could slip a lung breather

(Breath Intubator) down my throat and tie me down on the gurney and then wheeled me into a dark room. I realized my hands and feet were tied down on the gurney when I awoke suffocating with the breather being shut off on me and so I couldn't yell for help. I struggled because I didn't think the nurses realized I couldn't tell them I was suffocating! The male nurse who was at my side was laughing like a hyena and the female nurse, who was watching the monitor stated, "that acting like a wild man won't save me now." Because of how frantically I was trying to free my hands and feet from the gurney so I could pull out the intubator, that was suffocating me! IT WAS HOMICIDE! I had just enough time to commit my spirit into the hands of the Good Lord!

I WAS RESUSCITATED A SECOND TIME, and it's the only reason I'm still here! The second time I was deceased so long that it gave me partial amnesia, so that I couldn't remember what had just happened. They sent me home untreated, expecting me to die. I did what I could when I remembered what had happened to me and notified authorities.

The hospital had told my wife and I that I was gone the first time for five minutes and the second time for eight minutes and I was lucky to be alive. I later read the medical report and they denied the second time altogether and created a made-up story to explain the first one that had nothing to do with the reality that they had given me an incompatible blood transfusion. They had lied and said it was a rare cause that brought on the pulmonary edema instead of their three units of incompatible blood transfusion. It was so difficult for me to watch these people go free from what they did to me. I was too weak to defend myself and try to make citizen arrests for public safety.

In the time that followed I was so sick, I thought I would die at any moment for years, but I was so furious, I fought on to make certain these people were arrested! There were more crimes that took place against me that I have tried desperately to get an investigation but without success. I was so enraged but so sick, that for many years I thought I had to resort to vigilante justice against them all! But was too ill and too poor to do so. It was only as my knowledge grew about these crimes, I had to resolve that I must live to tell you all about them and then with the passage of time, God enable me to forgive them and pray that no one else suffers from these kinds of crimes I've endured. It's taken me all this time due to how ill I've been to learn how to self-publish on the Internet.

I want to convince you all that for your own safety and lives, ALL HOSPITALIZED DEATHS NEED TO BE

ROUNTINELY EXAMINED, and that all procedures MUST BE SUPERVISED with cameras linked to medical malpractice attorneys that represent the public from these kinds of crimes! The lab reports need to be examined as well; pre- and post-op lab reports given to medical experts that are to be used to prevent medical malpractice from continuing against the general population! Not just when loved ones inquire, BUT ALL DEATHS! Any time people die, there should be an investigation and hospitals and their staff held accountable for any intentional homicides!

I found out that our civilization is up against people that try to HIDE their crimes and many are just in plain sight. I determined I needed to warn others rather than go about anything such as vigilante style justice, even though it at one time seemed reasonable to me that if no one would help me arrest such corruption, I had to do it myself. Instead, what I came to realize that our nation has a God-sized problem, just one man incensed against these crimes, wouldn't even begin to stop them if I tried to handle it by vigilante justice. God Almighty has his day of reckoning for all who refuse to repent and learn to live righteously. For now, He ask of all His Sons and Daughters to be focused on Eternity and LIFE instead of death. It's just too many things are set against us and everyone needs to be FOR us, or they keep picking us off one at a time.

At the time I was actively reporting these crimes, I didn't know how many had conspired against me. The crimes involved more than just the doctors and nurses, and I imagine they considered me an ideal candidate since no one would miss me due to the circumstances that put me there in the hospital in the first place.

It was only afterward that I figured it all out and by then it would have been a difficult story for anyone to believe. I tried! hardly anyone would believe me! Most people who have met with serious evil in this world, seem to know that I'm telling the truth. I'm telling the world, to stop pretending! Stop looking the other way! And unite and do what you can to defend yourselves and each other. I was turned out of the hospital left to suffer and die, was too ill to ever regain lawful employment, so all that was left for me to do was to read and come up with what are these poorly written books based on all my research; these are the best I can do. I offer suggestions to make equality in America something that is in evidence and reality. Right now, economic inequality is so great (and increasing) that the poorest are dying from poverty, pushed out into the streets to suffer and die. Innocent people dying horrifically.

It was incredible for me to witness how many people just jumped on the bandwagon of corruption, it didn't need to be premeditated conspiracy when so many people were ready to commit crimes. If there had been any investigation, provided that they had medical experts, I believe I had sufficient evidence that I was telling the truth, not the doctors and nurses that tried to murder me and left me permanently disabled to date. Some people imagine that disabilities are always visible, but there are disabilities that injure you internally, that prevents you from ever being able to hold down anything like a 9-to-5 job again. I work on these books out of sheer determination whenever I can. So, it has taken me many years to get them into publication.

It was tragic for me to be in real estate here in the northwest, during one of the biggest migrations here and not capitalize on it. I lost MILLIONS of dollars in earnings, all my holdings, all my estate, and was left destitute because of these crimes. I had a promising career in residential, and commercial real estate and in emerging developments with city planning, it's too bad my career was cut so short before I even made it into my mid-thirties. To this date, while I can forgive those who made this my fate, I simply cannot allow this to happen to anyone else. I have witnessed terrible events in my lifetime and they are just part of the reasons for this book.

There is much more to my story than I'm relating here because I want the focus to be on how the state did not investigate and tried to cover up these crimes, and THAT NO ONE didn't even try to investigate my serious efforts in that regard. INSTEAD, I TOLD YOU THEY THREATENED ME WITH ARREST FOR TRYING TO REPORT THESE CRIMES! You can read the rest of the details if you want to on my website https://www.blastthetrumpet.org.

Consider these Crimes Against Humanity

https://www.youtube.com/watch?v=KHqdwmqu-h0&list=PLL4CV8_Rn74ru8kjD6DkLvl0zLZsdWOvh - research for yourselves these topics of just how many are dying due to procedures against them.

https://www.youtube.com/watch?v=2MQllpJ2lmM - there is much evidence.

http://www.truthandaction.org/former-darpa-director-wants-swallow-id-microchips/ - WE ARE NOT YOUR SLAVES! Brand yourselves, you insanely delusional, arrogant, greedy, globalists!

These are matters of life and death, and if you don't have a few moments to read or watch documentaries, then you need to recheck your priorities. I try and tell the short of it. Weather warfare, geo-engineering is a fact; it has been in research well over the past 50 years. IN ADDITION, monsanto has genetically modified food to ABSORB the toxins they are spraying like Round-up (not die off like other vegetation is all over the world) as a gambit to control food and water supplies. THE CHEMICALS are TOXIC; they cause brain and organ damage! REGARDLESS of whatever reasons ANYONE might use to justify this insanity it MUST BE STOPPED IMMEDIATELY!

https://www.google.com/search?client=opera&q=countries+where+monsanto+is+banned&sourceid=opera&ie=UTF-8&oe=UTF-8 - countries that have banned monsanto, why haven't we done the same?

https://www.youtube.com/watch?v=XCQ7rljcfdc - whistleblowers have been doing their best to sound the alarm. Chem-trails are a fact. At least there are footage of jets spraying our atmosphere. Our own government has authorized experiments on the general population. LOOK IT UP, DO YOUR OWN RESEARCH. Yes, there are more planes, more contrails (condensation), but there are documented experiments where our government authorized spraying drugs into the atmosphere to see the results on the general population.

https://www.youtube.com/watch?v=If9yzHwOeUc - there are alarming events taking place all over this world, that many need to become aware of. Everyone should be calling upon our Lord Jesus Christ and making sure they and their loved ones are all prepared for Heaven. Then ask Him what He wants them to do here on earth. Sound the alarm, preach the Gospel.

Besides the overt genocides going on under everyone's noses in local hospitals: https://www.blastthetrumpet.org/PublicLetters

/AAAUpdatedPublicAlertsMattersofLifeandDeath/Updates
053016/End%20Abortion.pdf   and all the open
procedures and policies of death and
destruction: https://www.blastthetrumpet.org/PublicLett
ers/AAAUpdatedPublicAlertsMattersofLifeandDeath/Upda
tes053016/Depopulation.pdf - depopulation by intent or
accident.

https://www.facebook.com/video.php?v=5641869870108
11 - I wish people would unite and depose the evil lunatics
attacking our lives and destroying our
planet! https://www.blastthetrumpet.org/PublicLetters/A
AAUpdatedPublicAlertsMattersofLifeandDeath/Updates05
3016/Strategies%20of%20War.pdf Strategies of War. War
is not just modern weapons, but warfare is accomplished
by social engineering, economically, biologically, and so
much more and
https://www.blastthetrumpet.org/PublicLetters/AAAUpda
tedPublicAlertsMattersofLifeandDeath/Updates053016/M
ost%20Wanted%20Criminals%20part%201.pdf - crimes
against humanity, makes the world's most wanted those
who are attacking us all and our planet!

https://www.facebook.com/photo.php?fbid=612203735
562678&set=a.50168379948006.1073742150.11489683
1960040&type=1&theater - the Georgia Guidestones, a
manifesto of alarming global depopulation -

https://www.google.com/search?client=opera&q=georgia+guidestones&sourceid=opera&ie=UTF-8&oe=UTF-8

https://www.facebook.com/photo.php?fbid=312558798874911&set=a.292070200923771.1073741828.289189664545158&type=1&theater - content that points out their crimes is routinely censored. You have to become aware and fight to maintain awareness as much as you can.

https://www.youtube.com/watch?feature=player_embedded&v=fsD7I9xENRQ - so it's been a plan to use bioweapons against the general population. Zoonotic viruses in recent history coincide with genetic modification.

https://www.youtube.com/watch?v=stGT6NcxVRQ&feature=youtu.be - too many people think that the world is overpopulated today and are expressing ways to decrease the population. So, my question is are they already implementing these procedures? which is why I've written this book.

Bio-engineering diseases to create pandemics (compliments of the satanic NWO, UN depopulation agendas, funding ultimately by the world bank of course)

- http://www.naturalnews.com/046412_pandemic_virus_US_scientist_biological_hazard.html#_citizens of the world must unite to recognize their most serious adversaries are so insane that they are a genuine threat to all life on the planet! https://www.blastthetrumpet.org/PublicLetters/AAAUpdatedPublicAlertsMattersofLifeandDeath/Updates053016/Strategies%20of%20War.pdf and https://www.blastthetrumpet.org/PublicLetters/AAAUpdatedPublicAlertsMattersofLifeandDeath/Updates053016/Most%20Wanted%20Criminals%20part%202.pdf

http://www.occupycorporatism.com/home/youll-never-guess-dangerous-ingredient-gates-contraceptive-implant/?utm_source=Top+US+World+News+|+Susanne+Posel+Daily+Headlines+and+Research&utm_medium=FB - I STILL get people who think there is no depopulation agenda among the global elite; despite the fact that overwhelming empirical evidence and their own statements and investments PROVE OVERWHELMINGLY otherwise!

http://sustainablepulse.com/2014/07/08/brazil-announces-dengue-fever-emergency-gm-mosquito-trials-region/ - genetically modified mosquitoes released into the general population without the desired effects. Releasing genetically modified creatures still has unknown ramifications on earth's ecosystem.

https://www.youtube.com/watch?v=u7yV0IG2MI4 - there is just too much evidence that a significant portion of our population is aggressively acting against the lives and quality of lives of the general population.

https://www.blastthetrumpet.org/PublicLetters/AAAUpdatedPublicAlertsMattersofLifeandDeath/Updates053016/Crimes%20Against%20Humanity%20Part%201.pdf - Crimes against humanity do not happen by mere chance, they are not just the results of greed, ignorance, and negligence BUT ARE CAREFULLY STUDIED AND IMPLEMENTED PREMEDITATED GENOCIDES! Read and click on the links below (watch the presentations, listen to the arrogance of those implementing policies of death against the masses in their own words) if you are in any doubt of that fact!

http://madworldnews.com/video-want-proof-high-treason-need-see-sea-arms/ - as long as the wealthy, who control the mints finance wars, the rest of humanity will suffer. I sure hope the poor and oppressed citizens on earth realize their real enemies are not each other but those who instigate the wars in the name of depopulation; while they soak themselves in the bloodshed and profit off the deaths of millions of innocent citizens. https://www.youtube.com/watch?v=YoimzqUqm

8E and https://www.youtube.com/results?search_query= rothschild+fund+wars

https://www.youtube.com/watch?v=CFyOw9lgtjY&list=PL 6A1FD147A45EF50D - this is the kind of thinking that is responsible for all the procedures and policies of death and destruction on earth. These kinds of intellectuals just can't look at the fact that our tiny planet is but one in a vast universe or simple solutions other than to complain about limited resources and too many people. If, INSTEAD OF THINKING HUMANITY IS CONFINED TO THIS SPHERE, they actually looked at reality; perhaps billions of us would not be getting murdered by such visionless minds.

https://www.youtube.com/watch?v=qiA2XCf9l2o - throug h more accurate statistics we DON'T see runaway explosive population growth; so the people of the world need to focus on cleaning up the oceans and the land, on improving aquaponics, agriculture and aquaculture NATURALLY (without genetic modification; instead use nutrient rich, composting, biological teas like https://www.youtube.com/watch?v=Uj4FL0u1wvg) AND STOP THE INSANITY of Agenda 21 and people that think that way!

https://www.youtube.com/watch?v=c34U0Pwz4_c - more and more videos exposing their crimes get suppressed. People should download and propagate them so that they cannot deny what they are doing to us.

https://www.youtube.com/watch?v=lf9yzHwOeUc - there are incredible events taking place all over the world that portend to end time events. We need to become aware of them and pray God Almighty has mercy on us and rights the wrongs.

By visionless I mean, no suggestions, just complaints, no solutions other than to reduce populations and quality of life. https://www.youtube.com/watch?v=ll96QkZaz1E and https://www.blastthetrumpet.org/PublicLetters/AAAUpdatedPublicAlertsMattersofLifeandDeath/Updates053016/End%20Times%20Verse%20By%20Verse.pdf He asks if anything will get better with more population. Is the man that clueless? take a look at history! increase in knowledge, technologies, etc. corresponds directly with population growth. (more minds, more solutions! his mind is limited to numbers and extreme pessimism, but not everyone's is - THANK GOD!) More population, more art, more inventions, more interaction = more accumulated knowledge = more viable solutions (provided the fools presently ruining the world stop brainwashing and dumbing down everyone in so many evil ways! (brainwashing, mind control propaganda, lies, drugs, etc.), each mind of each person is similar to merging many CPUs to handle HUGE computations! Knowledge LEAPS forward (provided you don't have persons like this thinking it is their purpose to increase death rates and reduce birth rates by evil means like poisoning everyone else on earth as their solution to the problem) They ignore a virtually infinite list of solutions and possibilities that doesn't involve murdering people. https://www.blastthetrumpet.org/PublicLetters/AAAUpdatedPublicAlertsMattersofLifeandDeath/Updates053016/SOLUTIONS.pdf (I get comments from people who have an instant aversion to even the mention of such words as "GOD", "religion", "Jesus", etc. thinking rather unconsciously (due to the NWO programming in public indoctrination and media) that it is not rational or intelligent to suggest or even mention; but I encourage everyone to consider the facts: https://www.blastthetrumpet.org/PublicLetters/AAAUpdatedPublicAlertsMattersofLifeandDeath/Updates053016/Evidence%20of%20GOD.pdf **THE VERY FIRST INSTRUCTION THAT CAME FROM OUR CREATOR AS FOUND IN THE HOLY BIBLE IS FOR EVERY MAN, WOMAN AND CHILD TO WISELY STEWARD THE EARTH! Directly from our Creator, He gave us the duty and responsibility to tend this planet we find ourselves on! MANKINDS NUMBER ONE DUTY AND RESPONSIBILITY; THE VERY FIRST INSTRUCTION LONG BEFORE THE TEN COMMANDMENTS CAME ALONG OR ANYTHING ELSE,**

WAS TO REPLANT! RESUPPLY! RESTOCK! TAKE CARE OF THIS WORLD WISELY!!!!!!!!! (If mankind actually followed that Divine Counsel given to us all for our welfare and focused on agricultural and aquacultural production; we wouldn't be facing this horrific depopulation agenda; of people who simply refuse to look at the FACTS! **GOD, our CREATOR, always has been and always will be THE ANSWER**)! - Life comes from our Creator. Persons like THE MINDSET OF THE ANTICHRIST should simply tell the whole world; "HEY! I am a visionless individual who thinks if you all have babies, your children will have nothing left to eat but each other!" And let the people decide how to handle the "facts". One of the greatest fundamental flaws in this man's presentation; is the assumption that once something is used on planet earth it simply vanishes and is completely gone POOF! I'm sure physicists would be interested in his so called "facts" in that regard. Truth is most still believe in "the law of conservation", but none of his calculations take that law into account. As such, every one of his so called "facts" are RUBBISH! and of course, therefore his conclusions equally unsound.

https://www.youtube.com/watch?v=fTznEIZRkLg - He's an idealist. What has happened is that wealth inequality has GROWN, making part of our cultures, poorer than ever. For many we are going BACKWARDS not FORWARDS.

https://www.youtube.com/watch?v=AqHX2dVn0c8 - it's mindsets that are the problem. Everyone needs to RECEIVE our LORD JESUS CHRIST, and LOVE EACH OTHER, then the world advance together! Focus on life and quality of life for everyone. Love God and each other.

I have seen thousands upon thousands of viable solutions from our Creator (solutions that come from our Creator are actual solutions unlike the lame example he used regarding the Nile). The solution from our Creator specifically in that regard was to chastise the Egyptians for cutting off the life blood of their own nation! Move a linear mile away from either side of the Nile all existing structures! Keep it perpetually open for agricultural purposes! Move out of the delta region for the same purpose! Build water precipitators inland for agricultural purposes. Or if your people starve understand it was because you were too stubborn to listen to the Wisdom of our Creator. The One True GOD has true solutions for all that mankind is facing THAT DOES NOT INCLUDE MURDERING OR HARMING ANYONE ON EARTH! of actually how to IMPROVE QUALITY OF LIFE for the global population! For example, by immediately crossing over to solar boosted hydro-electric power motors for all transit, mag-levs (magnetized, levitated transits) etc. AND BUILDING EVERYTHING FROM SMALL APPLIANCES TO BUILDINGS TO LAST; we can immediately cease BURNING fossil fuels (and save that resource strictly for molded uses of solid recyclable substances). Power generation can be made by giant solar collectors and concentrators that are mostly made from glass and silicon (sand)! In addition, improved nuclear reactors (molten salt, cold fusion etc.) and a cessation from coal burning! The list goes on and on. Gigantic recovery campaigns from landfills and the oceans in recycling. A trend back to glassware containers (which are best for beverages anyway and not toxic) and earthenware pots and pans, etc. Still high tech, still modern, but SMART, non-toxic, re-usable, non-polluting! Potable water precipitators, and desalination evaporators for independent and widespread usage to end water shortages. THE ENTIRE WORLD IS SUFFERING SIMPLY BECAUSE THE PEOPLE IN CHARGE HAVE NO VISION! THEY ARE SELFISH AND GREEDY AND EVERYTHING WE DO PRESENTLY IS BASED ON THE GREED OF CONSUMERISM AND WASTE (things made intentionally to break; not made to last, filling up landfills instead of being recycled or being dumped in the oceans while we rape the earth of more raw materials rather needlessly; due to such unconscionable waste and greed); instead of simply passing on long term reusable environmentally friendly tools and lifestyles! I can think of so many ways all the people on earth can be fed, watered, housed, virtually indefinitely! Why can't they? LACK OF VISION! http://biblehub.com/proverbs/29-18.htm As long as people look at the problem; instead of at the solution (our Creator, with His Wisdom, Knowledge and Understanding) they will have no hope. EVERYONE PLEASE CALL UPON OUR CREATOR TO TEACH AND MENTOR YOU; and stop this insanity of the visionless satanic NWO at once! http://biblehub.com/john/14-26.htm

https://www.facebook.com/photo.php?fbid=1015201870
2242011&set=a.401332512010.180522.112052962010&ty
pe=1&theater and https://www.google.com/search?q=je
ff+rothschild+speech+in+china&rlz=1C1GIGM_enUS535US
535&oq=jeff+roth&aqs=chrome.3.69i57j0l5.9266j0j8&sou
rceid=chrome&es_sm=93&ie=UTF-8

https://www.facebook.com/photo.php?fbid=1015242384
3945628&set=a.10150447008155628.418304.2114823806
27&type=1&theater - more and more content vanishes
regarding their crimes.

https://www.youtube.com/watch?v=VIlwRgSECcw#t=116
- thank God for everyone exposing the madness of the
satanic NWO! And praying God ends it soon!

http://www.secretsofthefed.com/nasa-the-end-of-
mankind-leaked-document-2013/ - more and more
disappears from the internet.

How can I convey the horrors of my personal life
experiences and my own personal deprogramming
through a decade of full-time research in mere words?

GOD help me. LORD, lift the blinds of all deceptions off the eyes of those all over the world now and unite the oppressed to stand up against the oppressors worldwide. Amen.

They are killing us in ways that make it seem as if it's a natural affliction rather than ways to shorten lifespans while making us all sick! Chronically ill! Yes, those in the know and have the means can prolong their lives, but the poor die on average 20 years sooner!

http://articles.mercola.com/sites/articles/archive/2000/07/30/doctors-death-part-one.aspx - the internet is under increasing censorship, wealthy individuals and corporations driving the public to their sites and creating policies that are private agendas. (censoring others from even being heard if they disagree with those policies and agendas)

https://www.google.com/search?q=codex+alimentarius+commission+depopulation&rlz=1C1GIGM_enUS535US535&oq=codex+alimentarius+commission+depopulation&aqs=chrome..69i57&sourceid=chrome&espv=2&es_sm=93&ie=UTF-8 - the elements of the UN have planned procedures for global depopulation. We have to decide if those plans and procedures constitute crimes against humanity.

http://www.youtube.com/watch?v=Znqxe-uNe8M - I am testifying of crimes that took place against me and have left me indigent and disabled. I am testifying that this kind of crime is routinely done against innocent citizens in hospitals across our nation, based on the lack of investigation and animosity I got from our government at all levels. Also based on the numbers of iatrogenic deaths for many decades.

http://www.naturalnews.com/043995_human_civilization_processed_food_stealth_war.html - food is being engineered to be harmful to our health and it's working just look at the rise in diabetes, cancers, digestive disorders, chronic and terminal conditions in industrialized nations, especially our own.

http://www.youtube.com/watch?v=jkCEOSgLRt4 - "today it is easier to kill a million people, than it is to control them".

https://www.facebook.com/photo.php?fbid=5368633930 09170&set=a.558128970882612.134988.27489751920576 0&type=1&theater - more incriminating content that has vanished from the internet.

https://www.youtube.com/watch?v=S3debDqi8sM so sad that important content seems to be vanishing which is why I encourage people to download my notes and videos and make certain they are available to each and every generation until the Return of our Lord Jesus Christ and https://www.blastthetrumpet.org/PublicLetters/AAA UpdatedPublicAlertsMattersofLifeandDeath/Updates0530 16/Conspiracy%20Theories%20or%20Plain%20Truth.pdf the satanic NWO has been increasing the heat on the boiling water over time; such that now people don't realize these maniacs have placed death squads in local hospitals that murder millions of innocent citizens worldwide each year (www.blastthetrumpet.org), they conduct human experiments such that they know exactly what toxins cause brain damage, exactly what toxins cause sterilization, exactly how far to push the envelope before causing a revolution against them. www.beyondtreason.com, so they put those toxins in our water, in our food and now in our air, all while brainwashing the public in media and education, such that they think what is happening against them isn't eugenic genocide; when that is exactly what it is! https://www.blastthetrumpet.org/PublicLetters/AAAU pdatedPublicAlertsMattersofLifeandDeath/Updates05301 6/Depopulation.pdf

When my life came under obvious and immediate attack, I still had not become aware that my life had already been under attack virtually from the time of my birth. I will hereby attempt with all my heart, mind, soul and strength to convey the shocking and horrifying awakening process of leaving my own snow globe world of wishful thinking into facing reality.

I tell my story in detail of how doctors and nurses tried to murder me during a routine minor surgery on https://www.blastthetrumpet.org/ . I know mass millions of souls are suffering intensely all over the world; so, I am not claiming mine exceeds anyone else's by saying I have been in so much excruciating pain for so long that even as a pro-life advocate; I understand why there are people who advocate for physician assisted suicide or euthanization under "compassionate end of life care". My journey of coming out of my own programming into enlightenment and facing reality followed my efforts at attempting to get these mass murderers arrested and meeting on all levels of our government and society only apathy, ignorance, wicked agreement, and psychological denial. I thought in my early attempts during the YEARS of thoroughly exhaustive efforts, affidavits, phone calls, faxes, by the thousands; even personal appearances while deathly ill; sacrificing the last of my financial reserves to do so, and culminating with a ten trillion dollar class action law suit

http://www.blastthetrumpet.org/iTestifytheTRUTH/USGov
EuthanizingUSCitizens.pdf; that I simply had failed to find
any competent and conscientious authorities. However,
my extreme pain and suffering persisted and I began to
ask HOW IS IT POSSIBLE that in an entire nation on ALL
levels of government, I could not find ANYONE
professional enough to arrest mass murdering doctors and
nurses; a very real, clear and present danger to citizens?
However, it is that very level of intense pain that has
caused me to dedicate the rest of my existence to the
cause of global public awareness that the lives of mass
billions of people are ALREADY under attack in the
following ways (this partial list is by no means exhaustive):

1) Whether you can face it or not, billions of us; all over
the world, are born into system of slavery and only told
(indoctrinated) that we are
free. http://www.utrend.tv/v/9-out-of-10-americans-are-
completely-wrong-about-this-mind-blowing-fact/

a) This system of slavery is primarily caused by the love
and even worship of money/mammon, materialism, things
of this world; as evidenced above and by ubiquitous
evidence globally. Greed that is so grievous it amounts to
economic genocide against the poorest people on
earth. https://www.blastthetrumpet.org/PublicLetters/AA
AUpdatedPublicAlertsMattersofLifeandDeath/Updates053

016/Treatise%20on%20Greed%20and%20Corruption.pdf
but it is intertwined with incredible arrogance
(undeserved, unwarranted, self-indulgent pride) otherwise
known as delusions of grandeur that enable the 1% to live
luxuriously while enslaving and maltreating all the rest of
us to the point of practicing eugenics and "population
management" upon the whole world.
http://hnn.us/article/1796 It enables them to dine
sumptuously and speculate on commodities (food) to
increase their wealth; even though by doing so, it causes
people to starve to death by the hundreds of millions and
in parts of the world be reduced to cannibalism and other
hellish
horrors. http://library.thinkquest.org/C002291/high/pres
ent/stats.htm and
http://www.youtube.com/results?search_query=starvatio
n+cannibalsim&page=3 and
https://www.google.com/#q=cannibalism+in+africa+due+t
o+modern+starvation and
https://www.google.com/search?q=africa+modern+starva
tion&source=lnms&tbm=isch&sa=X&ei=5L1iUrKKIsGDiQLk
voHgCw&ved=0CAcQ_AUoAQ&biw=1067&bih=702&dpr=1
   I watched an episode where these
guys http://traveltheroad.wordpress.com/aboutus/ wer
e traveling through an impoverished nation and
encountered starvation that was leading to cannibalism in
recent history. We hear people calling for an end to world
hunger and the 1% has the ability to do so easily; but they
don't. https://www.google.com/search?q=TBN+missionari
es+in+africa+witness+cannibalism&source=lnms&sa=X&ei

=b75iUoOvKqiYiQLcsoEg&ved=0CAYQ_AUoAA&biw=1067 &bih=702&dpr=1#q=rothschild+trillions So when you and your children are going hungry, please don't blame yourselves any longer; your lives are under attack! It is no wonder that Christ used such a person for the example of the type that would be burning in hellfire. http://www.biblegateway.com/passage/?search =Luke+16%3A19-31&version=KJV

b) "get a job" - IF you can find one; it more than likely pays below poverty level wages all over the world; yes, even in America; supposedly one of the wealthiest nations in all history. http://www.latimes.com/business/money/la-fi-mo-fast-food-minimum-wage-20131014,0,1971900.story and http://www.dailykos.co m/story/2013/10/15/1247468/-Workers-at-biggest-fast-food-companies-need-billions-in-public-assistance# simultaneously; https://www.google.com/# q=banks+report+record+profits and https://www.google.com/#q=oil+companies+make+record +profits and https://www.google.com/#q=ceo+earnings+at+an+all+tim e+high   so when you have to work two and three full time jobs and still can't pay your bills; don't blame yourself; it is NOT your fault. FACE IT; our lives are under attack INTENTIONALLY. On the one hand, people are so poor they are facing death and in some locations cannibalism and on the other hand, there are people so greedy that they blackmail us all to record profits! Oh, you are still not convinced? At first, I thought it was due to the "dumbing down" of our public education; that had caused an epidemic of seeming apathetic incompetence. I thought it was only an accidental result of people who had no real education; even though they thought they did. No problem, that's not your fault either; because like myself you were indoctrinated, brainwashed since you entered public education and by the controlled media/programming you watch on television lifelong. https://www.blastthetrumpet.org/PublicLetters/AAAUpdatedPublicAlertsMattersofLifeandDeath/Updates053016/PROPAGANDA.pdf

c) Satanic NWO Indoctrination of the Masses/Slave Mentalities -
https://www.google.com/#q=Behold+a+pale+horse+cia+orion+black+ops+brainwashing+The_1% eugenic fascists of the satanic NWO are responsible for this evil modern trend in public education (indoctrination/brainwashing) https://www.google.com/#q=rockefeller+public+education brought to you by the same people who view us all as expendable slaves and wants for the most part billions to die off of the planet https://www.google.com/#q=rockefeller+and+nwo+depopulation   It is these same 1% luxuriating while you go hungry that tell you whatever is in THEIR interest throughout virtually all mainstream media.

https://www.google.com/#q=6+corporations+control+90+of+the+media+in+america   That is why we have people that actually believe the universe came from nothing and all life has "evolved" by pure random chance despite all scientific and ubiquitous evidence to the contrary https://www.blastthetrumpet.org/PublicLetters/AAAUpdatedPublicAlertsMattersofLifeandDeath/Updates053016/Evidence%20of%20GOD.pdf   It is probably the hardest thing for atheists and evolutionists to face but they are absolute evidence of successful mass brainwashing through indoctrination and televised programming. https://www.blastthetrumpet.org/PublicLetters/AAAUpdatedPublicAlertsMattersofLifeandDeath/Updates053016/Evolution%20and%20Atheism%20Intertwined%20Cults%20of%20the%20Insane.pdf   Why? Why would the satanic NWO want to lie to the masses and keep you and us all from knowing the Creator and your own Divine Purpose? Because if they can control the way you think; they can control you! ... after all we're just "slaves" in their thinking.

d) So, you can't get a job, at least one that keeps up with the "cost of living"; so, now they tell you "GET TRAINING! GET AN EDUCATION!" And off you go to MORE INDOCTRINATION. https://www.blastthetrumpet.org/PublicLetters/AAAUpdatedPublicAlertsMattersofLifeandDeath/Updates053016/Brainwashing.pdf   What's worse is YOU ACTUALLY PAY for that indoctrination! It used to be apprentice programs were almost in all walks of life; such that you got paid while you were in training; but the greedy 1% studied brainwashing techniques and grew even greedier.

https://www.google.com/#q=mk+ultra and they reasoned that not only could they privatize all jobs (service for them and their wealthy rule and control of the world) but they could privatize "education" as well and still have you think it was public. They do so outright by founding "technical and vocational schools" and they do so not so obviously by funding grants to universities and colleges (firing any professors that do not practice their indoctrination agendas). https://www.google.com/#q=creation+scientists+fired+from+universities; again, despite all evidence to the

contrary: http://www.youtube.com/watch?v=mtBz1roiQR8 the biblical account of Creation has NEVER been disproven and has so much overwhelming scientific support; that it makes people look incredibly foolish who still don't acknowledge the facts; but the brainwashing has been so successful; victims actually refuse to even look at the evidence and whenever it is presented to them think it's a hoax; preferring to cling to the animations they were shown in grade school as fact over reality shown them like: http://www.youtube.com/watch?v=CEmnXV5Qs2Q&list=PLDD19870F568B7818 and cling to their childhood stories in the name of science so strongly that they think soft tissue can exist for hundreds of millions of years and throw a temper tantrum if you show them

otherwise: https://www.google.com/#q=soft+tissue+of+di nosaurs and soft tissue is not nearly as rare as the "missing links"; which are in fact non-existent.
https://www.google.com/#q=all+missing+links+to+date+p roven+hoaxes   If evolution were true transitory forms would be throughout the fossil record; but there are none despite desperate claims otherwise.
https://www.google.com/#q=no+transitory+forms+in+the +fossil+record even a child can see looking at those claiming there are transitional forms that they resort to drawings primarily to make those claims (imagination/fiction) and while showing a fossil of creatures still in existence all over the world claim it is a transitory form. Or they show a species that is extinct and make the same claim; even though all bones of an extinct species show is that life has died; it in no way proves "macro evolution" a change of kinds like a dog becoming a whale or a horse becoming a giraffe; which again, this guy proves how utterly ridiculous such a notion really is: http://www.youtube.com/watch?v=GjvuwneORrE It is difficult to face; especially because not only were you brainwashed thoroughly with complete fiction; but it was interwoven with marxist pride and arrogance to make you think people that know otherwise are just ignorant or worse stupid; when in fact sadly; even intelligent people can be fooled if they were lied to throughout the years of their education. It's not your fault that so many are presenting as if they are
https://www.blastthetrumpet.org/PublicLetters/AAAUpda tedPublicAlertsMattersofLifeandDeath/Updates053016/M

entally%20Challenged.pdf due to all the mass drugging: https://www.blastthetrumpet.org/PublicLetters/AAAUpdatedPublicAlertsMattersofLifeandDeath/Updates053016/Our%20Creator%20Told%20us%20in%20the%20Holy%20Bible%20Truth%20About%20Drugs.pdf mass brainwashing, propaganda of the satanic NWO (scientifically proven to cause brain damage so severe that people think fiction is fact and facts are fiction; because https://www.blastthetrumpet.org/PublicLetters/AAAUpdatedPublicAlertsMattersofLifeandDeath/Updates053016/Acknowledging%20the%20Eternal%20Creator%20Takes%20No%20Faith%20It%20is%20Scientific%20Fact.pdf Again, it is NOT your fault; you were victimized by very evil, very wicked people... the so called 1%; who tell anyone challenging their indoctrination to sit down, shut up, leave their classroom. https://www.google.com/#q=student+given+an+F+for+mentioning+God and https://www.google.com/#q=creationist+students+told+to+leave+the+classroom In fact, by censoring even the mention of GOD in public education both history and science has been rewritten to the point of teaching fiction; pure fantasy. http://www.youtube.com/watch?v=3HoHmSn5Gns and http://shop.wallbuilders.com/the-american-heritage-series-10-dvd-boxed-set and https://www.google.com/#q=catherine+millard+rewriting+american+history+pdf Again, your programming has been intentional by very evil persons funding it from the highest levels (the 1%) for very evil reasons http://www.youtube.com/watch?v=4mxXICZ9mXo&list=PL7F9B57EBDCCEECF8 and http://www.youtube.com/watch?v=j7XR9yH2ETk When you finally understand that their goal is depopulation (your death and that of your children; and prior to that enslavement; it all makes perfect sense). http://www.youtube.com/watch?v=kVeA07d2F_I and https://www.google.com/#q=satanic+nwo+linked+to+abortion,+euthanization,+depopulation - the Satanic New World Order is comprised of real persons who have slithered into our schools, our media, our police departments, our hospitals and have put these procedures in place. They LIE to us and cover up their crimes by their infiltration. Even corrupt judges that reverse historic decisions that once favored life and truth but now shows only policies of deceit and death. Some of them do not hold meetings hailing satan in public, but are just person that are susceptible to corruption, vice, or blackmail and that is how these things are taking place with no one I could find to stop them. So, it isn't necessarily an entire precinct, it just if certain crimes are not being investigated you probably have a satanic police chief to blame and so on up the chain of command. CHRISTIANS need to be in all places of public trust! People who KNOW God! Instead of persons who are still being deceived by the devil and his spirit of err.

e) So, you get your training/education/indoctrination and yet?
https://www.google.com/#q=half+of+college+graduates+unemployed+or+underemployed and so you listen to the programming tell you
https://www.google.com/#q=jobs+have+gone+overseas because the 1% are SO GREEDY
https://www.google.com/#q=corporations+looking+for+slave+labor+worldwide So, because they have created a world by being so arrogant and so selfish that people are starving to death by the hundreds of millions each year; which in turn makes life so hellish that mothers murder their own babies rather than watch them suffer (because by design they make having children EXPENSIVE; because in their eugenic thinking wealthy, cold-blooded killers like themselves deserve to breed; not poor, oppressed slaves) http://www.numberofabortions.com/   and so a hungry, poor slave, then volunteers their LIFE for food in their many mercenary arms of the satanic NWO
https://www.google.com/#q=abortion+clinics+and+military+recruiting+in+poor+neighborhoods   The socially engineered slave PAYS the 1% to get indoctrinated; often taking out exorbitant loans of indentured servitude; only to end up serving as an impoverished slave in one of their many agendas (global depopulation and control of the world's resources; including food and water). https://www.google.com/#q=farmers+paid+not+to+grow+cropsremember   the 1% invest in commodities and scarcity drives demand and PRICES up; whether people can face it or not the 1% are directly responsible

for setting prices worldwide (for their own profits and global

suffering) http://www.youtube.com/watch?v=bMm7QYI7 Bbg not just oil but they set the prices on virtually everything because they own virtually

everything! http://www.youtube.com/results?search_que ry=water+the+new+oil&oq=water+the+new+oil&gs_l=you tube.3..0.57143.61437.0.61772.17.11.0.6.6.0.178.1292.1j1 0.11.0...0.0...1ac.1.11.youtube.80-

eUty_r90 and https://www.google.com/#q=the+wealthy +own+most+real+estate+worldwide and

https://www.google.com/#q=who+owns+the+most+land+i n+the+world THEY'RE BUYING UP ALL THE LAND AND WATER ON EARTH! so just remember, when you're homeless, hungry, begging; that it's NOT your fault! These are the same people who are causing global poverty so terrible, that people starve, go naked, even turn to cannibalism so drastic they eat their own children; all while hoarding enough shoes and clothes to comfort those poor souls many times over

https://www.google.com/#q=owning+thousands+of+pair+ of+shoes Again, it may be difficult to face but the reason they are able to be that selfish and that greedy is that they look at the poor masses as expendable

slaves http://www.facebook.com/photo.php?fbid=60759 0239287670&set=a.478718612174834.110771.478715722 175123&type=1&relevant_count=1&ref=nf or worse as a plague that needs to be

eradicated. http://www.youtube.com/results?search_que ry=philip+come+back+as+a+deadly+virus&oq=philip+come

+back+as+a+deadly+virus&gs_l=youtube.3..33i21.400007.
407988.0.408589.34.34.0.0.0.0.234.3488.8j25j1.34.0...0.0.
..1ac.1.11.youtube.VnC1WJAfFHE

Still not convinced? please don't blame yourself; neither was I; this has been a horrifying experience for me of leaving my own chosen snow globe world of wishful thinking to face reality; because only by doing so can the poor, suffering, oppressed people of the world change it for the better.

f) The 1% show you constantly what to worship in their satanic programming
http://www.youtube.com/results?search_query=illuminati+exposed&oq=illuminati&gs_l=youtube.1.0.0l10.748169.750917.0.753592.10.6.0.4.4.0.194.643.1j5.6.0...0.0...1ac.1.11.youtube.35wMcQxLHMo commercials to develop your own worship of mammon http://biblehub.com/1_john/2-16.htm and http://biblehub.com/matthew/6-24.htm and yet, because you are a poor, oppressed slave and the 1% are selfishly hoarding the luxuries of the world; you cannot have those things they tell you to worship constantly through their brainwashing in all major media. So, you turn to "crime" (again, all socially engineered and predicted; where once again the 1% provide you with the tools of the trade; for their wealth and your exploitation... poor, oppressed slave.) https://www.google.com/#q=clinton+linked+to+illegal+drug+smuggling+in+america and then ALSO BY DESIGN AND

INTENT you find yourself wearing their all too predictable chains of forced labor which has now become highly profitable big business for the 1% and is most definitely engineered modern slavery!

https://www.google.com/#q=prisons+are+big+business and

https://www.google.com/#q=prisons+modern+day+slavery you end up making them lots of money in forced labor and in their prisons designed as a form of modern slavery; where you spend your life working in one of their corporations designed for prisoners.

g) I know, I know, but please tell everyone you know these conditions on planet earth are NOT your fault! https://www.google.com/#q=types+of+modern+day+slavery and

https://www.google.com/#q=slavery+worldwide+today WAKE UP, fellow oppressed and suffering citizens of the world! It is NOT your fault... it most definitely is theirs! https://www.google.com/#q=rothschild+and+rockefeller and all kissing up to them for some of their play money; that they make all the rest of us slave and die for our entire lives!

2) Wars are for profit, control of global resources and depopulation

a) http://www.youtube.com/results?search_query=wars+are+for+profit&oq=wars+are+for+profit&gs_l=youtube.3...289878.293980.0.294388.21.19.1.1.1.0.126.2036.1j18.19.0...0.0...1ac.1.11.youtube.CPmiWNy7dLE - wars are for profit and to serve their depopulation agendas.

b) http://www.youtube.com/watch?v=VM5Yv-TbzJU another unavailable video, perhaps youtube can drag these from their archives.

c) http://www.youtube.com/watch?v=Fuinalm-kd4 - Russo actually had interviews with people who are trying to re-forge our nations and create a one world government based on new currency.

d) https://www.google.com/#q=world+bank+in+recent+wars - wars often are not for what the public are thinking they are over, but are actually about control of the global population. The World Bank to put a central bank into the nations those wars are against. (Economic slavery)

e) http://www.fourwinds10.net/siterun_data/government/banking_and_taxation_irs_and_insurance/social_security/news.php?q=1320062234 - another defunct site, whenever you find data online be sure to store it for future posterity.

f) https://www.google.com/#q=rothschild+world+bank+nations+through - the world bank is about not just control of currencies worldwide, but those behind it want to control the world's resources and population.

g) https://www.google.com/#q=wars+are+invented+for+depopulation+and+control+of+resources so it's really about their greed, that so many people lives are lost.

h) https://www.google.com/#q=wars+are+incited+for+depopulation+and+control+of+resources - wars are for depopulation and control of resources.

i) https://www.google.com/#q=wwiii+planned+for+depopulation - it's incredible that people actually think Hitler was a Christian, when he persecuted Christians and Jews in the holocaust. His conversations published in "Hitler's Table Talk" revealed his antichristian sentiments. Politicians make public speeches all the time that they want the public to hear, but do not reflect their actual sentiments.

j) http://www.thepeopleshistory.net/2013/06/the-war-on-terror-is-fraud-how-west-has.html - if there was a real war on terror, islam would be banned worldwide. It has created the largest number of violent terrorist organizations in the history of the world. Read my book https://www.amazon.com/Save-World-islam-Michael-Israel-ebook/dp/B0D9C5PJ2H/ref=tmm_kin_swatch_0 Save the World from islam.

k) http://www.youtube.com/results?search_query=war+on+terror+hoax&sm=3 - the media is used by politicians to effect their plans regardless of the intentions behind them.

3) Your Water is Toxic/Poisonous
- https://www.youtube.com/watch?v=P7BqFtyCRJc

a) While the 1% buys up all the land and water of the world
https://www.google.com/#q=water+is+the+new+oil and
https://www.google.com/#q=water+is+the+new+gold and
https://www.google.com/#q=bush+buy+land+in+paraguay

and even though THEY have state of the art water filtration and rejuvenators https://www.google.com/#q=hi+tech+water+purifiers+and+revitalizers   and https://www.google.com/#q=the+very+best+hi+tech+water+purifiers+

YOUR water is full of so many toxins it's virtually impossible to list them all... https://www.google.com/#q=chemical+in+tap+water+across+the+u.s   like this one tells us over 2000 toxic chemicals found http://www.healthguidance.org/entry/14913/1/What-Chemicals-Are-in-Tap-Water.html   but intentional fluoridation is the obvious satanic NWO additive to make slave mentalities while simultaneously increasing the death rate.

b)
fluoridation https://www.google.com/#q=fluoride+toxicity to make your brainwashing through public education and media easier to swallow. https://www.google.com/#q=fluoride+toxicity+effects+on+the+brain   Scientific studies have been out for many years now telling us there is no benefit whatsoever to fluoride in our water and only harmful side effects. https://www.google.com/#q=fluoride+in+our+water Time to face the facts; you and your children are being INTENTIONALLY poisoned!

https://www.youtube.com/watch?v=tx0ROInM3C4 - keep in mind this presentation preceded COVID and other bioweapons against us. They are all concerned about the governments intentional lies all while harming us by their actions.

https://www.facebook.com/ASheepNoMore/photos/a.22 5932444186870.49466.225921714187943/526201954159 916/?type=1&theater - so many are suffering from increasing health maladies.

https://www.facebook.com/MarchAgainstMonstanto/pho tos/a.566016720083519.1073741828.566004240084767/ 797990803552775/?type=1&theater - monsanto was banned in numerous countries and should have been banned worldwide.

http://livefreelivenatural.com/proves-water-fluoridation-murder/ - chronic illnesses and mental disorders on the rise in our nation and in the industrialized world.

http://higherperspective.com/2014/05/wont-believe-found-75-air-rain-samples.html?utm_source=MAM - so many pollutants in water just from the air.

http://fluorideinformationaustralia.files.wordpress.com/2013/01/a-brief-primer-on-water-fluoridation_pollution-diane-drayton-buckland-8-oct-2013.pdf - more and more people are wanting healthier food and water because of how many are developing chronic and terminal conditions.

https://www.federalregister.gov/articles/2013/02/20/2013-03835/flavored-milk-petition-to-amend-the-standard-of-identity-for-milk-and-17-additional-dairy-products   petition to poison the public by redefining "milk" and milk related products

4) Your Food is Poisonous

https://www.indiegogo.com/projects/bought-the-hidden-story-behind-vaccines-big-pharma-your-food - watch this if you can.

https://www.facebook.com/photo.php?fbid=743373489026383&set=a.102928613070877.7109.10000061217127

7&type=1&theater whistle blower who found poison in America's food.

https://www.facebook.com/photo.php?v=1311609628978745&set=vb.1104995126306864&type=2&theater - another censored content. Facebook should be tasked with supporting the public anytime someone puts on an effort about exposing the public to crimes against humanity.

a) https://www.google.com/#q=known+toxins+in+our+food+and+beverage - as you can see much of my efforts to warn you have undergone censorship and is why I'm forced to use general references to alert you all to this problem.

b) https://www.google.com/#q=known+carcinogens+in+our+food+and+beverage - toxins and carcinogens in our foods and beverages, especially processed foods and beverages.

c) https://www.google.com/#q=arsenic+added+to+the+chicken+feed - poisons in our feed for the meats we eat.

d) https://www.google.com/#q=are+farm+raised+salmon+genetically+modified - more and more farm raised animals are increasing toxic, even farmed raised fish!

e) https://www.google.com/#q=gmo+food+killing+bees+and+other+animals - bees are in danger from the use of pesticides and herbicides on our crops, honey bee populations have been in decline.

f) https://www.google.com/#q=gmo+food+causing+cancer+lab+rats - genetically modified food causing cancer in lab rats.

g) https://www.google.com/#q=gmo+food+causes+diseases+infertility - genetically modified food causing sterilization

h) https://www.google.com/#q=monsanto+and+fda - just because the FDA approves something does not mean it's healthy, there is a corrupt link between regulators and corporations. Whenever people can be bribed drugs and foods get approved that are not good for us.

i)https://www.google.com/#q=monsanto+responsible+for+all+these+additives+and+preservatives&spell=1 - the more processed food becomes typically the more harmful due to all the chemicals, additives and preservatives.

j)https://www.google.com/#q=monsanto+developed+these+highly+toxic+additives+and+preservatives - with Monsanto's history of crimes against humanity, it boggles the mind that they are allowed to operate.

k) https://www.google.com/#q=monsanto+developed+these+highly+toxic+chemicals - corporate monocultures linked to genetic modification use herbicides and pesticides that are not being removed from our food, they are increasingly toxic. Wheat crops are harvested just after being sprayed to speed up browning, making them ready for it, and those toxins are processed right along with the wheat.

l) https://www.google.com/search?client=opera&q=monsanto+hoarding+seeds&sourceid=opera&ie=UTF-8&oe=UTF-8 GMOs are not just invasive, but monsanto sues farmers trying to put them out of business. In India farmers are committing record numbers of suicides.

m) https://www.google.com/search?client=opera&q=toxins+in+the+meatpacking+industry&sourceid=opera&ie=UTF-8&oe=UTF-8 toxins in our meats.

n) https://www.google.com/search?client=opera&q=ammonia+in+the+meat+packing+industry&sourceid=opera&ie=UTF-8&oe=UTF-8 - it's not just what we feed our animals that a problem but is the way we harvest meat in general.

o) https://www.google.com/search?client=opera&q=toxins+in+processed+foods&sourceid=opera&ie=UTF-8&oe=UTF-8 - toxins in processed foods.

p) https://www.google.com/search?client=opera&q=carcinogens+in+processed+meats&sourceid=opera&ie=UTF-8&oe=UTF-8 - carcinogens, cancer causing ingredients, in processed meats.

q) https://www.facebook.com/GMOFreeUSA/photos/a.468695639837571.108816.402058139834655/712895405417592/?type=1&theater - pigs with birth defects from GMO feed.

http://www.dcclothesline.com/2014/01/15/fema-seeking-contractors-can-supply-biohazard-disposal-facilitiestarps-housing-units-24-48-hours-notice/ - another censored site.

http://ecowatch.com/2014/02/27/yoga-mat-sandwich-bread/ - another censored site.

https://www.google.com/search?client=opera&q=bread+that+has+plastic+in+it+yoga+mat&sourceid=opera&ie=UTF-8&oe=UTF-8 - plastic in our bread.

http://www.inchem.org/documents/jecfa/jecmono/40abcj01.htm - World Health Organization TOXICOLOGICAL EVALUATION OF SOME ANTIMICROBIALS, ANTIOXIDANTS, EMULSIFIERS, STABILIZERS, FLOUR-TREATMENT AGENTS, ACIDS AND BASES

http://rt.com/usa/azodicarbonamide-ada-chemical-foods-263/ - plastic chemical found in nearly 500 foods products here in the USA.

https://www.youtube.com/watch?v=wshlnRWnf30 - no longer available video. With storage as cheap as it is, it's alarming how much incriminating evidence is getting removed.

http://www.nytimes.com/2013/10/02/business/fda-bans-three-arsenic-drugs-used-in-poultry-and-pig-feeds.html?_r=0 (these actions only occur AFTER the public demands it) while BGH, GMOs, and toxins are continued to be proliferated and widely used; causing slow and painful deaths of the unsuspecting masses.

https://www.google.com/search?q=reports+that+95%25+of+cancer+is+caused+by+diet+and+environmental+toxicity&rlz=1C1GIGM_enUS535US535&oq=reports+that+95%25+of+cancer+is+caused+by+diet+and+environmental+toxicity&aqs=chrome..69i57&sourceid=chrome&es_sm=93&ie=UTF-8 **WE NEED TO FIGHT THE CAUSE WHILE WE ARE HEALTHY; instead of fighting to live once we are sick and dying!**

I could go on endlessly on this topic, but I want people to stop believing the lies that these chemical additives are necessary when proper canning, packaging requires NONE of them. For generations, smoking or salting preserved meats so well that it lasted for YEARS not just months. For generations canning preserved heirloom foods with NO TOXINS whatsoever; food still nutritious after being stored for years; not just months. Once again, face it, your life is under attack intentionally and purposefully to increase the death rate due to the satanic NWO eugenic views that you and your children are expendable slaves and billions of us must die. Just look at the facts!

https://www.google.com/#q=cancer+rates+have+increased+globally diseases in general have increased recently due to these facts TOXINS/POISONS, in our food, water and even in the very air we breathe!

https://www.google.com/#q=toxins+are+causing+an+increase+in+disease+worldwide

5) Yes, with all the toxins in our food and water, hygiene products and medications, is it any wonder there's a conspiracy about even the AIR is being INTENTIONALLY POISONED (spraying our crops, and winds and air movement brings those herbicides and pesticides into our cities)

With human experimentation as a fact of history by our own government, it's isn't any wonder that people hold fast to chem-trails and labels all of them as conspiracy theories.

https://www.google.com/search?client=opera&q=government+experimentation+on+the+population&sourceid=opera&ie=UTF-8&oe=UTF-8 so you might be able to understand why some people are just not convinced that ALL of them are innocent contrails.

https://www.youtube.com/watch?feature=player_embedded&v=5k3Wrgevpel and

https://www.facebook.com/photo.php?fbid=676798885700138&set=a.478718612174834.110771.478715722175123&type=1&theater - more incriminating content disappearing.

https://www.youtube.com/watch?v=UdtLTyNOB0A - Chem-trails are a fact, at least according to people who give footage of jets SPRAYING the air.

http://www.healthyaeon.com/2013/10/chemtrails-planetary-catastrophe.html#.Uw_X330_XMI

https://www.gaia.com/article/chemtrails-versus-contrails - I can't believe they are still denying it! Chemtrails last for a very long time and cloud the atmosphere, whereas contrails do not, their just vapor! The skies NEVER looked like they do now when I was a child. Perhaps it is just that jets fly higher and there's more of them but can you blame some of us for thinking that it's a form of deliberately getting us accustomed to skies looking that way, so that they can do something in the future.

a) https://www.google.com/#q=chemtrails+traces+of+toxins+in+the+ground - yes, there is so much disinformation, it can be difficult to decide who is telling the truth. But what would be enlightening is if medical providers screened for glyphosate routinely and other ingredients the so-called conspirators allege in our systems.

b) there is no doubt whatsoever that planes are fitted with toxic chemicals and being sprayed over populations https://www.google.com/search?q=chemtrails+traces+of+toxins+in+the+ground&source=lnms&tbm=isch&sa=X&ei=x_FiUtrhAqSnigK3-4CYCg&ved=0CAcQ_AUoAQ&biw=1067&bih=702&dpr=1

c) https://www.google.com/search?q=inside+a+chemtrail+plane&tbm=isch&tbo=u&source=univ&sa=X&ei=XvJiUoPuOqLliAKP-YCYDQ&sqi=2&ved=0CCwQsAQ&biw=1067&bih=702&dpr=1 - yes I know they say they're just ballast tanks meant to simulate the weight of passengers, but there are still plenty of photos and footage of jets SPRAYING something into the air that are just NOT contrails.

d) http://www.youtube.com/watch?v=igFH0pAlcGY

e) https://www.ncbi.nlm.nih.gov/pmc/articles/PMC29020
97/

f) http://www.youtube.com/watch?v=j8NmzfjIkl0 - Yes, I know these are all conspiracy theories, because the official narrative is all just contrails. But their remains in history times when our government flew in our atmosphere chemicals designed to experiment on the general population. https://www.nbcnews.com/health/health-news/ugly-past-u-s-human-experiments-uncovered-flna1c9465329

g) Are you STILL not convinced that your lives and that of your children are ALREADY under attack? http://www.youtube.com/results?search_query=words+of+the+satanic+NWO+reduce+global+population&oq=words+of+the+satanic+NWO+reduce+global+population&gs_l=youtube.3...376658.389936.0.390255.49.46.0.3.3.1.233.5074.6j39j1.46.0...0.0...1ac.1.11.youtube.ykJ_SPGgLI
Y

h) https://www.google.com/search?client=opera&q=smog+air+pollution+at+dangerous+high+levels+in+cities+worldwide&sourceid=opera&ie=UTF-8&oe=UTF-8 - we should be concerned about having clean, nutritious food, clean, pure water and clean air enough to crossover to hydro-electric transit and enough to ban gmo's together with spraying our crops with herbicides and pesticides. Try to minimize fossil fuel burning for transportation of ourselves and our goods, and for energy. Instead embrace newer and cleaner sources of energy.

i) https://www.google.com/search?client=opera&q=Unethical+human+experimentation+in+the+United+States&sourceid=opera&ie=UTF-8&oe=UTF-8 - with all the illegal activities performed by our own governments against citizens, it's no wonder people form conspiracy theories. So, you decide if all these are just "conspiracy theories" or if our lives are actually under attack in all these ways.

6) So far those who own the world and the things in it are providing us POISONS in our WATER, FOOD, and possibly AIR with all the herbicides and pesticides, but it sure doesn't stop there; poisons are everywhere and especially in products to be absorbed through your skin; like consumer hygiene products and cosmetics.

a) https://www.google.com/search?client=opera&q=dangerous+chemicals+in+hygiene+products&sourceid=opera&ie=UTF-8&oe=UTF-8 - dangerous chemicals in our hygiene products

b) https://www.google.com/search?client=opera&q=dangerous+chemicals+in+cleaning+products&sourceid=opera&ie=UTF-8&oe=UTF-8 - dangerous chemicals in our cleaning products

c) https://www.google.com/search?client=opera&q=dangerous+chemicals+in+cosmetics&sourceid=opera&ie=UTF-8&oe=UTF-8 - dangerous chemicals in our cosmetics

d) https://www.google.com/search?client=opera&q=toxic+chemicals+in+mouthwash&sourceid=opera&ie=UTF-8&oe=UTF-8 - even toxins in our mouthwash

e) https://www.google.com/search?client=opera&q=toxic+chemicals+in+shampoo&sourceid=opera&ie=UTF-8&oe=UTF-8 - lists of toxic chemicals in our shampoos

f) https://www.google.com/search?client=opera&q=toxic+chemicals+in+shampoo&sourceid=opera&ie=UTF-8&oe=UTF-8 - some hair straighteners were so toxic they were recalled, but many remain on the market today

The top 1% KNOW exactly what they are putting in the products they want YOU to use; so please come out of your world of wishful thinking and realize when deadly poison is in our food, water, air, and virtually all products; especially those disguised to be for our health; it is by VERY EVIL INTENT!

http://www.rightwingnews.com/liberals/al-gore-we-really-need-to-control-africas-population/

7) You guessed it! POISONS are in our "healthcare products" and "medications"

a) https://www.google.com/search?client=opera&q=poison+added+to+medication+to+make+stomach+upset&sourceid=opera&ie=UTF-8&oe=UTF-8 - toxins added to medication to make your stomach upset so you don't overdose. Medication that is already so toxic, YOU CAN OVERDOSE, still has toxins added to it!

b) https://www.google.com/search?client=opera&q=virtually+all+medications+have+harmful+side+effects&sourceid=opera&ie=UTF-8&oe=UTF-8 - virtually all medications have harmful side effects, why is that mankind just can't make any that are inherently beneficial to us?

c) Do you really think if the 1% wasn't intentionally poisoning us; they could get their so-called bribed buddies in the Supreme Court to exempt them from liability for doing so?

https://www.google.com/search?client=opera&q=supreme+court+rules+drug+companies+exempt+from+lawsuits&sourceid=opera&ie=UTF-8&oe=UTF-8 - drug companies have injured or killed so many people, that now the generic versions are held guiltless, if the FDA approves the brand name substance. How do you feel about that? You or your loved ones suffer and perhaps die, and no one is held responsible?!

d) How do they get away with poisoning us on purpose? http://www.youtube.com/watch?feature=player_embedded&v=PVB6XSyBTVE

First of all; people don't even realize it until or unless something terrible happens to them like myself and even those people don't realize the extent of it until and unless they try to find out why there is NO RECOURSE for what was done to us! Then they find out the 1% hang out together, share the same worldview of disdain for the masses, and concoct their plans for global domination

(why they chime on about how wonderful the NWO is- for them when so many of us are sick and dying!)

http://www.youtube.com/results?search_query=NWO+be+their+slave+or+die&oq=NWO+be+their+slave+or+die&gs_l=youtube.3...1760193.1765867.0.1766147.25.25.0.0.0.0.358.3129.0j23j1j1.25.0...0.0...1ac.1.11.youtube.vGwOTICgICl WAKE UP! they tell us in stone they only want 500 million slave minions on earth! http://www.youtube.com/results?search_query=georgia+guidestones+population+down+to+500+million&oq=georgia+guidestones+population+down+to+500+million&gs_l=youtube.3...93793.111165.0.111518.54.41.2.11.12.0.168.4408.4j37.41.0...0.0...1ac.1.11.youtube.SAqVab0IpVo and how do they then get away with poisoning us to the extent they are getting rich off making us all sick and dying? Why of course big Pharma, the FDA, bribed politicians are all part of that 1%!

https://www.google.com/search?client=opera&q=fda+big+pharma+revolving+door&sourceid=opera&ie=UTF-8&oe=UTF-8 - when regulators have ties to the pharmaceuticals and so many drugs injure and kill mass millions of us, there needs to be some who REGULATES the regulators with JUSTICE!

e) just look at the numbers of permanently disabled HORRIFIC SLOW EXCRUCIATING DEATHS they are causing!

https://www.google.com/search?client=opera&q=hundred+of+thousands+suffering+from+big+pharma&sourceid=opera&ie=UTF-8&oe=UTF-8 and

https://www.google.com/search?client=opera&q=people+with+long+term+disabilities+from+big+pharma&sourceid=opera&ie=UTF-8&oe=UTF-8 - people with long term disabilities caused by the medications they took.

f) I have said it before and I'll say it here again; when you see some poor soul homeless, muttering and drooling on themselves; **that's not the way they went into a mental ward; full of modern day chemical lobotomizers... it's the way they came out!** https://www.google.com/search?client=opera&q=psychiatric+drugs+cause+permanent+brain+damage&sourceid=opera&ie=UTF-8&oe=UTF-8; those are the victims that didn't DIE in their "care". They suffered permanent brain damage from their psychiatric medications! https://www.google.com/search?client=opera&q=medical+practice+the+third+leading+cause+of+death&sourceid=opera&ie=UTF-8&oe=UTF-8 - medical malpractice is the third leading cause of death in the United States and https://www.google.com/search?client=opera&q=psychiatric+drugs+cause+organ+damage&sourceid=opera&ie=UTF-8&oe=UTF-8 - psychiatric drugs can cause not just brain damage but permanent damage to your vital organs and https://www.google.com/search?client=opera&q=parents+march+against+the+FDA+because+of+teen+suicides+linked+to+psychiatric+medications&sourceid=opera&ie=U

TF-8&oe=UTF-8 - parents contend that some of these medications caused suicides in their children. All these mind control drugs are developed with full knowledge of the satanic NWO black ops missions!

https://www.google.com/search?client=opera&q=psychiatric+medications+linked+to+satanic+NWO+depopulation&sourceid=opera&ie=UTF-8&oe=UTF-8 - drugs are linked to counterculture and rebellions, it's no wonder these drugs end up harming and even killing people. Who do you think funds such mind control devices to this day?

https://www.google.com/search?client=opera&q=leary+lsd+truth+serum+cia+involvement&sourceid=opera&ie=UTF-8&oe=UTF-8 So LSD was intended to be a truth serum made with the CIA involvement. It's all about developing manchurian candidates/mercenaries they control completely for their wishful rule of the world.

http://www.youtube.com/results?search_query=Department+of+Defense+in+MIT+neural+implants+for+mind+control&oq=Department+of+Defense+in+MIT+neural+implants+for+mind+control&gs_l=youtube.12...907007.907007.0.908352.1.1.0.0.0.0.377.377.3-1.1.0...0.0...1ac.2.11.youtube.eHxJhFW5Dzc and

http://www.youtube.com/results?search_query=mit+neural+implants+for+mind+control+manchurian+candidate&oq=MIT+neural+implants+for+mind+control+manchurian+cand&gs_l=youtube.1.0.33i21.23721.31111.0.33377.17.17.0.0.0.0.170.1957.1j16.17.0...0.0...1ac.1.11.youtube.aNwSBH

pwCcM and
http://www.youtube.com/results?search_query=implants
+for+mind+control+manchurian+candidate&oq=implants+
for+mind+control+manchurian+candidate&gs_l=youtube.1
2...24612.24612.0.26756.1.1.0.0.0.0.105.105.0j1.1.0...0.0..
.1ac.1.11.youtube.6SxidraYkV0 the **entire field of
psychiatry is steeped in some of the worst atrocities and
human rights violations the world has ever
known** https://www.youtube.com/watch?v=II96QkZaz1
E; but now through mass media
brainwashing https://www.blastthetrumpet.org/PublicLe
tters/AAAUpdatedPublicAlertsMattersofLifeandDeath/Upd
ates053016/PROPAGANDA.pdf
and https://www.blastthetrumpet.org/PublicLetters/AAA
UpdatedPublicAlertsMattersofLifeandDeath/Updates0530
16/Brainwashing.pdf; they have taken it to a global level
as just one of their many methods of global enslavement
and depopulation.

After all; if all this was happening by accident, why
would the Creator tell us plainly that all doing these things
are going to burn in the Lake of Fire?
https://www.blastthetrumpet.org/PublicLetters/AAAUpda
tedPublicAlertsMattersofLifeandDeath/Updates053016/O
ur%20Creator%20Told%20us%20in%20the%20Holy%20Bib
le%20Truth%20About%20Drugs.pdf

https://www.youtube.com/results?search_query=mercu ry+in+vaccines+cause+autism - **face it people; THEY KNOW WHAT THEY ARE DOING TO US AND ARE DOING THIS EVIL TO US ON PURPOSE!**

https://www.google.com/search?client=opera&q=human-fetal-dna-fragments-in-vaccines-are-a-possible-cause-for-autism-according&sourceid=opera&ie=UTF-8&oe=UTF-8 - pervasive toxins are causing LIFELONG DISABILITIES, SUFFERING AND PROLONGED AGONIZING DEATHS! Why hasn't the public united against these MOST EVIL CRIMINALS! more than this, the heavy metal toxins in our food, air, water, drugs, hygiene products, that are in high concentrations also in inoculations are leading to more and more chronic conditions, suffering, sterility, brain and organ damage and death WORLDWIDE; AND IT IS TIME FOR THE PUBLIC TO UNITE FORCEFULLY AGAINST THE GENOCIDAL, EUGENIC FASCISTS DOING THIS PERVASIVE EVIL OF GLOBAL GENOCIDE, TORTURE AND ENSLAVEMENT DELIBERATELY TO US ALL!

http://www.truthandaction.org/epa-tested-deadly-pollutants-people-obama-administrations-agenda/

Psychological denial is a powerful thing; so powerful that keep in mind, I myself have spent thousands upon thousands of hours of my life looking into these things before finally facing reality and in all it's terrible wickedness; all the evil deeds of these people that are so horrific most people can't even imagine the things they do; let alone bring themselves to do such things. (and is how they have been getting away with all these things and worse) The truth about just how truly evil these people are is so disturbing; that just hearing about what they do causes trauma; sometimes so severe that the mind blocks it out, to most decent citizens on earth. http://www.youtube.com/results?search_query=SRA+trauma+causes+mind+blocks&oq=SRA+trauma+causes+mind+blocks&gs_l=youtube.3...3074.18992.0.19364.7.7.0.0.0.0.192.924.1j6.7.0...0.0...1ac.1.11.youtube.AnUgnxqPFpo and http://www.youtube.com/results?search_query=SRA+trauma+causes+mind+blanks&oq=SRA+trauma+causes+mind+blanks&gs_l=youtube.3...15625.16957.0.17402.4.4.0.0.0.0.125.430.0j4.4.0...0.0...1ac.1.11.youtube.u4YkFazypDA and http://www.youtube.com/results?search_query=SRA+ted+gunderson&oq=SRA+ted+gunderson&gs_l=youtube.12...15405.17722.0.19385.12.12.0.0.0.0.122.1152.3j9.12.0...0.0...1ac.1.11.youtube.w6VLDaCoi_0 and http://www.youtube.com/results?search_query=SRA+the+franklin+scandal&oq=SRA+the+franklin+scandal&gs_l=youtube.3...16538.22072.0.22365.20.20.0.0.0.0.194.2126.4j16.20.0...0.0...1ac.1.11.youtube.WFOOTxKFsvM

worse their satanic influence leads to http://www.youtube.com/results?search_query=satanic+ritual+abuse+cannibalism+and+vampirism&oq=satanic+

ritual+abuse+cannibalism+and+vampirism&gs_l=youtube.
3...2627.8201.0.8419.22.21.1.0.0.0.111.2102.5j16.21.0...0.
0...1ac.1.11.youtube.ymSp3yj5Nkc

but you've ALREADY been programmed to look the other
way and call anyone who tells you of these things, liars or
conspiracy theorists; because your psyche has been
developed to live in denial of just how evil these people
really are; ALL BY DESIGN and
DECEPTION. https://www.google.com/search?client=oper
a&q=occultism+in+the+government&sourceid=opera&ie=
UTF-8&oe=UTF-8   and
https://www.google.com/search?client=opera&q=satanis
m+in+the+military&sourceid=opera&ie=UTF-8&oe=UTF-
8 and
https://www.google.com/search?client=opera&q=occultis
m+and+the+nazis&sourceid=opera&ie=UTF-8&oe=UTF-
8 who then entered our own government
https://www.google.com/search?client=opera&q=occultis
m+and+the+Nazis+adopted+by+the+United+States&sourc
eid=opera&ie=UTF-8&oe=UTF-8   and
https://www.google.com/search?client=opera&q=the+Naz
is+assimilated+by+the+United+States&sourceid=opera&ie
=UTF-8&oe=UTF-8   and
https://www.google.com/search?client=opera&q=project
+paperclip&sourceid=opera&ie=UTF-8&oe=UTF-8   All of
these elitists have common satanic ties and secret
societies and flash their satanic allegiance openly to one
another constantly.
https://www.google.com/search?client=opera&q=the+sat

anic+hand+signals+of+secret+societies+of+governments&
sourceid=opera&ie=UTF-8&oe=UTF-
8 and http://www.youtube.com/results?search_query=t
he+satanic+connection+hand+signals+secret+societies+of
+governments&oq=the+satanic+connection+hand+signals
+secret+societies+of+governments&gs_l=youtube.12...511
662.511662.0.512658.1.1.0.0.0.0.0.303.303.3-
1.1.0...0.0...1ac.2.11.youtube.UIJsVyyDq1g which is why
I point out the following:
https://www.blastthetrumpet.org/PublicLetters/AAAUpda
tedPublicAlertsMattersofLifeandDeath/Updates053016/PR
OPAGANDA.pdf

8) Abortion
- https://www.blastthetrumpet.org/PublicLetters/AAAUp
datedPublicAlertsMattersofLifeandDeath/Updates053016/
End%20Abortion.pdf - it's astonishing that people would
choose to murder their own babies. I attribute it that so
many people are having such a hard life, they just can't
imagine bringing a child into this world and I attribute that
fact to the masses are suffering from OPPRESSION!

a) planned and propagated through public indoctrination
in schools and media
http://www.youtube.com/watch?v=j7XR9yH2ETk and ht
tp://www.youtube.com/results?search_query=satanism+i
n+hollywood&oq=satanism&gs_l=youtube.1.2.0l10.16345.

21069.0.25305.10.9.1.0.0.0.177.1085.0j9.9.0...0.0...1ac.1.1
1.youtube.-4VqRJjMpLA_ Hollywood plays a role in our
culture and it's more and more not so admirable and
http://www.youtube.com/results?search_query=satanism
+sex+and+abortion+in+music+and+media&oq=satanism+s
ex+and+abortion+in+music+and+media&gs_l=youtube.3...
19037.29412.0.29892.49.48.1.0.0.0.409.5434.6j41j4-
1.48.0...0.0...1ac.1.11.youtube.Tv-VMuKldAs - so much of
music and Hollywood has very dark messages from the
devil. The devil is real.

b) the greatest numbers of innocent babes slain in the
history of the world as a result
http://www.numberofabortions.com/

c) child sacrifice is satanic
worship http://www.youtube.com/results?search_query
=abortion+child+sacrifice&oq=abortion+child&gs_l=youtu
be.1.0.0l2.140401.145449.0.147900.22.15.4.3.3.0.161.189
0.0j15.15.0...0.0...1ac.1.11.youtube.Byd35iHfSQE and

and
http://www.youtube.com/results?search_query=abortion
+satanic+worship&oq=abortion+satanic+worship&gs_l=yo
utube.3...17938.25712.0.26121.30.28.0.2.2.0.123.3036.2j2
6.28.0...0.0...1ac.1.11.youtube.gDaeXDOsXz0

http://www.youtube.com/watch?v=BtpdYlcbVRQ - brutal! baby comes out in pieces; there are graphic images that show us the babies feel PAIN during that time! https://www.youtube.com/watch?v=YrEFZDHbSL4 - I watched a video of baby in the womb having an abortion that clearly cringed and moved away painfully from the forceps that ripped that child apart! I recently noted how hard it was to find that footage; because abortion is still being promoted by the powers that be.

I have shown you plainly that you and your children are being intentionally brainwashed, poisoned and treated like slaves and worse. I have shown you that your lives and that of your children are ALREADY under attack; that at any moment it could break forth into outright massive genocides worldwide if these people (that 1%) are not arrested immediately for their many, many crimes against humanity. PEOPLE ARE STARVING TO DEATH RIGHT NOW! https://www.blastthetrumpet.org/PublicLetters/AAAUpdatedPublicAlertsMattersofLifeandDeath/Updates053016/Crimes%20Against%20Humanity%20Part%201.pdf and http://www.youtube.com/watch?v=IPBotpbZ1v8 and they have already shown us they will murder their own citizens in false flag operations many times over. https://www.google.com/search?client=opera&q=911+just+another+false+flag+in+a+long+list&sourceid=opera&ie=UTF-8&oe=UTF-8 and even more recently, a new false flag is underway

http://www.snopes.com/politics/conspiracy/charleston.as
p   living in denial that there are many "missing nukes"
worldwide   https://www.google.com/search?client=opera
&q=missing+nukes+worldwide&sourceid=opera&ie=UTF-
8&oe=UTF-8
and   https://www.google.com/search?client=opera&q=ho
w+many+nukes+are+missing+worldwide&sourceid=opera
&ie=UTF-8&oe=UTF-8   is hardly reassuring by a "Snopes"
denial. Especially, when we currently have an Islamic
infiltrator with no legal right to hold the office of president
of the United States, currently running the show.
http://www.youtube.com/watch?v=mOHJKrxhBME   and
http://shoebat.com/2013/05/28/confirmed-barack-
obamas-brother-in-bed-with-man-wanted-by-
international-criminal-court-icc-for-crimes-against-
humanity/   and there is so much on this topic you could
spend at least a year full time looking into just how this
person succeeded infiltration into the highest office of our
land and has illegally held office this long. If you think
having an islamic infiltrator is no big deal; you really need
to educate yourself on the history on up to current events
of islam! https://youtu.be/AxB524T53xI?t=65 Obama
spent several years in Indonesia and heard the call to
islamic
prayer.   https://www.blastthetrumpet.org/PublicLetters/
AAAUpdatedPublicAlertsMattersofLifeandDeath/Updates0
53016/Truth%20Sets%20and%20Keeps%20Us%20Free.pdf
   Ultimately, it is because the satanic NWO has no regard
whatsoever for Americans or our Constitution
https://www.google.com/search?client=opera&q=un+taki

ng+control+of+the+world&sourceid=opera&ie=UTF-8&oe=UTF-8 UN is a private organization but seeks to have governance of the world and https://www.google.com/search?client=opera&q=emerging+"New+World+Constitution"&sourceid=opera&ie=UTF-8&oe=UTF-8 and https://www.google.com/search?client=opera&q=daniel+estulin+Bilderberg+group&sourceid=opera&ie=UTF-8&oe=UTF-8 but that whole discovery leads to the fusion centers and Fema concentration camps (the wicked have already begun desensitizing people by rounding up the homeless! (that they CAUSED BY THEIR GREED!) https://www.google.com/search?client=opera&q=homeless+in+Fema+camps&sourceid=opera&ie=UTF-8&oe=UTF-8); awaiting martial law when they collapse the dollar (underway currently) and mandate RFID implants as the new world digital currency and control of the masses. http://www.youtube.com/results?search_query=war+on+terror+fraud+for+nwo&oq=war+on+terror+fraud+for+nwo&gs_l=youtube.12...441418.449494.0.451594.29.22.1.6.6.0.192.2397.2j20.22.0...0.0...1ac.1.11.youtube.rALYeNbRRNc and http://www.youtube.com/results?search_query=rfid+implants+when+dollar+collapse&oq=rfid+implants+when+dollar+collapse&gs_l=youtube.3...17339.25176.0.25617.34.34.0.0.0.0.159.3701.3j31.34.0...0.0...1ac.1.11.youtube.iulxxBsh38s and http://www.youtube.com/results?search_query=fusion+centers+and+fema+camps&oq=fusion+centers+and+fema+camps&gs_l=youtube.3...23056.29910.0.30174.33.30.1.2.2.0.187.3036.5j25.30.0...0.0...1a

c.1.11.youtube.mxnst13_Sps_ - fusion centers on American soil.

You can either ignore the fact the 1% has spent huge amounts; of all their play money they mint out of thin air to do whatever they want; on all these things for no particular reason; or whatever lie(s), they come up with or look at the evidence real hard right now; so, you don't end up like the victims of all the holocausts in history. I am praying and hoping that my efforts to save lives and souls, by God's Grace are not in vain.

https://www.blastthetrumpet.org/PublicLetters/AAAUpdatedPublicAlertsMattersofLifeandDeath/Updates053016/Crimes%20Against%20Humanity%20Part%201.pdf - crimes against humanity

http://www.lifesitenews.com/news/breaking-belgium-parliament-passes-law-allowing-children-to-be-euthanized - people are going right past killing babies in the womb to infanticide!

https://www.blastthetrumpet.org/PublicLetters/AAAUpdatedPublicAlertsMattersofLifeandDeath/Updates053016/En d%20Abortion.pdf - How did murder of the unborn become legal.

https://www.blastthetrumpet.org/PublicLetters/AAAUpdatedPublicAlertsMattersofLifeandDeath/Updates053016/Treatise%20on%20Greed%20and%20Corruption.pdf and https://www.blastthetrumpet.org/PublicLetters/AAAUpdatedPublicAlertsMattersofLifeandDeath/Updates053016/satanism%20is%20a%20danger%20to%20everyone%20even%20those%20who%20practice%20it.pdf

https://www.blastthetrumpet.org/PublicLetters/AAAUpdatedPublicAlertsMattersofLifeandDeath/Updates053016/islam%20is%20Evil%20part1.pdf - we still have openly ILLEGAL PRACTICES going on worldwide, despite that is now the over 2000 years since GOD CAME AND TOLD US TO STOP THIS EVIL! Every day mankind refuses to repent of all these wicked ways is one day closer to His Wrath! EVERYONE MUST REPENT NOW!

www.blastthetrumpet.org - mass millions around the world have been slaughtered in local hospitals in the USA and all around the world for DECADES now; it is a real and ongoing holocaust (not just abortions but adults murdered and hacked up for their organs as yet one of many depopulation procedures already in full force as stated in above links) Illegal organ harvesting, causes some doctors to weigh out murder as an option to the millions of dollars in organ transplant revenue. Even if ALL iatrogenic deaths are due to accidents by doctors and nurses, it still amounts to MILLIONS of dead citizens that shouldn't have died prematurely. I assure you that many deaths are NOT all accidents!

http://www.huffingtonpost.com/2014/02/12/beijing-smog_n_4777506.html?ncid=edlinkusaolp00000009 - we have to be concerned with ceasing to burn fossil fuels for our own health and welfare. There are cars and bicycles that run on WATER, with no pollution! We need to cross over to that technology!

These people are so evil words fail to describe just how vile they really are; as they intentionally make everyone sick and dying; purely to profit from our suffering and deaths. The poor suffer and die; while they extort others who can afford the cures:

http://thinkprogress.org/health/2014/01/26/3205861/pharmaceutical-ceo-cancer-drug-westerners-afford/ - another article no longer available.

http://www.youtube.com/watch?v=HgiMqgjS-zM -
bioweapons are disguised as naturally occurring diseases!
Yes of course, the criminals are going to deny their
crimes, but the truth is COVID was first diagnosed in
China in 1976. And patents of records show that research
began thereafter. Research to make it more contagious,
research that causes the reasonably minded individuals
to realize that virtually all these "zoonotic pandemics"
were bio-engineered weapons! And yes, "fact finders"
are employed by them to deny their conspiracies. Such
"fact finders" are known to disseminate misinformation
on purpose. Finding reputable reporting today, is a
matter of due diligence based on the evidence, and
frankly, that needs to be done by us all.

http://higherperspective.com/2013/10/8-foods-even-
experts-wont-eat.html?utm_source=MAM - yet another
link showing criminal activities, gone missing.

        Please take this time to make certain your soul and
that of your loved ones are at peace with GOD, our LORD
and
SAVIOR. https://www.blastthetrumpet.org/PublicLetters/
AAAUpdatedPublicAlertsMattersofLifeandDeath/Updates0
53016/Are%20You%20A%20Christian.pdf and https://w
ww.blastthetrumpet.org/PublicLetters/AAAUpdatedPublic

AlertsMattersofLifeandDeath/Updates053016/You%20MU
ST%20Be%20Born%20Again.pdf

and thereafter PRAY FERVENTLY and please choose to LIVE
and if necessary, die with a clear conscience!

https://www.blastthetrumpet.org/PublicLetters/AAAUpda
tedPublicAlertsMattersofLifeandDeath/Updates053016/Th
e%20Dangers%20of%20Remaining%20Ignorant%20About
%20the%20Times%20We%20Are%20Living%20In.pdf

https://www.blastthetrumpet.org/PublicLetters/AAAUpda
tedPublicAlertsMattersofLifeandDeath/Updates053016/sa
tanism%20is%20a%20danger%20to%20everyone%20even
%20those%20who%20practice%20it.pdf - some people
just don't realize that when you are not acknowledging
and bowing before our Lord Jesus Christ, the One True
God, you are, by default, being deceived by the devil.

...**19We know that we are of God, and that the whole
world is under the power of the evil one. 20**And we
know that the Son of God has come and has
given us understanding, so that we may know Him who
is true; and we are in Him who
is true— in His Son Jesus Christ. He is the TRUE God and et

ernal life. **21**Little children, keep yourselves from idols....
https://biblehub.com/1_john/5-19.htm

EVERYONE MUST REPENT AND RECEIVE OUR LORD
JESUS CHRIST, who then sets us FREE from the devil! (so,
you are no longer a slave to his deceptions and evil ways!)

The Truth will Set You Free
...**35**A slave is not a permanent member of the family, but
a son belongs to it forever. **36**So if the Son sets you
free, you will
be free indeed. https://biblehub.com/john/8-36.htm

https://www.blastthetrumpet.org/PublicLetters/AAAUpda
tedPublicAlertsMattersofLifeandDeath/Updates053016/PR
OPAGANDA.pdf - the devil will have a much harder time in
deceiving you with propaganda. Because you can check
everything with GOD and His Words in the Holy Bible!

https://www.blastthetrumpet.org/PublicLetters/AAAUpda
tedPublicAlertsMattersofLifeandDeath/Updates053016/Tr
uth%20Sets%20and%20Keeps%20Us%20Free.pdf - The
Truth keeps us free!

https://www.blastthetrumpet.org/PublicLetters/AAAUpdatedPublicAlertsMattersofLifeandDeath/Updates053016/The%20Sufferings%20of%20Christ.pdf - Jesus paid it ALL! and He gives us the strength to FOLLOW HIM!
https://www.preceptaustin.org/tetelestai-paid_in_full

https://www.blastthetrumpet.org/PublicLetters/AAAUpdatedPublicAlertsMattersofLifeandDeath/Updates053016/My%20Most%20Dangerous%20Situation.pdf - it's a real danger to us all when so many people still do not KNOW the LORD JESUS CHRIST, and are not practicing living righteously before Him.

https://www.blastthetrumpet.org/PublicLetters/AAAUpdatedPublicAlertsMattersofLifeandDeath/Updates053016/What%20is%20Happening%20to%20America.pdf - as more and more people become corrupt because we are not teaching the Holy Bible in our schools any longer, our nation as a whole begins to suffer.

https://www.blastthetrumpet.org/PublicLetters/AAAUpdatedPublicAlertsMattersofLifeandDeath/Updates053016/THE%20PLANNED%20DEMORALIZATION%20OF%20AMERICA.pdf - enemies have crept into our nation and are intentionally corrupting it because that is how empires fell in the past. WE MUST RETURN TO JESUS CHRIST AND OUR AMERICAN CHRISTIAN HERITAGE!

https://www.youtube.com/watch?v=u7Ca7iPC_2o   The satanic NWO peddling their enslavement tool. They want chips to track you just like cattle, just like goods in a warehouse; you will be branded as their personal property. And if you fail to do as they command; boom your chip will no longer access your credits at their bank. you will starve in a world where it is unlawful to be poor and homeless; where such persons are exterminated by the NWO head shrinks like they're been doing for so many years already. (and will get worse unless people unite to stop these madmen!) https://www.youtube.com/watch?v=II96QkZaz1E - more and more people are under psychiatric medication when some of them are so toxic they carry lethal side effects!

https://www.google.com/search?client=opera&q=homeless+fully+eradicated+government+assessment+camps+staffed+now&sourceid=opera&ie=UTF-8&oe=UTF-8 - making it illegal to be poor, disabled and elderly and reduced by our civilization to just dying on the streets.

It is at times like this we need to hear the words of our patriotic founders; words like https://www.blastthetrumpet.org/PublicLetters/AAAUpdatedPublicAlertsMattersofLifeandDeath/Some%20Quotes%20and%20Thought1.pdf   and of course: https://www.youtube.com/watch?v=XvJrSdr34co and http://www.youtube.com/watch?v=ucduNh4FFvE

This is a time on earth when people everywhere think they alone determine what is right and wrong and, in the disagreement, as a result bloodshed ensues. I cannot tell how many will come to their senses prior to our Lord's Glorious Return but I can guarantee that when He does, all will agree and understand https://www.blastthetrumpet.org/PublicLetters/AAAUpdatedPublicAlertsMattersofLifeandDeath/Updates053016/Why%20We%20All%20Need%20Instructions%20From%20Our%20Creator%20to%20Live%20By.pdf

I have said throughout this note of alarm to all citizens everywhere; that it is NOT your fault; but if you don't take the time to look into these topics diligently; if you don't care enough to stand up for your own lives and that of your children and demand the arrests of all persons doing these things to us globally; if you don't spread the word (share this information) with others; then it will no longer be only their fault... it will also be yours!

https://www.youtube.com/watch?v=OwaV2snnc5I -
another suppressed documentary.

https://www.youtube.com/watch?v=VIlwRgSECcw - Allan
Watt has some interesting comments on our civilization.
Whenever I cite someone, it is not that I completely agree
with them and their opinions, it's just that I found portions
of what they are trying to communicate worthy enough to
think on.

https://www.youtube.com/watch?v=KHqdwmqu-
h0&list=PLL4CV8_Rn74ru8kjD6DkLvl0zLZsdWOvh -
removed, I tend to think the public should demand the
retrieval of what youtube in removing these days because
it does seem like government censorship regarding
sensitive information.

It has been said and it sadly is
true... http://www.goodreads.com/quotes/423016-all-
that-is-necessary-for-evil-to-triumph-is-for

**"All that is necessary for evil to triumph is for good men
to do nothing."**

But if you are persuaded that you will not be one of those who will allow yourself and your loved ones to be rounded up and slaughtered; who will not stand by while you and your loved ones are poisoned to death and completely enslaved;
then https://www.blastthetrumpet.org/PublicLetters/AAA UpdatedPublicAlertsMattersofLifeandDeath/Updates0530 16/GAIN%20AND%20RESTORE%20FREEDOM.pdf

I want to draw attention to the not so obvious ones or as yet well known enough to stop them (as should be done immediately by any and all sane citizens that care about their own lives, that of their children and all life on the planet).

1) Genetically Modified Organisms -
https://www.facebook.com/ExposeTheTPP.USA/photos/a. 559197950803491.1073741828.557710050952281/72659 2800730671/?type=1&theater

https://www.facebook.com/ExposeTheTPP.USA/photos /a.559197950803491.1073741828.557710050952281/723 127274410557/?type=1&theater   Very evil persons are attempting to takeover food and water supplies to enslave citizens; this is a MUST FIGHT BACK CAUSE for all who love life and liberty! https://www.facebook.com/FarmageddonTHEMO VIE   The persons engaging in this activity are either so evil they deserve to be locked up or so ignorant as to need dramatic re-

education. https://www.google.com/search?q=kissinger+ control+the+food&rlz=1C1GIGM_enUS535US535&oq=kissi nger+control+the+food&aqs=chrome..69i57&sourceid=chr ome&es_sm=0&ie=UTF-8   It is an obvious move of the satanic NWO and unless you intend to be enslaved or exterminated, THEY HAVE GONE TOO FAR!

Corporations, such as youtube, engage in censorship for just about any reason and couch it all under things that they have no knowledge to defend. Such as medical misinformation or hate speech, when people are just alerting other citizens of medical malpractice. Both of those topics remain highly subjective and so anyone can be censored by them for any reason. THEY ACT AS IF THEY ARE ARBITRATORS OF ALL TRUTHFUL INFORMATION, when in fact MANKIND DOES NOT KNOW IT ALL and as such, censoring free speech, especially truthful information, is violating the highest laws of our nation; whether they do it in their ignorance or deliberately, such persons/corporations should be held accountable, both civilly and criminally. So, if anything you say in a video they can even remotely consider as violating their policies, they CENSOR THE ENTIRE VIDEO for maybe one thing that they just disagreed with. David Wood had very informative videos, that you-tube censored so much they simply wore him out trying to defend TRUTHFUL INFORMATION. So youtube is increasingly an arm of the satanic NWO order, censoring those of us shedding light on the fact our lives are under attack. THEY SHOULD BE SUED as an American corporation UNILATERALLY CENSORING Americans based on whatever policies they can drum up! So much for first amendment rights. And when youtube is marketed as a public forum to consider it privately protected legally, to get away with CENSORSHIP of important information, is just a way for private corporations to usurp the highest laws of our land! (Corporations founded in America, existing still in America, that dominate public forums on the internet, should be considered as public forums legally such that they must adhere to our national laws, otherwise they are engaging in subversive and even treasonous acts.) As far as I'm concerned YouTube is currently run by subversive citizens to our constitution. It would be interesting to note how many people working for these corporations engaging in such censorship of truthful information are muslims and if these corporations have received funding from muslims. FREEDOM ENDS WHEN CENSORSHIP BEGINS! CITIZENS SHOULD DEMAND THAT CENSORSHIP ENDS ON THE INTERNET, IT'S THE LAST BASTION OF FREE SPEECH AFFORDED US! The rich have bought up mainstream media, but the poor don't have a way to exercise their free speech, except through the internet. When rich corporations are actively censoring what we post on the internet, it only leads to the need of poor people to defend themselves and their freedoms, with violence. CENSORSHIP MUST BE AVOIDED AT ALL COSTS! It's has caused revolutions in the past! All of the persons involved in this evil can be properly arrested for crimes against humanity if the public would only unite and demand it! Our Creator has carefully designed life on the planet, such that it is interwoven in a complex web of interdependence.

Plants consist of genetic structures to be bioavailable to herbivores and omnivores; but altering that genetic structure even slightly is making them toxic and indigestible. If microbes don't eat it; can't live on it; if insects don't eat; can't live on it; it is not bio-available to other higher life forms; but toxic and is causing an increase in chronic diseases in such populations where GMOs are rampant. A disruption in the web of interdependency is fundamentally a danger to all life on the planet. Currently, GMOs represent one of the most, if not the most serious threat to all life on the planet. They are genetically similar enough to invade organic varieties and disrupt entire ecosystems. They are not controllable in that fashion.

Designed to be toxic or indigestible to lower life-forms; makes these genetically altered foods toxic to humans and other higher life forms causing ailments from food allergies and malnutrition thereby; to more serious chronic conditions; cancers and such. The science overwhelmingly shows that GMO monocultures disrupt ecologies in a most harmful manner wherever they have been introduced and are a leading cause of the rise in chronic ailments today. The danger is severe; such corporations and persons on earth meddling in altering the designs of our Creator are in fact so dangerous they must be put under arrest immediately. The genetic alteration of Intelligent Design by the LORD GOD ALMIGHTY is among the worst of all crimes against humanity and all of creation.

https://www.minds.com/blog/view/315466343296012288/the-era-of-chimeras-scientists-fearlessly-create-bizarre-humananimal-hybrids

Life is sustained on this planet in an interwoven cycle of bio-availability from the most basic life-forms to the most complex; that cycle is being disrupted globally now by the presence of GMOs! http://livefreelivenatural.com/dna-gmos-can-pass-directly-humans-study-confirms/ Putting an end to this practice should be one of the highest worldwide concerns and among the very chiefest priorities. Citizens are advised to keep their own organic seed supplies and grow their own food until these persons are properly put under arrest for their crimes against humanity (and all life on the planet).

http://www.pachamama.org/hawaiians-fight-monsanto-and-gmos

Some people don't understand what I am saying; so, let me clarify. Genetic modification of plant life, vegetables, etc. whether eaten by insects or higher life forms have been proven to CAUSE illnesses and premature deaths. Some might think that I am exaggerating though when I say this is not the worst danger of GMOs. GMOs have a very real possibility of causing runaway extinction events. How? you ask. Simply because people that are so greedy they want to control the world's seed and food supply decided it was a good idea to modify the plants in such a way as to produce natural toxins in increased amounts. The idea was to make plants more pest and disease resistant. (seems at first like a good idea) but what is the result? massive widespread die offs of lower life forms (INCLUDING POLLINATORS). http://berkeley.edu/news/media/releases/2006/10/25_pollinator.shtml It has been the cause of law suits that organic crops are being invaded by GMOs; proving that GMOs can spread beyond control and continue to cause extinction events of essential species necessary for life on the planet (including mankind). Like killer bees, genetic modification has yet to produce one positive result when objectively analyzed. The goal of these people to control food supplies is EVIL, the process is EVIL, and the results are anything from chronic ailments, mass suffering and premature deaths to causing runaway extinction events! (and all because the rest of the world is failing to arrest greedy persons who are so insane they want to control the entire world's food supply and are ignoring all the studies showing what they are doing is not just harmful but is leading to global catastrophes and the real possibility of uncontrollable runaway extinctions).

Pesticide resistant crops or crops that actually produce their own pesticides! GMOs are POISONING US! And the ecosystem of earth!

https://www.youtube.com/watch?feature=player_embedded&v=Njd0RugGjAg - rats developing cancer from being fed GMO crops.

http://covvha.net/monsanto-exposed-the-biggest-secrets-of-one-of-the-worlds-most-hated-corporations/#.U7ILa_IdU9R - the reputation of monsanto should have had that corporation shut down.

https://www.youtube.com/watch?v=wA2GhOCtmBE - GMOs are NOT Healthy!

https://www.youtube.com/watch?v=MJfLw2XXdBU - no longer available. We have to download incriminating evidence when we can because it appears they are actively censoring such information.

http://sustainablepulse.com/2014/07/28/indian-farmer-suicide-testimonials-show-huge-gmo-community-damage-watch-yield/#.U9aKBvIdU9R

https://www.facebook.com/MarchAgainstMonstanto/photos/a.566016720083519.1073741828.566004240084767/764814693537053/?type=1&theater

http://www.healthy-holistic-living.com/governments-ignore-definitive-proof-monsantos-roundup-causes-birth-defects.html

http://www.naturalnews.com/043995_human_civilization_processed_food_stealth_war.html

http://www.activistpost.com/2014/05/genetic-engineers-agree-gmos-neither.html

https://www.indiegogo.com/projects/bought-the-hidden-story-behind-vaccines-big-pharma-your-food

http://www.wesupportorganic.com/2014/04/10-scientific-studies.html

https://www.facebook.com/GMOFreeUSA/photos/a.4686 95639837571.108816.402058139834655/8163939950677 32/?type=1&theater

http://expandedconsciousness.com/2014/05/09/new-study-links-gmo-food-to-leukemia/ - more and more

GMOs are linked to diseases and yet no one is banning them in our nation!

http://www.collective-evolution.com/2014/01/09/confirmed-dna-from-genetically-modified-crops-can-be-transfered-to-humans-who-eat-them-2/

https://www.facebook.com/MarchAgainstMonstanto/photos/a.566016720083519.1073741828.566004240084767/767946229890566/?type=1&theater how many have to suffer and die before we ban GMOs?

http://www.collective-evolution.com/2014/04/25/how-monsanto-annihilated-a-paradise-turned-it-into-an-island-of-illness/ - if any of these links are no longer active just use your favorite search engine on the subject line. Like google: "how monsanto annihilated a paradise and turned it into an island of illness".

http://wewillblowyourmind.blogspot.com/2013/05/800-scientists-demand-global-gmo.html

http://www.collective-evolution.com/2013/08/03/american-scientists-confirm-pesticides-are-killing-honey-bees/ - honey bees play a critical role in pollination; their decline is an ecological disaster that could cause runaway extinction events of many species; besides a radical decline in our own food supply.

https://www.facebook.com/photo.php?fbid=584458791652337&set=a.453856594712558.1073741828.4481773319 47151&type=1&theater

https://www.facebook.com/MarchAgainstMonstanto/photos/a.566016720083519.1073741828.566004240084767/764814693537053/?type=1&theater

http://www.naturalcuresnotmedicine.com/2014/01/dna-gmo-can-transferred-person-eats.html - Genetically modified DNA can transfer into our cells.

http://wisemindhealthybody.com/cancer-deaths-double-gmos-agrochemicals/ - GMOs causing cancer rates to escalate.

https://www.facebook.com/photo.php?fbid=7782387755 49268&set=a.482231601816655.113449.47898155880832 6&type=1&theater - content censored.

https://www.facebook.com/photo.php?fbid=7588005774 85763&set=a.364218226944002.95415.356680184364473 &type=1&theater - patenting seeds was one of the worst mistakes our government and nations of the world ever made. NO ONE SHOULD BE MEDDLING WITH DIVINE DESIGNS! God Created and Made this planet to be bio-dependent on each other to sustain life, and yet GMOs are like viruses messing up the ecosystem of earth! They didn't make the seeds, GOD did, all they did was meddle with to make them toxic to life!

http://covvha.net/usda-admits-gmo-crops-may-cause-major-environmental-risks/#.U27H9_IdU9R

http://www.collective-evolution.com/2013/05/31/monsanto-found-guilty-of-chemical-poisoning-in-france/

https://www.facebook.com/photo.php?fbid=6230667744 35275&set=a.182339481841342.43482.182336115175012 &type=1&theater - letting people control food supplies rather than just growing heirloom varieties in bio-diverse ways as it was done for thousands of years is making mankind subject to those who greedily want to control us.

http://ecowatch.com/2014/03/06/nyu-gmos-destroy-planet/

http://www.healthy-holistic-living.com/biotech-companies-dont-want-us-know-gmo-fields.html - I remember when I grew up on a small farm and we would harvest our produce each year, how that all our food MADE ME FEEL HEALTHY, was NUTRITIOUS! And now, when I go to the market, the produce may look good, but makes me feel nauseous. Not all, but more and more, I'm wondering WHAT IS MAKING OUR FOOD SO UNHEALTHY! And then I studied it, AS MUCH AS 70% of our food is Genetically Engineered, GMOs or GMO ingredients are in so many things nowadays, it almost impossible to avoid them all.

https://www.facebook.com/Vegiheal.Life/photos/a.10150268990183706.348651.123021718705/10151269351683706/?type=1&theater - yet another broken link.

https://www.facebook.com/thefoodbabe/photos/a.20838 6335862752.56063.132535093447877/768281679873212 /?type=1&theater - some companies like craft spent huge amounts of money refusing to label GMO products. We should be wary of people and corporations who value dollars over our lives.

https://www.facebook.com/155935376162/photos/a.446 196711162.238598.155935376162/10152399311891163/ ?type=1&theater - what companies like monsanto are doing is causing extinction events. We need to be very concerned with what GMOs are doing to us and the earth's ecosystem.

https://www.facebook.com/MarchAgainstMonstanto/pho tos/a.566016720083519.1073741828.566004240084767/ 862081653810356/?type=1&theater

http://covvha.net/the-world-according-to-monsanto-full- length-video/#.U0C3BfldV5Z   Another video taken down! https://www.currentaffairs.org/news/2022/02/deny-until- we-die

https://www.google.com/search?client=opera&q=the+wo rld+according+to+monsato+full+length+documentary&sou rceid=opera&ie=UTF-8&oe=UTF-8 - watch this video.

If governments don't realize the danger to all life on the planet; everyone else needs to! THESE PEOPLE ARE EITHER TOO GREEDY OR TOO EVIL TO BE ALLOWED TO CONTINUE WITH THEIR EPIC FAILS IN PERVERTING THE GENETIC DESIGNS PROVIDED FOR US BY THE GOD OF ALL CREATION!!!!!!!! THEY OBVIOUSLY EITHER ARE OBLIVIOUS TO THE EXTINCTION EVENTS THEY ARE CAUSING, THE SUFFERING, DEATH AND DESTRUCTION OR THEY ARE INTENTIONALLY DOING SO! EITHER WAY, THE PUBLIC MUST STOP THESE PERSONS ANY WAY THEY CAN!!!!!!!!

I am astonished at how many people will try to argue against COMMON SENSE! your body, your physical form is comprised of what you eat (and drink and absorb by breathing or through your skin)! Our bodies need proper nourishment, not things that have been modified to be harmful to us, or poisoned! The devil is called the deceiver and destroyer because following him and his wicked schemes destroys mankind. So why would you argue that genetically modified food isn't harmful WHEN IT HAS BEEN ALTERED IN SUCH A WAY as to be fundamentally incompatible with the micro-biome in your digestive tract! They have FACTUALLY altered plants that reject metals inherently because too much metals would make them toxic (heavy metal toxicity leads to all kinds of ailments -
https://www.google.com/webhp?sourceid=chrome-

instant&rlz=1C1GIGM_enUS535US535&ion=1&espv=2&ie=UTF-8#q=heavy%20metal%20toxicity%20causes%20all%20kinds%20of%20diseases) They altered plants that would normally die in the presence of too much metals to actually be able to live and incorporate excessive amounts of metals into their foliage. (read the citations and study the details of what they have already modified and HOW!) LOOK AT THE FACTS! If for some reason common sense is failing you in this regard. (of knowing that genetically altering food to be toxic to lower life-forms is inherently HARMFUL to higher life forms; TO US; most OBVIOUSLY and INTRINSICALLY!)

http://eatlocalgrown.com/article/11524-the-monsanto-71-senators-who-betrayed-constituents-in-favor-of-biotech-dollars.html

https://www.facebook.com/photo.php?fbid=10152391654064388&set=a.10150644870149388.450934.162878479387&type=1&theater - professor says GMOs are a potential threat to our planet! I agree!

https://www.facebook.com/222092971257181/photos/a.223219014477910.57895.222092971257181/4481080286

55673/?type=1&theater - GMOs cause cancers in lab rats and kill human embryo cells!

https://www.facebook.com/GMOFreeUSA/photos/a.4686 95639837571.108816.402058139834655/7267714173633 24/?type=1&theater - money is influencing scientific findings that GMOs are harmful.

https://www.facebook.com/GMOFreeUSA/photos/a.4686 95639837571.108816.402058139834655/7380907428980 58/?type=1&theater - monsanto, is a company that's engaged in crimes against humanity and yet it's allowed to go on operating. What does that tell you about our government?

https://www.facebook.com/GMOFreeUSA/photos/a.4686 95639837571.108816.402058139834655/7284452905292 70/?type=1&theater - GMOs harming pigs, and so many life forms on our planet.

https://www.facebook.com/GMOFreeUSA/photos/a.4686 95639837571.108816.402058139834655/7300611237010 20/?type=1&theater - GMOs are invasive, they are like a virus to life on our planet!

https://www.facebook.com/connfact/photos/a.14688006 40001443.1073741830.1436001076614733/14749354360 54630/?type=1&theater - Doesn't anyone see anything wrong with meddling with DIVINE DESIGNS! We are not God! We can't see the full ramifications of what we do! It often isn't apparent to us until so many have died!

https://www.facebook.com/photo.php?fbid=6768149856 98528&set=a.478718612174834.110771.47871572217512 3&type=1&theater - another link no longer functional.

https://www.facebook.com/photo.php?fbid=1015234571 4164388&set=a.10150644870149388.450934.1628784793 87&type=1&theater - GMOs are invasive! they are already costing innocent farmers!

https://www.facebook.com/GMOFreeUSA/photos/a.4686 95639837571.108816.402058139834655/7205803813157 61/?type=1&theater - another broken link.

https://www.google.com/search?q=GMOs+causing+extinc tion&rlz=1C1GIGM_enUS535US535&oq=GMOS&aqs=chro

me.3.69i57j69i65j0j69i59j0l2.5155j0j8&sourceid=chrome&espv=210&es_sm=93&ie=UTF-8 and

https://www.facebook.com/GMOFreeUSA/photos/a.468695639837571.108816.402058139834655/718027994904333/?type=1&theater - genetically modified babies! Don't Do It!

https://www.google.com/search?q=gmos+cause+cancer&rlz=1C1GIGM_enUS535US535&oq=gmos+&aqs=chrome.4.69i57j0j69i59j69i65j0l2.4155j0j8&sourceid=chrome&espv=210&es_sm=93&ie=UTF-8 and

http://finance.yahoo.com/q/mh?s=MON+Major+Holders and

https://www.facebook.com/GMOFreeUSA/photos/a.468695639837571.108816.402058139834655/720946947945771/?type=1&theater - farmers in the Philippines are speaking out against GMOs.

https://www.facebook.com/GMOFreeUSA/photos/a.468695639837571.108816.402058139834655/717425338297932/?type=1&theater - Herbicides have been linked to causing damage to amphibians, we must stop using toxins that cause harm to our lives and our planet.

https://www.facebook.com/GMOFreeUSA/photos/a.4686 95639837571.108816.402058139834655/7198054513932 54/?type=1&theater - corporate GMO monocultures' farming practices are using so much herbicides and pesticides that it's contaminating our water supply.

https://www.facebook.com/photo.php?fbid=6051150095 63785&set=a.182339481841342.43482.182336115175012 &type=1&theater - another broken link.

http://en.wikipedia.org/wiki/Hugh_Grant_(business_exec utive)_ and

http://www.youtube.com/watch?v=Zbzcj321m1s GMOs cause harm!
and http://www.youtube.com/watch?v=OMQ07IN5khE the company makes false statements regarding their product and

https://www.facebook.com/photo.php?fbid=6678447332
62220&set=a.478718612174834.110771.47871572217512
3&type=1&theater - broken link.

https://www.facebook.com/348939748204/photos/a.349
138773204.154870.348939748204/10151688257238205/
?type=1&theater how many must suffer and die before
companies like monsanto are shut down permanently!
and

http://www.youtube.com/watch?v=a6OxbpLwEjQ (GMO'
s and their impact is unhealthy, death!)
and http://www.youtube.com/watch?v=-BYy6-
K3OJk another video removed, and

http://www.youtube.com/watch?v=omtYlsG1P5U and ht
tp://www.youtube.com/watch?v=UcwmpC9KQzo and
(two more removed!)

https://www.youtube.com/watch?v=ztwUXqGZXaY&featu
re=youtu.be - people need to be tested to determine if
they have glyphosate in their systems.

https://www.facebook.com/photo.php?v=1311609628978745&set=vb.1104995126306864&type=2&theater - another broken link. The problem with the Internet is that important information can disappear suddenly. Corporations as large as facebook, should consider making the posts permanent and perhaps even implement a database that can be searched.

http://www.youtube.com/watch?v=B_XtCcMeWrw - Seed's of Death full movie and https://fbcdn-sphotos-e-a.akamaihd.net/hphotos-ak-prn1/1512801_677948462245620_755031833_n.jpg - another broken link.

http://vimeo.com/58863554 - people just don't realize that what they're eating is contributing to chronic and terminal conditions!

http://www.cornucopia.org/2013/12/genetically-modified-wheat-lawsuits-monsanto-transferred-kansas-federal-court/ - read up on this lawsuit.

https://www.facebook.com/photo.php?fbid=691459884227811&set=a.468695639837571.108816.40205813983465

5&type=1&theater - male infertility linked to monsanto and round-up.

https://www.facebook.com/photo.php?fbid=6954856971
58563&set=a.468695639837571.108816.40205813983465
5&type=1&theater - with cancer on the rise, do we really want GMOs?

https://www.facebook.com/photo.php?fbid=6965491170
52221&set=a.468695639837571.108816.40205813983465
5&type=1&theater - independent researchers have determined that our farming practices with GMOs and roundup are incredibly dangerous to our health and the environment!

https://www.facebook.com/photo.php?fbid=6969582503
44641&set=a.468695639837571.108816.40205813983465
5&type=1&theater - pesticides are killing honey bee populations.

http://eatlocalgrown.com/article/12483-new-study-links-gmo-food-to-leukemia.html - another report linked GMOs to leukemia, has since been removed.

https://www.facebook.com/photo.php?fbid=7007711766 30015&set=a.46869563983757.108816.40205813983465 5&type=1&theater - crops are being modified, sprayed with herbicides and pesticides and sold to us. There is a rise in chronic and terminal conditions among Americans.

https://www.facebook.com/photo.php?fbid=1015201780 0504934&set=a.10150142479999934.291724.1334187993 3&type=1&theater - instead of GMOs, we need to resupply wild salmon and don't overfish our seas!

https://www.facebook.com/photo.php?fbid=6174064983 08399&set=a.358524584196593.73711.358517274197324 &type=1&theater - even with gloves on farmers still get herbicides and pesticides in their systems!

https://www.facebook.com/photo.php?fbid=7033425763 72875&set=a.46869563983757.108816.40205813983465 5&type=1&theater - God does it BEST! Organic biodiversity for all our fruits and vegetables; NO GMOs!

https://www.facebook.com/GMOFreeUSA/photos/a.4686 95639837571.108816.402058139834655/7072088326529 16/?type=1&theater - the use of GMOs resistant to herbicides and pesticides is that they are creating weeds that are as well! Meaning ever increasing toxicity to try and manage them.

https://www.facebook.com/photo.php?fbid=591910274219078&set=a.337387396338035.74405.327002374043204&type=1&theater - geneticist telling the world GMOs are harmful to us!

https://www.facebook.com/GMOFreeUSA/photos/a.468695639837571.108816.402058139834655/712895405417592/?type=1&theater - glyphosate a chemical in roundup causing birth defects in pigs by feeding them GMO crops sprayed with roundup.

https://www.facebook.com/GMOFreeUSA/photos/a.468695639837571.108816.402058139834655/713532398687226/?type=1&theater - GMOs crops can be drowned in herbicides and pesticides because they have been modified to withstand the toxins, WE HAVEN'T so the toxins are causing us harm!

http://www.truth-out.org/news/item/21917-gmos-are-killing-the-bees-butterflies-birds-and - colony collapse disorder - all the pesticides and herbicides are just harming us by life on earth!

http://ecowatch.com/2014/02/20/study-differences-gmo-non-gmo-foods/ - more and more people are claiming gluten intolerance, cancer increases, and yet even though studies show GMOs are to blame and herbicides and pesticides related to GMOs crops, still the FDA approves. Sometimes other people are just not registering the facts; due to how much corruption there is linked to money.

https://www.facebook.com/photo.php?fbid=10152308678019388&set=a.10150644870149388.450934.162878479387&type=1&theater - poisons on our food drains into our water supplies and gets into our systems. Makes me want to live far away from civilization, anywhere people still practice pure living.

https://youtu.be/4NQ6Tw7KXUk -

The World According to Monsanto (Full Documentary) - The hype is undermined by the facts!

http://earthweareone.com/monsanto-ordered-to-pay-93-million-to-small-town-for-poisoning-citizens-2/ - it would be interesting to find out if the victims ever see one penny. This was a post that monsanto had been ordered to pay 93 million for poisoning a town.

https://www.blastthetrumpet.org/PublicLetters/AAAUpdatedPublicAlertsMattersofLifeandDeath/Updates053016/Not%20One%20Thin%20Dime.pdf

All the above links are reasons why GMOs are crimes against humanity! And are yet still in practice and still portrayed as harmless by our government, when the facts show they are lying and that our regulators are subject to falsifying reports due to corruption. Too many are caving into money, financial incentives allowing harmful substances to be marketed to OUR HARM and the HARM OF THE PLANET!

Glucosamine sensitivities are on the rise. It's due to our wheat which is now grown with herbicides and pesticides throughout its growing process then right before harvest they use them again to make the wheat ready for harvesting. It's no wonder people are developing "Glucosamine" sensitivities. Those who migrated to a part of the world where the wheat was not grown with any herbicide and pesticides reported that they did NOT have their glucosamine sufferings. Research this fact online.

http://www.activistpost.com/2011/06/chemtrails-monsanto-olgacom-connection.html   - herbicides and pesticides some call "chemtrails" are NO DOUBT TOXIC to organic life-forms, INCLUDING HUMANS, therefore IT REALLY DOESN'T MATTER ALL THE THEORIES AS TO WHY so much use of toxins/poisons EXIST! They are KILLING PEOPLE! and other life-forms as a result! BUT after studying all the many theories about them, I conclude that the FACTS are there ARE TOXIC CHEMICALS AND METALS in the mass spraying (whether for weather control, crop control or other reasons) THESE CHEMICALS ARE IN FACT TOXIC! IT IS ALSO A FACT that Monsanto has genetically modified crops to continue to grow EVEN WITH THOSE TOXINS AND METALS. https://www.google.com/search?client=opera& q=gmo+heavy+metal+plants&sourceid=opera&ie=UTF-8&oe=UTF-8 and plants that contain heavy metals are able to pass on their contents to those who consume them! IT IS A WELL-KNOWN AGENDA OF THE NWO TO ATTEMPT TO CONTROL FOOD AND WATER SUPPLIES! http://www.democraticunderground.com/disc uss/duboard.php?az=view_all&address=389x2578928 Kis singer has been involved in the NWO most all of his life. Publicly the NWO refers to the trend of globalism and a global economy, but privately the NWO refers to enslavement of the masses, through such global control by the wealthiest citizens of the world. Together with the Global Depopulation agenda http://www.depopulation.newworldorderuniversi ty.com/Wordpress/ that the OBVIOUS result of using toxins on our food is it makes humans very ill; it harms organic crops and most all life forms (that alone is enough to arrest all involved with chemtrails for crimes against humanity); BUT the chemicals being sprayed have been tested on Monsanto's GM crops! (they intentionally modified plants to keep growing even with the heavy metal toxins that would otherwise kill them off). As such, is evidence of DEPOPULATION AND CONTROL FOOD SUPPLY; DESTROYING ORGANIC CROPS BY AEROSOL SPRAYING OF TOXIC CHEMICALS on our food and taints our water supply. It's what is occurring in present day reality! NOW IT'S UP TO THE PEOPLE OF THE WORLD TO UNITE AGAINST THESE MANIACS AND STOP THEM, before these unbelievable INSANE IGNORAMUSES CAUSE RUNAWAY EXTINCTION EVENTS WORLDWIDE! The scientists that are not corrupt (haven't accepted bribes from Monsanto) are speaking out trying to warn the world.

https://www.youtube.com/watch?v=4NQ6Tw7KXUk

If you're wondering why I have included spraying with herbicides and pesticides, manufactured poisons, in the exposure of the threat of GMOs; it is because those responsible for GMOs have intentionally modified their seeds, plants to live in the toxins that are being sprayed in the atmosphere, tainting our water supplies, destroying other vegetation and organisms; PROVING collaboration! (or as some aptly call it conspiracy) So the unbelievable greed of these people and desire to control the world's food supply currently is showing evidence that they have FOREKNOWLEDGE that what is being sprayed worldwide is toxic to life-forms all over the planet; that they have INTENTIONALLY modified their seeds to survive those toxins; in an effort to monopolize food and seed supply for the world! THESE ARE CRIMES AGAINST HUMANITY OF THE WORST KIND; WHAT THEY HAVE DONE ALREADY IS SUFFICIENT TO WARRENT THEIR ARRESTS MANY TIMES OVER!!!!!!!! (living in denial will not save you and your children from these wicked people; look at the evidence)

THESE CRIMINAL IDIOTS ARE A SERIOUS THREAT TO ALL LIFE ON THE PLANET!!!!!!!! https://www.facebook.com/GMOFreeUSA/photos/a.468695639837571.108816.402058139834655/719536294753503/?type=1&theater - harming the environment of the earth. GMOs are not harmless and the poisons (herbicides and pesticides) are not harmless, they're killing us and causing extinction events on earth!

The FDA should be using organic fruits and vegetables and noting which are herbicide and pesticide free! FREE FROM TOXIC CHEMICALS BEING SPRAYED ON THEM! Making sure that our stores are stocked with healthy food! Instead of things that are causing chronic ailments, food that is deadly for us.

http://health.usnews.com/health-news/articles/2014/05/07/scientists-create-1st-living-organism-from-artificial-dna?src=usn_tw   seriously, these people are intellectual idiots! The entire world is a complex web of interdependent species, (cycle of life depends on bio-availability, bio-compatibility, ecological harmony) THESE GENETIC ABERRATIONS INTERRUPT that fabric of designed interdependency, and have the potential to easily cause runaway extinction events! https://www.google.com/search?q=genetic+modification+causing+extinction&rlz=1C1GIGM_enUS535US535&oq=genetic+modi&aqs=chrome.2.69i57j0j69i59j0l3.3673j0j8&sourceid=chrome&es_sm=93&ie=UTF-8 intentionally making something that is indigestible, poisonous, harmful, toxic, biologically different from all known life forms IS INSANE! I suppose they didn't learn from those meddling and produced the killer bees, or other destructive nightmares to date. BUT NOT ONE GMO has produced any GOOD benefit; all have been varying degrees of harmful to deadly! Corn has become increasingly indigestible, it looks good, but it's not the same as unmodified corn, nutritionally. **TIME TO ARREST THESE PEOPLE SINCE THEY JUST CAN'T SEEM TO THINK BEYOND TO SEE THE CONSEQUENCES OF THEIR ACTIONS!**

https://www.google.com/search?client=opera&q=the+world+according+to+monsanto&sourceid=opera&ie=UTF-8&oe=UTF-8 - Watch this documentary, money is obviously corrupting our regulators, FDA, when the science tells us GMOs and toxins/poisoning our food are HARMFUL!

All of those committing the worst crimes against humanity are focused on their personal profits; amassing wealth; regardless of the consequences to our planet and all life on it; including other human beings. http://library.uniteddiversity.coop/More_Books_a nd_Reports/Silent_Spring-Rachel_Carson-1962.pdf - Herbicides and pesticide use is found in increasing amounts in our soils and water supplies with harmful results. When you become informed and see the connections between their personal greed, their attitudes toward humanity and global depopulation, their arrogant disdain for God our Creator and His Instructions for Life contained in the Holy Bible, their evil, selfish, greedy commonalities result in massive suffering and deaths on earth; then you; AS I DO NOW, will call for their immediate arrests worldwide. https://www.blastthetrumpet.org/PublicLette rs/AAAUpdatedPublicAlertsMattersofLifeandDeath/Updat es053016/Treatise%20on%20Greed%20and%20Corruptio n.pdf and

https://www.blastthetrumpet.org/PublicLetters/AAAUpda tedPublicAlertsMattersofLifeandDeath/Updates053016/D epopulation.pdf - when companies are causing widespread illness and early death, just in the name of profits, why are they not under arrest for crimes against humanity?

https://www.google.com/search?client=opera&q=two+reporters+fired+for+gmo+related+health+concerns+to+milk&sourceid=opera&ie=UTF-8&oe=UTF-8 - When monsanto somehow wields power to fire people who are reporting their conscience, they are obviously controlling our regulators as well. More evidence that those in power are funding genocides; rather than arresting those committing them.

Genetic modification of the designs encoded by our Eternal Creator for His Creation represents one of the most serious threats to all life on the planet. The only thing more dangerous is a human being that does not know and learn from our Creator directly; thereby capable of every kind of evil; including genetic modifications done either by intent or ignorance and which are already having devastating consequences worldwide. If I were empowered by the people; I would be IMMEDIATELY arresting all persons involved in these atrocities and assaults on our world and all life therein; including human life. Since, I am not empowered to do so and have not the means to individually place all such wicked, depraved, ignorant, and insane persons under arrest that are doing these things, I CALL FOR ALL PEOPLE

AROUND THE WORLD TO UNITE AND MAKE THAT HAPPEN!!!!!!!! Genetic modification of anything is a most serious threat to YOUR LIVES! (STOP BELIEVING THE LYING PROPAGANDA of anyone who claims otherwise; most everyone that does so is directly and/or indirectly making millions to billions of dollars to lie to you and commit these offenses against humanity and all life on the planet).

https://www.facebook.com/AGENTORANGE1/photos/a.505024272926127.1073741827.222449644516926/671835666244986/?type=1&theater

God almighty tells mankind how to farm the land:

Sabbath Laws
10For six years you are to sow your land and gather its produce, 11but in the seventh year you must let it rest and lie fallow, so that the poor among your people may eat from the field and the wild animals may consume what they leave. Do the same with your vineyard and olive grove. 12For six days you are to do your work, but on the seventh day you must cease, so that your ox and your donkey may rest and the son of your maidservant may be refreshed, as well as the foreign resident....
https://biblehub.com/exodus/23-11.htm

For so long we have not returned to organic farming which uses composts from farm animals instead of herbicide and pesticides and for too long we have not let the land rest every seventh year, and so our soils are depleted. We have got to return to God's Instruction for how to tend the planet. Since no one knows the day or hour of sabbath rest, one farm could take it and the next farmer take in next year, and so on so the land all has it rest and the people too, until we can all agree when is the sabbath rests for all. Or one farmer might divide his acreage into seven parcels and just make every seventh one rest a particular year. Composting organically with organic heirloom seeds, NO GMOs! No herbicides! No pesticides! One of those years the farmer should rest every seventh year.

In addition, we all must lively godly lives, or the pests will destroy our crops. People who farm, should speak over their crops and ask that they grow fruitful to God's glory in Jesus Mighty Name! In Jesus Name, command that the pests will not harm your crops! As long as people are living godly lives you will have bountiful harvests, just remember to let the land rest every seventh year. People act like we are to ignore the Lord who gave us the Sabbaths, and just honor: thou shalt not murder, thou shalt not commit adultery, or desire anything that is your neighbors but they ignore the FIRST

COMMANDMENT and that is to HONOR GOD, and particularly to rest as he commands and to worship Him on the Sabbaths. We all should have lives of toil yes, but also lives of rest! If everyone honored God the way He says to, we would all have a day of rest every week, and weeks of rest like every other month, year of rest every seventh year, and JUBILEE every 50th year when all our debts are erased! But mankind is rebelling and we are SUFFERING! Now God taught us that the Sabbaths ARE FOR US, that is lawful to do GOOD and RIGHT always! But otherwise, the Sabbaths are for REST and to GIVE THANKS to Him! It is not an oppressive measure! It is for your REST!

In the Name of Jesus Christ, let the curse pass away as we all come into obedience to our Divine Creator, and let His Blessings and Kingdom Come!

2) Intentional toxins in our food, water, air, hygiene and cosmetic products, and medications. (fluoridation, geoengineering, bioengineering, systematic toxic poisoning in food processing/manufacturing industries, and GMOs are all linked to policies of death and destruction, sterilization, mind control, enslavement, global depopulation, crimes against humanity) https://www.google.com/search?q=toxins+in+our+food%2C+water%2C+air%2C+hygiene+and+cosmetic+products%

2C+and+medications&rlz=1C1GIGM_enUS535US535&oq=t
oxins+in+our+food%2C+water%2C+air%2C+hygiene+and+c
osmetic+products%2C+and+medications&aqs=chrome..69i
57.3704j0j8&sourceid=chrome&espv=210&es_sm=93&ie=
UTF-8 and

https://www.google.com/search?q=toxins+in+our+food%
2C+water%2C+air%2C+hygiene+and+cosmetic+products%
2C+and+medications&rlz=1C1GIGM_enUS535US535&oq=t
oxins+in+our+food%2C+water%2C+air%2C+hygiene+and+c
osmetic+products%2C+and+medications&aqs=chrome..69i
57.3704j0j8&sourceid=chrome&espv=210&es_sm=93&ie=
UTF-
8#es_sm=93&espv=210&q=toxins+in+our+food+causing+c
hronic+illness and

https://www.google.com/search?q=toxins+in+our+food%
2C+water%2C+air%2C+hygiene+and+cosmetic+products%
2C+and+medications&rlz=1C1GIGM_enUS535US535&oq=t
oxins+in+our+food%2C+water%2C+air%2C+hygiene+and+c
osmetic+products%2C+and+medications&aqs=chrome..69i
57.3704j0j8&sourceid=chrome&espv=210&es_sm=93&ie=
UTF-8#es_sm=93&espv=210&q=fluoride+added+to+water

And when you are all getting sick of all kinds of so
many ailments such that even the doctors can't name all
the diseases or diagnose you, such that they tell you, "It's
all in your head" or claim you are not truly ill other than
mentally; then it is time to face the facts **YOU HAVE BEEN**

POISONED! YOU AND YOUR CHILDREN ARE DYING BECAUSE OF TOXIC POISONING! Try to find any facilities that will test for glyphosate and other common toxins in our civilization, carcinogens and more than likely these poisons are to blame!

https://www.blastthetrumpet.org/PublicLetters/AAAUpdatedPublicAlertsMattersofLifeandDeath/Updates053016/Depopulation.pdf   **AND**

https://www.blastthetrumpet.org/PublicLetters/AAAUpdatedPublicAlertsMattersofLifeandDeath/Updates053016/Our%20Creator%20Told%20us%20in%20the%20Holy%20Bible%20Truth%20About%20Drugs.pdf   TOXINS IN YOUR BODY CAUSE EVERY KNOWN SERIOUS TO TERMINAL CONDITION KNOWN TO MANKIND! (INCLUDING INGESTING GMOs THAT ARE DESIGNED TO DAMAGE DNA (CAUSES CANCER AND DEATH IN MANY FORMS - https://www.google.com/search?q=gmos+cause+cancer&rlz=1C1GIGM_enUS535US535&oq=gmos+&aqs=chrome.4.69i57j0j69i59j69i65j0l2&sourceid=chrome&espv=210&es_sm=93&ie=UTF-8) AND IS WHY EVERYTHING FROM INSECTS AND RODENTS TO HUMANS DIE THAT EAT SUCH DEATH FOOD)!!!!!!!!

https://www.google.com/search?client=opera&q=Dr.+John+Rengen+Virapen&sourceid=opera&ie=UTF-8&oe=UTF-

<u>8</u> - whistle blowers try to warn us about the harm we are doing to ourselves and the environment.

https://www.youtube.com/results?search_query=fluoride +documentary&sm=1 - Thankfully more and more people are warning about things that our civilization is doing that are harmful to us.

GMOs are causing diseases, farmers are telling us that corn is affected by GMOs, so we need to preserve non-modified seeds!
https://youtu.be/4NQ6Tw7KXUk?t=5644

http://www.geoengineeringwatch.org/chemtrails-killing-organic-crops-monsantos-gmo-seeds-thrive/ - it's understandable that people imagine chemtrails are being sprayed at high levels, when there are so much use of herbicides and pesticides that ground water is affected, that they just aren't properly recognizing the cause. The herbicides and pesticides that GMOs have been engineered to absorb and still grow are causing problems to us and the world.

https://www.facebook.com/photo.php?fbid=5368734663 41496&set=a.558128970882612.134988.27489751920576

0&type=1&theater - where are all these pollutants coming from, or are they just disinformation statistics.

https://www.youtube.com/watch?feature=player_embedded&v=NlWjkLPanes - people seem to have footage of Chemtrails, not contrails.

http://esa.un.org/unpd/wpp/index.htm - http://www.geoengineeringwatch.org/undeniable-footage-of-jet-aircraft-spraying/ crop dusting people is just one of many depopulation measures now underway. There is footage of something being sprayed that are not contrails, so something is going on.
https://www.facebook.com/notes/michael-swenson/depopulation-by-intent-or-accident/544721958940101

and http://www.livescience.com/37123-fluoridation.html

https://www.facebook.com/photo.php?fbid=760001300700156&set=a.320871874613103.83525.190818870951738&type=1&theater - chemtrails might not be a conspiracy theory after all; there are some who are speaking of geoengineering seriously.
https://www.google.com/search?client=opera&q=bill+gat

es+admits+to+chemtrails&sourceid=opera&ie=UTF-8&oe=UTF-8

https://www.facebook.com/222092971257181/photos/a.223219014477910.57895.222092971257181/454443821355427/?type=1&theater - with all the things harming our heath, can you understand why some people imagine there are harmful pollutions and chemicals in our air?

https://www.google.com/search?client=opera&q=new-study-reveals-children-being-vaccinated-with-toxic-levels-of-aluminum-causing-neurological-damage-and-autism&sourceid=opera&ie=UTF-8&oe=UTF-8 - inoculations linked to neurological damage and autism.

https://www.youtube.com/watch?feature=player_embedded&v=F4R21kZt0rw - herbicides and pesticides are poisoning us.

https://www.google.com/search?client=opera&q=fluoride+linked+to+autism&sourceid=opera&ie=UTF-8&oe=UTF-8 - fluoride linked to autism.

http://humansarefree.com/2014/02/exclusive-leaked-photos-of-chemtrail.html#more - a suspended account?

http://foodbabe.com/2014/05/13/shocking-why-are-doctors-recommending-this-toxic-drink/ - there are just too many harmful ingredients in our processed foods and beverages that don't need to be added there to make the argument that they're there by accident.

http://fluoridealert.org/articles/50-reasons/ - people are suffering!

https://www.google.com/search?client=opera&q=fluoride+lowers+intelligence&sourceid=opera&ie=UTF-8&oe=UTF-8 - fluoride lowers intelligence in studies.

https://www.google.com/search?q=effects+of+fluoride+on+lab+rats&rlz=1C1GIGM_enUS535US535&oq=effects+of+fluoride+on+lab+rats&aqs=chrome..69i57.8908j0j8&sourceid=chrome&espv=210&es_sm=93&ie=UTF-8 - fluoride has harmful effects on lab rats.

http://12160.info/m/blogpost?id=2649739%3ABlogPost%3A1284856 - chemtrails conspiracy has a lot of footage that makes their theories seem quite reasonable despite all the denials. https://www.youtube.com/watch?v=lZaD-H_j3pU

https://www.facebook.com/photo.php?fbid=7228291010 90801&set=a.466484540058593.101715.46621758675195 5&type=1&theater - massive amounts of roundup in our groundwater.

https://www.facebook.com/photo.php?fbid=1434934776 757493&set=gm.615999261829939&type=1&theater - cloud seeding, geoengineering are real, what is controversial is that some are flying chemtrails that are putting harmful chemicals in our atmosphere. http://12160.info/m/blogpost?id=2649739%3ABlogPost% 3A1284856 - chemtrails conspiracy has a lot of footage that makes their theories seem quite reasonable despite all the denials. https://www.youtube.com/watch?v=lZaD-H_j3pU

https://www.facebook.com/photo.php?fbid=1435525430 031761&set=gm.618143754948823&type=1&theater - https://ntrs.nasa.gov/citations/20050214696 that experiments have been done seeming granting chemtrails theorists some credibility.

Do I really have to call for the arrests of all persons who are doing these evils to you and your children? ARREST THEM AT ONCE!!!!!!!! ARREST ALL OF THEM WHO FUND IT, WHO MAKE IT, WHO USE IT TO INTENTIONALLY POISON FOOD, WATER, AIR, etc.! THAT'S RIGHT ARREST ALL the use of herbicides and pesticides PILOTS that are poisoning our food and water supplies! **ARREST THEM ALL! EVERY LAST ONE OF THEM; THEY ARE MURDERING YOU AND YOUR CHILDREN!!!!!!!! AND THEY ARE DOING IT IN GENOCIDAL FASHION!!!!!!!! Just because some of you are not dying immediately, doesn't mean that your life spans aren't being shortened by these practices. We have to make it illegal when it is shortening our lifespans causing chronic ailments such that we really suffer before we die!**

Ted Gunderson told us plainly of the satanic infiltration in our nation and around the world and gave us a couple base locations of those launching poisons against us. https://www.youtube.com/watch?v=gR6KVYJ73AU and if you want to know more:

https://www.google.com/search?q=CHEMICAL+SPILL+IN+FEMA+3+INTENTIONAL&rlz=1C1GIGM_enUS535US535&oq=CHEMICAL+SPILL+IN+FEMA+3+INTENTIONAL&aqs=chrome..69i57.11900j0j8&sourceid=chrome&espv=210&es_sm=93&ie=UTF-8 - when chemicals harm our environment, it's a wonder that round-up get a pass.

https://www.fema.gov/cbrn-tools/key-planning-factors-chemical/prologue/1 - It would seem these laws protects us and ensure poisons would not be used and so deliberately sprayed on our food and into our water supplies.

http://panacea-bocaf.org/chemtrails.htm - there are those that document chemtrails that are not the common contrails.
https://www.youtube.com/watch?v=bmYyvk9Lp-A - those that say they are all contrails are denying the evidence.

http://globalskywatch.com/stories/my-chemtrail-story/chemtrail-information/chemtrail-types.html#IronType - conspiracy theorists have attributed ailments; all their evidence, just can't be explained by contrails, there are just too many videos showing spraying going on.

https://www.youtube.com/watch?feature=player_embedded&v=L5is16A8pfw - so why is the mainstream media saying chemtrails are just a conspiracy theory and that they're all just contrails, when geoengineering through spraying chemicals into our atmosphere is a fact!

https://www.cbsnews.com/news/geoengineering-treatment-stratospheric-aerosol-injection-climate-change-study-today-2018-11-23/ - there are reasons to believe in chemtrails. The public denial that they are all contrails is just a means for them to continue to spray our atmosphere.

https://www.facebook.com/ASheepNoMore/photos/a.225932444186870.49466.225921714187943/562954193818025/?type=1&theater

Apparently, Chemtrails are a global phenomenon. WHEN HAVE YOU KNOWN IN ALL OF HISTORY ALL NATIONS ON EARTH TO AGREE TO ANYTHING? LET ALONE UNIVERSAL GLOBAL RELEASE OF TOXINS AND METALS INTO THE EARTH'S ATMOSPHERE? Chemtrails APPEAR TO SURPASS even the UN membership and authority. WHO ON EARTH CAN MUSTER SUCH A CONCERTED EFFORT? How can ALL NATIONS BE ALLOWING TOXINS AND METALS TO BE GENEROUSLY SPRAYED INTO THE AIR OF THE WHOLE WORLD?! What meeting took place? HOW WAS UNIVERSAL AGREEMENT REACHED ON THIS ISSUE? So far NO ONE IS CLAIMING RESPONSIBILITY, BUT CHEMTRAILS ARE PROLIFICALLY IN USE! As I see it, this should be a very high priority for the public and of a most urgent nature! HOW HAS THIS UNIVERSAL PHENOMENON HAPPENED IN A WORLD WHERE NATIONS FIGHT EACH OTHER

CONSTANTLY! How and why are militaries and governments allowing chemicals and metals to be sprayed generously over the entire world? If ANYONE knows answers to these questions PLEASE COMMENT; even if you only have some theories as to how this can even happen (global spraying of the entire world's atmosphere - WHO HAS THE POWER OR AUTHORITY TO COORDINATE SUCH AN OPERATION? AND HOW DID THEY GET ALL NATIONS ON EARTH TO AGREE TO IT?) - Yes, the rational conclusion is that the vast majority are all CONTRAILS, but it doesn't change the facts that there is so much footage (posted videos) of jets SPRAYING *something* into our atmosphere!

https://www.theguardian.com/environment/2013/sep/19/russia-un-climate-report-geoengineering   AND

https://www.google.com/search?client=opera&q=chemtrails+seen+globally&sourceid=opera&ie=UTF-8&oe=UTF-8 - notice how the media denies chemtrails despite all the evidence and despite our politician's comments on geoengineering:
https://www.youtube.com/watch?feature=player_embedded&v=L5is16A8pfw

But is universal agreement really necessary to spray the entire world with toxic chemicals and metals? http://www.un.org/en/sc/members/ there are only a few world superpowers on earth and all of them UN members; the rest of national air-forces are insufficient to fight against the superpowers (at least in the thinking of the superpower bullies of the world - the rest of humanity COULD and SHOULD stand up to them; at least if they value their own lives and that of their children, friends and the innocent masses on earth); so this could easily be a mandate of the few against the many and still adversely affect the whole world. (thus, universal agreement isn't necessary to implement such a global strike; just agreement of the most powerful). So, if the most powerful are using global warming as an excuse and weather control as a cover for global depopulation; even if other nations disagreed, it could continue. So, then I go on to think are the most powerful nations on earth ruled and governed by people so mentally challenged they would intentionally poison earth's atmosphere; risking not just human life but many species worldwide? Are they so mentally challenged they would poison their own air? As difficult as it is to believe some of the most diabolical maniacs currently ruling/ruining the world right now are elderly; so, they know they are about to die regardless, but would they be that heartless against their own progeny? The wealthy can buy the best food and drink and can even filter the air they breathe, but the poor masses are dying off on average 20 years sooner than those of means. https://www.google.com/search?client=opera&q=poverty +kills+people+20+years+sooner+according+to+statistics&s ourceid=opera&ie=UTF-8&oe=UTF-8

More and more people are presenting with more and more illnesses. When will it be enough? How many must die? How many know that in certain polluted cities, oxygen bars have emerged. Not to long ago we all had safe water to drink, healthy food to eat, and fresh air to breath, but those things are vanishing so quickly today. Replaced with filtered water, increasingly toxic food, and like I said more and more people filtering their air and requiring oxygen from all the pollution.

https://www.youtube.com/watch?v=9wMMJkk6feY - some people imagine the world is overpopulated, some of them are powerful, rich and can have the methods to reduce it.

https://www.youtube.com/watch?v=4EVodX6lCWA - we can build transit that burns seawater and has very little global impact, cooler running motors with no pollution. We can shift the population to clean up the world, mostly recycle and also toward replenishing the world in the form of increased agriculture and aquaculture for more people to contribute to our food supplies.

https://www.youtube.com/watch?v=1T-62uxbMBM - more removed videos detailing crimes against humanity.

Poisoning the air is about the most self-destructive thing I have ever seen; but there is no doubt it is occurring. God tells us that poisoning our planet only results in having poison to drink. (Jer 9:14,15) GET YOURSELF

TESTED! Glyphosate for one, and known carcinogens for two! REGARDLESS of the reason, the so-called global ruling elite ARE CLEARLY DEMONSTRATING they are too incompetent or too greedy to hold office. Even if it's a depopulation agenda, would they be so insane as to poison their own food, water and air (or so mentally challenged that they don't realize they are doing so)? Sadly, with blunders like Chernobyl and Fukushima we see people do things all the time that are a real danger to their own existence and life on the planet. But I want to know just HOW ANYONE convinced them to POISON OUR ATMOSPHERE in ANY amount (ROUNDUP IS POISONOUS), and themselves in the process. How could someone say GLOBAL WARMING! and scare ANYONE so badly, that they agree POISONING OUR AIR AND WORLD is a good idea? If the nations of the world (so called ruling elite) don't stop spraying our food and ground water immediately, STOP MODIFYING DIVINE DESIGNS- NO GMOs!, the citizens of the world should depose those self-destructive persons who are doing so by force ASAP and demand herbicide and pesticide free produce worldwide. Even if more people have to grow our crops to make it happen! I don't know about you all, but I like farming, living in the country, growing food!

http://www.geoengineeringwatch.org/how-do-we-stop-the-spraying/ - Dane Wigington is maintaining undeniable footage of chemtrails and that the media and government is denying it's taking place. Geoengineering is a fact! How often has these two entities lied to the public?!

http://www.truthandaction.org/epa-tested-deadly-pollutants-people-obama-administrations-agenda/ - ever noticed how that lab tests routinely DO NOT TEST FOR POISONS like glyphosate, AND other POLLUTANTS that are harmful to us? WHY NOT! Our health is adversely affected by all these toxic substances!

Citizens of the world! The so called ruling elite are so https://www.blastthetrumpet.org/PublicLetters/AAAUpdatedPublicAlertsMattersofLifeandDeath/Updates053016/Mentally%20Challenged.pdf that they THINK the SOLUTION is to KILL BILLIONS OF CITIZENS WORLDWIDE! Apparently, they ALL don't KNOW our CREATOR! (most likely because they have ignored the plethora of ubiquitous https://www.blastthetrumpet.org/PublicLetters/AAAUpdatedPublicAlertsMattersofLifeandDeath/Updates053016/Evidence%20of%20GOD.pdf and https://www.blastthetrumpet.org/PublicLetters/AAAUpdatedPublicAlertsMattersofLifeandDeath/Updates053016/The%20Sufferings%20of%20Christ.pdf as such, IN THEIR ARROGANCE, they THINK there are no other https://www.blastthetrumpet.org/PublicLetters/AAAUpdatedPublicAlertsMattersofLifeandDeath/Updates053016/SOLUTIONS.pdf When I personally have received methods directly from our CREATOR how to address all the major problems facing humanity worldwide! If people would just come to know our Eternal Creator, He would provide solutions for everything mankind is facing from generation to generation! As such, I can tell you THEIR POLICIES OF DEATH AND DESTRUCTION ARE THE ABSOLUTE WORST IDEAS (MOST EVIL) EVER TO MANIFEST ON EARTH AND THESE WICKED PEOPLE MUST BE ARRESTED WHEREVER AND WHENEVER THEY ARE FOUND! https://www.blastthetrumpet.org/PublicLetters/ AAAUpdatedPublicAlertsMattersofLifeandDeath/Updates0 53016/Depopulation.pdf   and   https://www.blastthetrum pet.org/PublicLetters/AAAUpdatedPublicAlertsMattersofLi feandDeath/Updates053016/Treatise%20on%20Greed%20 and%20Corruption.pdf   and https://www.blastthetrumpet.org/PublicLetters/AAAUpda tedPublicAlertsMattersofLifeandDeath/Updates053016/Br ainwashing.pdf   and https://www.blastthetrumpet.org/PublicLetters/AAAUpda tedPublicAlertsMattersofLifeandDeath/Updates053016/PR OPAGANDA.pdf and   https://www.blastthetrumpet.org/PublicLetters/AAA UpdatedPublicAlertsMattersofLifeandDeath/Updates0530 16/satanism%20is%20a%20danger%20to%20everyone%2 0even%20those%20who%20practice%20it.pdf   and   https ://www.blastthetrumpet.org/PublicLetters/AAAUpdatedP ublicAlertsMattersofLifeandDeath/Updates053016/Evoluti on%20and%20Atheism%20Intertwined%20Cults%20of%20 the%20Insane.pdf   They obviously have chosen complete https://www.blastthetrumpet.org/PublicLetters /AAAUpdatedPublicAlertsMattersofLifeandDeath/Updates 053016/STUPIDITY.pdf   and INSANITY! BUT THAT IS NO REASON THE REST OF THE POPULATION ON EARTH

SHOULD SUFFER AND
DIE!!!!!!!! https://www.blastthetrumpet.org/PublicLetter
s/AAAUpdatedPublicAlertsMattersofLifeandDeath/Update
s053016/Acknowledging%20the%20Eternal%20Creator%2
0Takes%20No%20Faith%20It%20is%20Scientific%20Fact.p
df and https://www.blastthetrumpet.org/PublicLetters/
AAAUpdatedPublicAlertsMattersofLifeandDeath/Updates0
53016/HOW%20TO%20KNOW%20TRUTH%20IN%20A%20
WORLD%20OF%20LIES.pdf and https://www.blastthetr
umpet.org/PublicLetters/AAAUpdatedPublicAlertsMatters
ofLifeandDeath/Updates053016/Creation%20V%20Evoluti
on%20Use%20Your%20Intelligence%20to%20Recognize%
20INTELLIGENCE.pdf

https://www.google.com/search?client=opera&q=fluoride
+linked+to+alcoa&sourceid=opera&ie=UTF-8&oe=UTF-8 -
the release of metric tons of toxic chemicals into our
breathable atmosphere is our water systems is an overt
attack on all of our lives. It's only after we develop chronic
and terminal conditions that we then realize it was what
we did, thinking there was nothing wrong until we got ill.
It's then we realize what our civilization is doing to us, is
harming us! When will we fight back?! Please pray this
incredible evil stops IMMEDIATELY. Thank you.

http://www.geoengineeringwatch.org/geoengineeringwat
ch-weather-update-september-13th-2014/ -

Geoengineering is still experimenting on our weather, we don't know what we're doing and still forging ahead regardless of the consequences.

http://www.geoengineeringwatch.org/monsanto-and-the-geoengineers-a-lethal-mix-for-humanity/ - Roundup, herbicides and pesticides need to cease, we need to go back to seed the way God made, (NO GMOs) and more people labor for biodiversity. We need to resume growing crops and use farming methods in ways that are not harmful to us!

http://www.geoengineeringwatch.org/dialog-with-a-geoengineering-insider/

http://www.geoengineeringwatch.org/dialog-with-a-geoengineering-insider-part-2/ - one has to decide just how much information on the internet is disinformation and examine their reported evidence for themselves.

I wish people would unite and depose the evil lunatics attacking our lives and destroying our planet! https://www.blastthetrumpet.org/PublicLetters/AAAUpdatedPublicAlertsMattersofLifeandDeath/Updates053016/Strategies%20of%20War.pdf and https://www.blastthetrumpet.org/PublicLetters/AAAUpdatedPublicAlerts

MattersofLifeandDeath/Updates053016/Most%20Wanted%20Criminals%20part%201.pdf - part 1 of 3 read them all.

DON'T LET BRIBE TAKING propagandists or "scientists" convince you that geo-engineering; spraying of toxic particulates into our atmosphere, is in any way acceptable! ARREST THE LIARS WITH THE MURDERERS! http://www.geoengineeringwatch.org/cooling-towers-for-weather-modification-absolute-nonsense/ (Thank you Dane for standing up against these liars and mass murderers!) Too often these days, whistle blowers are being ignored by a naive and trusting (albeit sick and dying) populace; who think there is no way those who own the mints are this evil or that they could find people willing to sell their souls for their blood soaked bills, but the people who are the multi-trillionaires of the world are so evil and arrogant that they INTENTIONALLY create depressions and recessions to make people DESPERATE enough to violate their own consciences for some of their "money" that THEY mint on demand. Geoengineering has footages of aircrafts spraying substances into our atmosphere, we would like an explanation as to what those jets are disposing upon us!

Are we really going to let egomaniacs who want to play with our atmosphere and thereby all life on planet earth continue to demonstrate their incredible ignorance and/or evil insanity to our harm? http://www.geoengineeringwatch.org/geoengineeringwatch-weather-update-september-6th-2014/

http://www.geoengineeringwatch.org/climate-engineered-dustbowl-in-the-west/

https://www.blastthetrumpet.org/PublicLetters/AAAUpdatedPublicAlertsMattersofLifeandDeath/Updates053016/Depopulation.pdf - Depopulation, when you calculate all the ways it's occurring, it just doesn't seem to ALL be by accident.

https://www.blastthetrumpet.org/PublicLetters/AAAUpdatedPublicAlertsMattersofLifeandDeath/Updates053016/Most%20Wanted%20Criminals%20part%202.pdf - part 2 of 3

https://www.blastthetrumpet.org/PublicLetters/AAAUpdatedPublicAlertsMattersofLifeandDeath/Updates053016/Conspiracy%20Theories%20or%20Plain%20Truth.pdf - conspiracy theories or plain truth!

https://www.blastthetrumpet.org/PublicLetters/AAAUpdatedPublicAlertsMattersofLifeandDeath/Updates053016/Police%20State%20Prison%20State%20Big%20Business%20Modern%20Slavery.pdf - if you're a hired mercenary of the genocidal oppressors of the world the time has come for you to choose sides! either you will continue to accept the blood-soaked bills as your pay from the satanic NWO psychopaths OR you will side with humanity and save our world and mass billions from slavery, death and destruction by helping us depose these evil, selfish, greedy, arrogant, wicked, perverse; so-called wanna-be "rulers of the world"!

Let us suppose that these chem-trails are not harmful in the least, even though that's doesn't seem to be the case at all, what's to keep someone from putting something harmful instead? The way Jim Jones assassinated all his cult members was to get them to habitually drink the Kool-Aid until the day it was POISONED to their doom! I DON'T WANT ANYONE SPRAYING ANYTHING OVER MY HEAD REGARDLESS IF THEY CLAIM IT ISN'T HARMFUL!

3) Fracking and the seemingly endless quest of greedy, corrupt persons to burn non-renewable, polluting fossil fuels (crude and coal mostly) as opposed to crossing over to non-polluting renewable energy like solar preferably and hydro-electric motors for all transit purposes.

https://www.facebook.com/photo.php?fbid=1015209982 0827708&set=a.136077452707.110998.12185972707&typ e=1&theater - when will people quests for money stop trumping our health. States are reporting water contamination from fracking.

https://www.google.com/search?q=FRACKING+dumping+c ontaminated+waste+water+in+our+oceans&rlz=1C1GIGM enUS535US535&oq=FRACKING+dumping+contaminated+ waste+water+in+our+oceans&aqs=chrome..69i57.18760j0 j8&sourceid=chrome&es_sm=93&ie=UTF-8 - Fracking is just not worth the environmental damage done to our planet!

https://www.facebook.com/ncconservationnetwork/phot os/a.186094151477.139245.17270171477/101521210834 26478/?type=1&theater - fracking is not harmless.

https://www.facebook.com/photo.php?fbid=1015220975 4447708&set=a.136077452707.110998.12185972707&typ e=1&theater - what's going to happen when we kill off the planet by all this pollution? We need to keep the earth clean and green for our children and their children! Stop focusing so much on money and instead focus on life and quality of life, for us all.

https://www.google.com/search?client=opera&q=north+dakota+waste+water+fracking&sourceid=opera&ie=UTF-8&oe=UTF-8 - toxic waste water from fracking is enormous!

https://www.youtube.com/results?search_query=gasland&sm=1 - Watch this documentary.

http://ecowatch.com/2013/12/06/3-islands-go-100-renewable-energy/ I say use solar powered waste incinerators and refineries and

http://www.popularresistance.org/rural-ny-communities-use-fracking-waste-to-de-ice-roads/ and stop polluting our ground water; poisoning us and our planet.

http://commonsensecanadian.ca/bcyukon-first-nation-bans-fracking-finds-impacts-outweigh-benefits/ some people are taking care of lives instead of profits and

https://www.google.com/search?q=aerial+view+of+fracki
ng&rlz=1C1GIGM_enUS535US535&espv=210&es_sm=93&
tbm=isch&tbo=u&source=univ&sa=X&ei=TqSoUovrPIv4oA
SO7IBI&ved=0CC4QsAQ&biw=1067&bih=701 take a good
look at fracking and see if it's worth the desolation to our
planet and

https://www.google.com/search?q=aerial+view+of+fracki
ng&rlz=1C1GIGM_enUS535US535&oq=aerial+view+of+fra
&aqs=chrome.2.69i57j0l5.10342j0j8&sourceid=chrome&e
spv=210&es_sm=93&ie=UTF-
8#es_sm=93&espv=210&q=fracking+chemicals+found+in+
groundwater - we're killing our planet and if it goes, we
go.

http://www.youtube.com/watch?feature=player_embedd
ed&v=dzx7UXzK_z4 - it's about LIFE, not money!

http://www.youtube.com/watch?feature=player_embedd
ed&v=n4HYZQDgQbM - it's about LIFE, not money!

http://vimeo.com/65533675 - stop fossil fuel burning.
Build solar powered waste incinerators and refineries.

Giant magnifying glass that follows the path of the sun and heats turbines for power! These same structures can melt our waste; so, no more dumps on land and in oceans! The refineries can be built so that they heat from solar magnification goes into a sealed glass enclosure and any waste can be recycled and reused or can be filtered before it's emitted into our atmosphere. KEEP OUR WORLD CLEAN AND GREEN FOR OUR LIVES AND THE LIVES OF ANY FUTURE GENERATIONS!

http://www.youtube.com/results?search_query=flammable+tap+water&sm=1 - toxic tap water! flaming!

http://www.usatoday.com/story/money/business/2014/01/05/some-states-confirm-water-pollution-from-drilling/4328859/ - water pollution in four states from fracking.

http://www.dailykos.com/story/2014/01/15/1269879/-Spill-proves-again-that-cozy-ties-between-government-and-coal-corporations-sticks-it-to-people - regulators in our government should not have ties to the markets they regulate! Too many shows that corruption costs our lives.

https://www.google.com/search?client=opera&q=Alberta +reluctant+to+treat+poor+health+conditions+fracking&so urceid=opera&ie=UTF-8&oe=UTF-8 - people lives are being compromised by fracking! We don't need fossil fuels for transit any longer!

https://www.google.com/search?client=opera&q=limo+th at+runs+on+salt+water&sourceid=opera&ie=UTF-8&oe=UTF-8 - sports cars that run on water!

https://www.google.com/search?client=opera&q=sports+ car+that+run+on+water&sourceid=opera&ie=UTF-8&oe=UTF-8

https://www.facebook.com/photo.php?fbid=7341090566 02034&set=a.170189839660628.41537.159993367346942 &type=1&theater

https://www.facebook.com/photo.php?fbid=7365326563 59674&set=a.170189839660628.41537.159993367346942 &type=1&theater - more and more important information keeps disappearing from the Internet. Babies with deformities linked to fracking.

http://ecowatch.com/2014/01/31/investing-dirty-fuels-bad-idea/ - people have to stop investing in outdated technology that's BAD FOR US, CAUSES POLLUTION, and shortens lifespans! Invest in the CLEAN AND GREEN

TECHNOLOGIES that are being suppressed by these people!

https://www.youtube.com/watch?feature=player_embedded&v=Be9XncS8tiA - corruption in the courts, enables the oil companies to get away from properly paying for the harm and deaths they cause to other people. GET OFF OF PETROL DEPENDENCY! It's outdated technology! It HARMS our earth and ourselves!

https://www.google.com/search?client=opera&q=coal+ash+drained+dan+river&sourceid=opera&ie=UTF-8&oe=UTF-8 - more harm to the environment.

https://www.google.com/search?client=opera&q=oil+sands+tailings+in+water&sourceid=opera&ie=UTF-8&oe=UTF-8 - fracking leaves behind a huge amount of toxic waste, it isn't worth it!

https://www.facebook.com/dailykos/photos/a.416444264254.190398.43179984254/10152231145919255/?type=1&theater - hypocrite!

https://www.facebook.com/photo.php?fbid=8314788068
78212&set=a.293872007305564.89304.138121286213971
&type=1&theater - more death and environmental
damage due to our unnecessary dependence on fossil
fuels. LET'S CROSSOVER TO CLEAN AND GREEN
TECHNOLOGIES NOW!

ONLY THOSE MAKING MONEY FROM THIS ASSAULT
ON OUR WORLD AND HUMANITY AND ALL LIFE ON THE
PLANET FALSELY CLAIM THERE IS NO DANGER OR
POLLUTION FROM THIS PRACTICE. USE YOUR EYEBALLS!
The toxic liquids are out in the open in large pools of death
to evaporate into the air; to seep into the ground; leakage
and seepage waste not only inadvertently destroys land
and water and life therein but it is INTENTIONALLY being
poured onto streets! Proponents for this rape of our land
in the endless pursuit of crude and coal constantly hide
behind "the economy" but **I list ways to employ people
and build a strong economy many times over by doing
things that DO NOT DESTROY THE WORLD AND ALL LIFE
ON THE PLANET here:**
https://www.blastthetrumpet.org/PublicLetters/AAAUpda
tedPublicAlertsMattersofLifeandDeath/Updates053016/S
OLUTIONS.pdf - We have got to cross over to from fossil
fuel burning now while we still have the manpower to
effectively change our manufacturing processes. Too
much manufacturing is occurring elsewhere on earth.
Hydro-electric transits, burning pollution free water!

PEOPLE NEED TO REALIZE THAT MONEY IS GENERATED BY WHOEVER IS IN POWER! Always has been that way, so there is enough money to do whatever good things the people decide to do. Clean water by building water precipitators and evaporators. So, we have more than enough potable water! Crossover to hydro-electric motors for all transit so no more pollution from exhausts. Employ people to build solar-powered waste incinerators/refineries to end dumping into oceans. Clean up the oceans via self propelled tug boats that clean the waste from the oceans via solar powered collectors as discussed in https://www.youtube.com/watch?v=du5d5PUrH0I and https://www.youtube.com/watch?v=ROW9F-c0kIQ

http://www.theguardian.com/environment/2013/dec/14/fracking-hell-live-next-shale-gas-well-texas-us?commentpage=1 - too many people are irresponsibly POLLUTING OUR PLANET! We have got to stop toxic waste or the planet could end up with so much toxic pollution, all of us could be suffering from POISONS in our ecosystem! We have got to demand a higher standard of toxic free living! Most consumers have no choice but to burn fossil fuels because manufactures are not giving them affordable options, so harm to our environment needs to be dealt with by the suppliers to consumers. Consumers will stop using fossil fuels when manufacturers provide clean and green affordable alternatives. Hydro-electric motors are affordable alternatives.

IF THE REST OF HUMANITY WANTS TO GIVE THE MOUNTAIN TOP REMOVERS AND FRACKING EXPLOITERS A HUGE BREAK THEN THEY SHOULD OFFER THEM LIFETIME IMPRISONMENT FOR THEIR CRIMES AGAINST HUMANITY AND ALL LIFE ON THE PLANET OR TO SPEND ALL THOSE GREEDY PROFITS THE REST OF THEIR NATURAL LIVES PURIFYING THE RIVERS THEY HAVE POLLUTED, REPLANTING THE FORESTS THEY HAVE DEMOLISHED, AND DETOXIFYING EVERYTHING THEY CONTAMINATED IN THEIR UNBELIEVABLE GREED!!!!!!!! Remember there is enough money in the world to hire people to do ANY GOOD THING WE ALL DECIDE TO DO!

https://www.google.com/search?client=opera&q=the-coal-industry-a-bad-santa-leaving-lumps-of-coal-in-your-lung-and-nothing-in-your-stocking-absurdity-today-ep-47&sourceid=opera&ie=UTF-8&oe=UTF-8 - coal industry, lumps of coal in your lungs.

Activists who have fought against these wicked persons, should be promoted to paying jobs in the EPA who have the oversight of all the people in these companies who have assaulted our world and all life on the planet! The greedy persons in these companies should have to clean every slew, every pond, every river to the satisfaction of these activists by scientific testing until such environs and ecologies are suitable for life (potable water) once again.

Methods of public service I suggest for all these companies that have devastated our earth and oceans include things like: black to white water filtration naturally, creating new rivers in the mountains and arid regions, even deserts by constructing huge water precipitators, ending the concern for potable water by building huge aqueducts that bring saline waters from the ocean into places like death valley and there build inexpensive huge evaporators that use the natural sunlight and heat to separate the salt and fresh water. (many continents can do this as there are hot regions that are at or below sea level all around the world) desalination evaporators can be constructed around shorelines all over the world, I go on to suggest that these companies can fund huge solar concentrators and collectors as well as participate in the crossover from the archaic fossil fuel burning engine to solar boosted hydro-electric motors available today. (Automobiles that do not need to be plugged into their greedy grid, that do not pollute in any way) and I further detail that the sea of plastic waste in our oceans can be gathered and recycled (as well as new methods of maximizing waste recycling and refinement). I get very specific of how the consequences for their evil actions could be rectified and they could even end up feeling good about themselves when they realize their actions have changed from sowing death and destruction to sowing life, peace and

prosperity. http://www.godempowersyou.com/documentation/Ideas.pdf

LET ME BE VERY CLEAR IF YOUR LEADERS, GOVERNMENTS, ARE NOT FOR THE ARRESTS OF ALL SUCH PERSONS IN ALL SUCH COMPANIES THEN THEY HAVE BECOME YOUR MORTAL ADVERSARIES! THEIR GREED HAS REACHED SUCH A LEVEL THEY ARE THREATENING YOUR LIVES AND ALL LIFE ON THE PLANET! IT THEN FALLS TO CITIZENS TO UNITE AND ARREST THEM ALL AND HOPEFULLY THEN PUT IN PLACE SUCH CITIZENS FROM AMONG YOURSELVES THAT WILL IMPLEMENT THESE SANE REFORMS TOWARD LIFE AND LIVING IN PROSPERITY AND GOOD HEALTH!

People MUST be for HEALTH for us all and for the planet! It is past time for the greed that is suppressing new tech to be REMOVED. If the greed of the few is preventing them from crossing over to hydro-electric, then they must be removed. It is a CRIME when your greed threatens the lives of others NEEDLESSLY!

4) soft-kill slow death technologies - experiments in weather modification are taking place by governments all over the world. https://www.google.com/search?client=opera&q=soft+kill+slow+death+technologies+conducted+by+military&sourceid=opera&ie=UTF-8&oe=UTF-8 and https://www.google.com/search?client=opera&q=weather+manipulation+is+a+fact&sourceid=opera&ie=UTF-8&oe=UTF-8

What can I say to convince you if your own eyes don't? The military has tested these weapons and the results are clear, they are lethal. Invisible directed RF energy weapons that penetrate your wood houses can be aimed at anyone on planet earth and most do not have the equipment necessary to detect it. These weapons result in all kinds of deaths, mostly cancers, but also mental delusions (can cause insanity and other so called "mental illnesses" as a result of damage to the brain.

https://www.google.com/search?client=opera&q=soft+kill+slow+death+technologies&sourceid=opera&ie=UTF-8&oe=UTF-8 - governments seemed to be preoccupied with sowing death and destruction, so there are new technologies harming us that many are not even aware exist.

These weapons damage organs and cause chronic conditions. They are invisible to the naked eye and can be used from satellites and towers on earth toward unsuspecting "enemies of state" they are a method of assassination that makes the death seem like "natural causes". Hence those using them refer to them as "soft kill, slow death" weapons. I have seen persons in the US government; by remote viewing and by dreams and revelations from our Creator, who want these murderers exposed and these weapons destroyed, referring to their murders/assassinations in this manner (soft kill, slow death) as opposed to hard kills (assassinations by sniping, explosives, drones and such). When they don't want to make a martyr of someone, poisoning, seduction leading to poisoning www.blastthetrumpet.org, and these directed energy weapons are the preferred methods of death by these evil persons. When an enemy of state (the greedy lunatics who profit from their warmongering ways- https://www.google.com/search?client=opera&q=soft+kill+slow+death+technologies&sourceid=opera&ie=UTF-8&oe=UTF-8) reaches a level of influence that actually poses a real threat then the hard kill methods are employed (as in the past: JFK, Martin Luther King Jr. etc.).

https://www.blastthetrumpet.org/PublicLetters/AAAUpdatedPublicAlertsMattersofLifeandDeath/Updates053016/False%20Flags.pdf - false flags to manipulate the public to going to war against each other to facilitate the greed of the few at the expense of our lives.

https://www.blastthetrumpet.org/PublicLetters/AAAUpdatedPublicAlertsMattersofLifeandDeath/Updates053016/Current%20Technologies.pdf - current technologies being suppressed by people who just want to leave things the way they are because of GREED! they're rich, who cares what happens to all the rest of us!

LOOK! I HAVE SHOWN YOU JUST SOME OF THE WAYS YOUR LIVES AND ALL LIFE ON THE PLANET ARE ALREADY UNDER ATTACK AND WARRANTS THE IMMEDIATE ARRESTS OF THE PEOPLE CURRENTLY RULING/RUINING THE WORLD!!!!!!!! IT IS TIME HUMANITY UNITED AGAINST ALL OF THEM BECAUSE THEY HAVE OPENLY STATED THEY ARE FOR YOUR DEATHS AND ARE IMPLEMENTING PROCEDURES TO MAKE THAT HAPPEN WORLDWIDE!!!!!!!!

From crime and corruption at the highest levels, down to municipalities. It is a lack of conscientious people with integrity that all these things are taking place. We MUST Return to Our Lord and Savior, JESUS CHRIST, or our nation and the world is failing due to CORRUPTION.

https://www.blastthetrumpet.org/PublicLetters/AAAUpda
tedPublicAlertsMattersofLifeandDeath/Updates053016/Ba
d%20Cops.pdf   - Thank God for all the ones doing their
best to do their jobs with integrity!

Perhaps the very worst crimes against humanity
fall under the category of brainwashing, indoctrination,
intentional deception, LIES!
https://www.blastthetrumpet.org/PublicLetters/AAAUpda
tedPublicAlertsMattersofLifeandDeath/Updates053016/Br
ainwashing.pdf   that is causing people to present
themselves as if they
are https://www.blastthetrumpet.org/PublicLetters/AAA
UpdatedPublicAlertsMattersofLifeandDeath/Updates0530
16/Mentally%20Challenged.pdf   Evidence mounts that
deceiving little children in public education and media
leads to criminal behavior that adversely affects all life on
the planet; as the information in the following links plainly
show:

https://www.blastthetrumpet.org/PublicLetters/AAAUpda
tedPublicAlertsMattersofLifeandDeath/Updates053016/PR
OPAGANDA.pdf   and
https://www.blastthetrumpet.org/PublicLetters/AAAUpda
tedPublicAlertsMattersofLifeandDeath/Updates053016/Tr
eatise%20on%20Greed%20and%20Corruption.pdf

and https://www.blastthetrumpet.org/PublicLetters/AAA UpdatedPublicAlertsMattersofLifeandDeath/Updates0530 16/satanism%20is%20a%20danger%20to%20everyone%2 0even%20those%20who%20practice%20it.pdf that brings

about https://www.blastthetrumpet.org/PublicLetters/AA AUpdatedPublicAlertsMattersofLifeandDeath/Updates053 016/STUPIDITY.pdf and https://www.blastthetrumpet. org/PublicLetters/AAAUpdatedPublicAlertsMattersofLifea ndDeath/Updates053016/Blasphemy%20and%20Idolatry. pdf for the purpose of https://www.blastthetrumpet.org/PublicLetters/AAAUpda tedPublicAlertsMattersofLifeandDeath/Updates053016/D epopulation.pdf and the only remedy

is https://www.blastthetrumpet.org/PublicLetters/AAAU pdatedPublicAlertsMattersofLifeandDeath/Updates05301 6/Why%20We%20All%20Need%20Instructions%20From% 20Our%20Creator%20to%20Live%20By.pdf to be taught everywhere; especially to the children; so they mature into such persons of integrity; necessary for a peaceful, strong, stable, prosperous society; as I propose: https://www.blastthetrumpet.org/PublicLetters/AAAUpda tedPublicAlertsMattersofLifeandDeath/Updates053016/S OLUTIONS.pdf and until then all who love freedom and especially all who love GOD need to https://www.blastthetrumpet.org/PublicLetters/AAAUpda tedPublicAlertsMattersofLifeandDeath/Updates053016/Th ere%20is%20No%20PreTribulation%20Rapture%20Prepar e%20for%20War.pdf teach the Truth!

https://www.blastthetrumpet.org/PublicLetters/AAAUpda
tedPublicAlertsMattersofLifeandDeath/Updates053016/Ev
idence%20of%20GOD.pdf Evidence of God

and https://www.blastthetrumpet.org/PublicLetters/AAA
UpdatedPublicAlertsMattersofLifeandDeath/Updates0530
16/The%20Sufferings%20of%20Christ.pdf   The Sufferings
of Christ

and https://www.blastthetrumpet.org/PublicLetters/AAA
UpdatedPublicAlertsMattersofLifeandDeath/Updates0530
16/Truth%20Sets%20and%20Keeps%20Us%20Free.pdf   T
ruth sets and keeps us free

and https://www.blastthetrumpet.org/PublicLetters/AAA
UpdatedPublicAlertsMattersofLifeandDeath/Updates0530
16/islam%20is%20Evil%20part1.pdf   islam is evil and any
worldview that calls for nonstop murder and
maltreatment of other citizens

and   https://www.blastthetrumpet.org/PublicLetters/AA
AUpdatedPublicAlertsMattersofLifeandDeath/Updates053
016/The%20Dangers%20of%20Remaining%20Ignorant%20
About%20the%20Times%20We%20Are%20Living%20In.pd
f the dangers of living in ignorance about the times we are
living in and

https://www.blastthetrumpet.org/PublicLetters/AAAUpda
tedPublicAlertsMattersofLifeandDeath/Updates053016/Bl
asphemy%20and%20Idolatry.pdf   blasphemy and idolatry

and https://www.blastthetrumpet.org/PublicLetters/AAA
UpdatedPublicAlertsMattersofLifeandDeath/Updates0530
16/Warning%20America%20Has%20Been%20Infiltrated%2

0and%20Invaded.pdf America, we've been invaded and our nation is under attack and (THE WARNING IF IT FAILS TO SHOW IS COVERED REDUNDANTLY) https://www.blastthetrumpet.org/Public Letters/AAAUpdatedPublicAlertsMattersofLifeandDeath/U pdates053016/THE%20PLANNED%20DEMORALIZATION%2 0OF%20AMERICA.pdf   - our nation is under attack ideologically, America's Christian Heritage is targeted because of personal greed and corruption; in order to get us to fail and fall.

https://www.blastthetrumpet.org/PublicLetters/AAAUpda tedPublicAlertsMattersofLifeandDeath/Updates053016/G AIN%20AND%20RESTORE%20FREEDOM.pdf - gain and restore freedom!

Do you understand what makes all these things so especially heinous is not that they all are causing disease, death and destruction; but brain and organ damage INTENTIONALLY DESIGNED AND COUPLED WITH https://www.blastthetrumpet.org/PublicLetters/AA AUpdatedPublicAlertsMattersofLifeandDeath/Updates053 016/Brainwashing.pdf
and https://www.blastthetrumpet.org/PublicLetters/AAA UpdatedPublicAlertsMattersofLifeandDeath/Updates0530 16/PROPAGANDA.pdf
for https://www.blastthetrumpet.org/PublicLetters/AAAU

pdatedPublicAlertsMattersofLifeandDeath/Updates05301 6/Depopulation.pdf **and enslavement of mind controlled societies by evil psychotic, megalomaniacs who think it is their right to maltreat everyone else on earth in these horrific ways!** https://www.blastthetrumpet.org/PublicLetters/AA AUpdatedPublicAlertsMattersofLifeandDeath/Updates053 016/Most%20Wanted%20Criminals%20part%201.pdf

They are making the population sick and dying and then they profit from it by giving us toxic medications in the name of healthcare! PROFITING FROM MAKING US SICK AND DYING! SICK, CHRONICALLY AND TERMINALLY ILL!

http://www.geoengineeringwatch.org/climate-engineering-toxic-fallout-and-northeastern-us-tree-die-off/ **- the people in charge are morbidly fascinated with death and destruction, but their delusions of grandeur prevent them from reigning in their own insanity!** Desires to rule the world, control the weather, and other ambitions to play like gods and goddesses, blinds them to the fact that their endeavors are destroying our planet and are a real threat to all life! We, the people, MUST unite to depose these ignorant lunatics before they succeed in causing runaway extinction events and killing off billions of us in the process!

If you agree that the persons doing these horrible things to mass millions of us on earth must be arrested immediately; empower me to do so in the United States! At the very least, make a flyer, a meme, share my notes, tell your neighbors, SPREAD THE WORD UNTIL THE WHOLE NATION IS DEMANDING THE ARRESTS OF THESE INSANELY EVIL PERSONS! If your governments won't arrest these criminals, ARREST THEM! PEOPLE OF THE WORLD YOUR LIVES ARE UNDER ATTACK! YOU AND YOUR CHILDREN ARE ACTIVELY BEING POISONED AND ENSLAVED! Please research all my notes they have loads of evidence, documentaries, scientific studies, etc. etc. etc. until you are as ready as I am to arrest the people responsible for the satanic NWO depopulation agenda; not by standing around in a disgruntled crowd but by arming yourselves in massive unity and deposing these insanely evil persons by force!

The attacks on my life, led me to discover that the lives of the general population are under increasing attacks in all these ways. People go into hospitals and die at the hands of doctors and nurses and no one investigates! Millions go missing each year and when their corporations commit crimes in which people are injured or dead, they do not get compensated. Wealthy people consider that they are above our laws. The poor basically have no recourse. If we lived in a moral and ethical society, instead of one built on greed, there would be no way other citizens can just kick any other citizens out of their homes into the streets just by their exorbitant demands for rent. Primary landlords are able to extort people who cannot pay their greedy demands and are turned out homeless to die in the elements! Everyone needs to be protected by law to be home owners by right or other people cannot kill you or endanger your lives and that of your children just by increasing your rent beyond want you can afford. WAGES ALL OVER THIS WORLD ARE NOT KEEPING UP WITH "THE COST OF LIVING" greedy globalism (wealthy people buying up all the real estate and resources of the world) causes inflation to kill of the poorest among us in economic genocides!

https://www.blastthetrumpet.org/PublicLetters/AAAUpdatedPublicAlertsMattersofLifeandDeath/Updates053016/The%20Weapons%20of%20our%20Warfare.pdf - the weapons of our warfare, keep them all until our Lord Jesus Christ returns!

More and more they are developing unmanned drones that are capable of dealing out death to anyone they are programmed against. So, it only takes a few lunatics to deal out death and destruction against anyone on earth. If you are developing robots or drones for the military, just imagine if such was not just against your enemies but against your loved ones and then stop enabling this technology for anyone!

What to do when the world is run by greedy, corrupt, ignorant, incompetent, wicked, delusional, diabolical psychopaths

LET ME BE VERY CLEAR, YOU AND YOUR CHILDREN, AND THE LIVES OF BILLIONS WORLDWIDE IS CURRENTLY and INCREASINGLY UNDER ATTACK RIGHT NOW!!!!!!!! If you and your children are not already sick, it will happen to you in the future if we don't change these things poisoning us and our planet NOW!

Those that have socially engineered the word by controlling the issuance of national currencies worldwide. (these persons are wealthier than the multi-billionaires of the world, because they issue the credits that nations, politicians included work for) These ARE the families of the satanic NWO and their agendas and plans ARE CURRENTLY UNDER IMPLEMENTATION WORLDWIDE. This is not a "conspiracy theory"; these are the FACTS, the OBSERVABLE FACTS! We need people in power that value the lives of us all! That do not sell us out for money! That do not cover up scandals, and skew scientific findings that tell us they are killing us whether it's in slow ways or by dangerously poisoning the environment. We have to find people that value our lives and cease in all these ways that are killing us in the name of "population management"

to govern = to control

The insidious part of these slow kill, soft death methods are their ability to assassinate citizen under the guise of plausible denial. The ability to target people of their choosing and make them look as if they died of natural causes, gives murderers and assassins reasons to try to get away with their crimes, until God brings EVERYONE to Justice. People who are working on these technologies need to be aware that anyone can be victimized, even them and should stop developing them!

I ENCOURAGE READERS WHO KNOW THESE THINGS ARE FACTS ABOUT PSYCHOLOGICAL, CHEMICAL AND BIOLOGICAL WARFARE BEING USED ON THE MASSES WORLDWIDE TO PROVIDE ADDITIONAL LINKS IN THE COMMENTS SECTION OF THESE NOTES OF REFERENCES AND DOCUMENTARIES ON THESE TOPICS. THANK YOU.

https://www.blastthetrumpet.org/PublicLetters/AAAUpdatedPublicAlertsMattersofLifeandDeath/Updates053016/Conspiracy%20Theories%20or%20Plain%20Truth.pdf - conspiracy theories or plain truth.

https://www.blastthetrumpet.org/PublicLetters/AAAUpdatedPublicAlertsMattersofLifeandDeath/Updates053016/St rategies%20of%20War.pdf - strategies of war comes in many different ways.

https://www.blastthetrumpet.org/PublicLetters/AAAUpdatedPublicAlertsMattersofLifeandDeath/Updates053016/Depopulation.pdf - depopulation

The ultra wealthy and their global agendas for RADICAL depopulation are in black and white, in the media and even set in stone. The REST OF THE WORLD NEEDS TO TAKE THEIR PLANS FOR EXTERMINATING BILLIONS GLOBALLY MOST SERIOUSLY!!!!!!!!

http://vigilantcitizen.com/latestnews/new-strange-2014-addition-georgia-guidestones/ - monument calling for radical depopulation.

https://www.google.com/search?client=opera&q=agenda+21+united+nations&sourceid=opera&ie=UTF-8&oe=UTF-8 - sustainable future includes depopulating the world.
https://www.google.com/search?client=opera&q=agenda+21+united+nations+depopulation&sourceid=opera&ie=UTF-8&oe=UTF-8

https://www.google.com/search?client=opera&q=project+paperclip&sourceid=opera&ie=UTF-8&oe=UTF-8 - how the Nazis came into our nation.

Social Engineering under antichrists is oppressive, cruel, and when examined their crimes against humanity are unconscionable; but what is more amazing than these crimes is the fact the population on earth suffering under this madness hasn't united against the people responsible and deposed them worldwide.

psy-ops - psychological warfare - mass brainwashing - mass programming:

https://www.google.com/search?q=Dod+psyops+experiments+to+control+the+public&rlz=1C1GIGM_enUS535US535&oq=Dod+psyops+experiments+to+control+the+public&aqs=chrome..69i57.11295j0j8&sourceid=chrome&es_sm=93&ie=UTF-8 - not just our military have been subjected to it, but the public.

https://www.google.com/search?q=Dod+psyops+experiments+to+control+the+public&rlz=1C1GIGM_enUS535US535&oq=Dod+psyops+experiments+to+control+the+public&aqs=chrome..69i57.11295j0j8&sourceid=chrome&es_sm=93&ie=UTF-8#q=Dod+MIT+mind+control - research the ways mass pys-ops have been implemented against the masses.

chemical and biological warfare:

https://www.facebook.com/photo.php?fbid=1020262216
6732006&set=a.1746188891180.99333.1132505953&type
=1&theater - "Lyme Disease" is named after the town of
"Lyme, Connecticut," where the 1970s outbreak began --
across the "Long Island Sound" from Lab257.

"Lyme" is just a bacterium (aka Borrelia burgdorferi (Bb)) --
akin to syphilis.

https://science.howstuffworks.com/science-vs-
myth/what-if/lyme-disease-bioweapon.htm - what people
don't understand about diseases now as opposed to the
naturally occurring ones that existed in the past, is that
now some of these diseases have been ALTERED to be
MORE CONTAGIOUS, MORE HARMFUL. It's not that
mankind is creating these diseases from scratch, they are
MODIFYING THEM! into bio-weapons. There are patents
of record on virtually all pandemics currently harming us!
THEY ALLEGE they were only experimenting on these
viruses AFTER they became pandemics with an agenda to
create vaccines BUT THE PATENTS SHOW THEY examined
and altered the viruses BEFORE they became pandemics.

PEOPLE NEED TO DO THEIR OWN RESEARCH
BECAUSE THE POWERS THAT BE LIE TO US! The media also
tends to report what the wealthy conglomerates tell them
to. YOU HAVE TO INVESTIGATE THE PATENTS! And
companies like you-tube censoring people for so called

medical misinformation NEED TO STOP DOING THAT, because the FDA and WHO are NOT TO BE TRUSTED as 100% giving us INFALLIBLE INFORMATION, ONLY GOD ALMIGHTY IS PERFECT! What is considered "medical misinformation" by them ISN'T necessarily so! Antidotes for poison are administered both intravenously, topically and by ingestion, SO PEOPLE WHO ARE SUFFERING FROM CHRONIC CONDITIONS MAY WELL IMPROVE THROUGH internal and external hydro-therapies, especially if they test positive for carcinogens in their systems! People take medications with water and so everyone already takes a method of internal hydro-therapy, I'm just saying that it needs to be NON-TOXIC! Beneficial medications! and to address any TOXINS in our system! Perhaps by chelation or some other kind of antidotes, so you-tube STOP CENSORING ME and other citizens who are only speaking truthfully and according to our own God-given conscience!

http://www.nytimes.com/2013/06/15/us/researchers-find-biological-evidence-of-gulf-war-illnesses.html?_r=2 - Please don't be among the boneheads who CHOOSE to remain ignorant about this fact. BIOLOGICAL WARFARE CANNOT BE CONTAINED; governments engaging in biological warfare are in fact committing the most heinous acts of all time; as it is genocide against the entire human race on earth!

LOOK INTO THESE PATENTS!

https://nypost.com/2023/11/16/news/pathogens-labeled-hiv-and-ebola-found-inside-illegal-chinese-owned-biolab-in-california/ - researching deadly diseases on American soil.

http://www.naturalnews.com/046290_Ebola_patent_vaccines_profit_motive.html - not so naturally occurring diseases are killing us!

http://www.rense.com/general13/inve.htm - doesn't anyone else find it fascinating that with the advent of GMOs there are suddenly zoonotic pandemics attacking us in record fashion?

https://www.google.com/search?q=biological+warfare+plum+island&rlz=1C1GIGM_enUS535US535&oq=biological+weapons+plum+isl&aqs=chrome.1.69i57j0.9953j0j8&sourceid=chrome&es_sm=93&ie=UTF-8 - why does the people of the world allow these maniacs to run loose on earth? people so deranged they are creating biological weapons against the entire global population belong confined; if not executed for their crimes against humanity!

http://www.rense.com/general38/made.htm - There are many researchers who claim all of these "zoonotic pandemics" in recent history are just bio-engineered weapons designed to depopulate the world. They claim the patents of record and government documents prove it.

greed and corruption:

http://www.amazon.com/Population-Control-Corporate-Owners-Killing/dp/0062359894 - another book pointing out how corporations greedy for profits are harming and killing us!

https://www.blastthetrumpet.org/PublicLetters/AAAUpdatedPublicAlertsMattersofLifeandDeath/Updates053016/Treatise%20on%20Greed%20and%20Corruption.pdf - Greed and Corruption are attacking many worldwide, not just in America as more and more people cannot keep up with the cost of living. Economic warfare against the vast majority on earth is causing them to die prematurely.

DO PEOPLE COMPREHEND MY FURY AS YET?! I and hundreds of millions on earth are/have been SUFFERING INTENSELY due to people so VILE, so GREEDY, so INSANELY DEGENERATE and CORRUPT, they have constructed a global network of oppression, destruction and death! THIS

IS WHY these wicked persons are called satanists! When you focus on death and destruction, that a sure sign the devil is ruling your life! THIS IS WHY their policies of destruction, suffering, death, oppression against the masses is referred to as the satanic NWO. **IT IS EVIL ALMOST BEYOND DESCRIPTION!!!!!!!!**

Like islam and so called muslim extremists who murder people not belonging to their cult, simply because there are not enough decent citizens to ARREST them all! (or who aren't being armed and empowered to do so by governments) That's satanic! and if the devil succeeds in making any population so corrupt that law and order fails, then it is a sad day for everyone, because anyone can be murdered and is how genocides occur!

These persons are ACTUALLY INTENTIONALLY attacking the global population with poisons in our food, water, air, hygiene products, cosmetics, VIRTUALLY EVERYTHING WE INGEST OR PUT ON OUR SKIN OR EVEN BREATH, and doing it in a way THEY ACTUALLY PROFIT from our slow and painful demises due to the chronic sicknesses THEY ARE CAUSING in modifying our food so much that people are suffering from gastrointestinal complications; cancers; weakening and overtaxing our immune systems such that we develop painful chronic conditions that lead to severe and terminal illnesses (THEY

ARE CAUSING A LIFE OF PAIN AND SUFFERING AND PREMATURE DEATH AND TRICKING THE MEDICAL PRACTITIONERS INTO HELPING THEM ACHIEVE IT, THROUGH DRUG PROMOTIONS AND MEDICAL PROCEDURES THAT ARE NOT DESIGNED TO HEAL OR EVEN ADDRESS THE ROOT CAUSES which is in fact that the population is sick due to poisoning, GMOs, toxins (chemical/biological warfare) that are killing us all. They're all just trusting in their ability to hide behind the public's ignorance and claim all of these are just the way of our civilization, trying to claim they didn't engineer it this way.

The psychological warfare is accomplished through brainwashing in public education making all these people THINK they are "educated" when in fact they have been subjected to clever mass mind control techniques that make them THINK they are doing a good thing pushing toxins in medications, toxins in inoculations, toxins in chemo and radiation therapies (ALL OF WHICH LEADS TO MORE SUFFERING AND A PREMATURE DEATH). And further tricking the public into thinking GMOs are supposed to be a good thing when they KNOW perfectly well it causes DEATH, suffering and death! So, when I say the public is under direct psychological, biological and chemical attack worldwide, I mean it!

https://www.youtube.com/watch?v=P7BqFtyCRJc -
water that kills. Fluoride-gate!
https://www.google.com/search?client=opera&q=Fluoride
-gate&sourceid=opera&ie=UTF-8&oe=UTF-8

https://www.youtube.com/watch?v=KNCGkprGW_o -
food that kills.

     GMOs that cause insects bellies to burst and die!
and Americans wonder why they get instant bloating after
eating that crappy toxic frankenfood! IT IS TOXIC BY
GENETIC ENGINEERING!!!!!!!! IT KILLS LIVING
ORGANISMS, THESE IDIOTS ARE DESTROYING LIFE ON
EARTH!!!!!!!! THEY ARE CORRUPTING THE FOOD
SUPPLY!!!!!!!! If I could I would mount an army right now
and PERMANENTLY SHUT DOWN monsanto and all
GENETIC MODIFICATION on earth! These nearly brain-
dead ignoramuses actually think they can mess with the
fabric of life and not have it destroy the complex web of
Divinely designed bio-interdependence on earth! totally
MAD!!!!!!!! corrupting the food supply on earth SO THAT
IT CAUSES DEATH is about the most self-destructive thing
ANYONE CAN DO!!!!!!!!

https://www.youtube.com/watch?v=A_YWwCCXGPk - time and again studies show that these GMOs are causing us harm!

PEOPLE STOP THESE GMO's BEFORE THEY SUCCEED IN CORRUPTING THE ENTIRE FOOD CHAIN ON EARTH!!!!!!!!

http://articles.mercola.com/sites/articles/archive/2015/03/08/altered-genes-twisted-truth-gmo.aspx - GMOs are destroying organic crops worldwide due to crosspollination. They are not containable! We don't want the world's food corrupted by these bio-hazardous seeds!

http://www.naturalnews.com/048892_Altered_Genes_Twisted_Truth_biotech_science_fraud_Jane_Goodall.html - Altered Genes, Twisted Truth by Steven M. Druker. Biotech and corrupt governments are harming us, provably.

WHEN POLICIES OF DESTRUCTION AND DEATH ARE BEING IMPLEMENTED, THE GOVERNMENTS OF THE WORLD ARE RUN BY PEOPLE EITHER TOO EVIL OR TOO CORRUPT TO BE IN POWER!!!!!!!! When they write laws devaluing the lives of others, they are too ignorant to realize it devalues their own life! When they fund research into chemically poisoning and biologically attacking others with illnesses, THEY THINK they will hold antidotes and cures, while the billions suffer and die. Realize that chemical and biological warfare CANNOT BE CONTAINED the world itself becomes a quarantine zone when so much toxins and bio-engineered weapons start causing runaway extinction events!!!!!!!!

https://www.law.cornell.edu/uscode/text/50/chapter-32 - chemical and biological warfare is a fact. And yet with the advent of GMOs suddenly pandemics are increasing among us worldwide!

PANDEMICS are spreading worldwide!!!!!!!! SUFFERING, DISEASE and DEATH THEY CAUSED!!!!!!!! WHY HASN'T the public united to stop these idiots before they destroy life on earth!!!!!!!!

https://www.google.com/search?q=HIV%2C+lyme+global+epidemics&rlz=1C1GIGM_enUS535US535&oq=HIV%2C+lyme+global+epidemics&aqs=chrome..69i57.12031j0j8&sourceid=chrome&es_sm=93&ie=UTF-8 - There are people claiming all these recent pandemics are bio-engineered in keeping with depopulation agendas.

https://www.google.com/search?q=releasing+genetically+modified+mosquitoes&rlz=1C1GIGM_enUS535US535&oq=releasing+genet&aqs=chrome.0.0j69i57j0l4.4935j0j8&sourceid=chrome&es_sm=93&ie=UTF-8 - in the guise of stemming pandemics, they have actually increased ailments. It may seem like a good idea, to release genetically modified mosquitoes that are designed not to bite us and spread diseases and tend to breed only males but HAS ANY PROOF OF THESE CLAIMS BEEN DONE AND STUDIED?! What I don't understand is why can't we trap mosquitoes en masse. Instead of insecticides, build a device that lures them into it with their favorite food, and make it like a giant solar powered bug zapper for mosquitoes. Strictly the mosquito's favorite food so it only traps them! What impact does it have if we eliminate them such that fish and birds that eat them have to find another food supply? When mankind meddles with the ecosystem of earth, through poisons, pesticides, herbicides, focusing on death and destruction, it has shown that the unseen ramifications only result in more death and destruction. We all have to focus on life, and returning to our Eternal Creator and living righteously. He tells us plagues, pestilences, diseases, are a result of Divine Consequences for disobedience. In other words, people trying to play god or goddesses on earth are causing increasing death and destruction. The entire world needs to repent and return to our Eternal Creator. He is the only one Wise and Knowledgeable enough to control the entire ecosystem on earth in a good way. Even so, this world is subject to decay because we all have sinned. Our Creator can and will perfect His Creation just as He tells us in the Holy Bible. Until then, we need to focus on Life and quality of life, and stop sowing death and destruction in rebellion against Him and His Commandments.

PEOPLE THEY ARE TELLING US THEY INTEND TO DEPOPULATE THE WORLD AND THEY ARE ATTACKING US AND OUR CHILDREN AND YOU ARE NOT FIGHTING FOR YOUR OWN LIVES, WHY NOT! STAND UP SPEAK OUT UNITE SO THAT YOU AND YOUR PEOPLE ARE HEARD! THOSE WHO CONTROL THE WORLD BANK, THE PERSONS AT THE HIGHEST LEVELS THAT CONTROL NATIONAL CENTRAL BANKS WITH THEIR TIES TO THE satanic mad, maniacs of the world - the Rockefellers, Rothschilds, ALL THE FAMILIES THAT HAVE UNLIMITED WEALTH DUE TO THEIR CONTROL OF ISSUING NATIONAL CURRENCIES ARE RESPONSIBLE FOR THE FUNDING OF THESE PROGRAMS. All of these things responsible for our illnesses NEED TO BE HELD RESPONSIBLE by those MAKING THESE THINGS harming us and our children. Billions of lives are at stake.

DEATH ON A GLOBAL SCALE IS INCREASING, SHORTENED LIFE SPANS OF SUFFERING AND OPPRESSION, INTENTIONAL STERILIZATION OF THE MASSES, these WICKED PEOPLE ARE ATTACKING YOU AND YOUR CHILDREN RIGHT NOW!!!!!!!!

https://www.google.com/search?q=mass+sterilization+pr
ograms+conducted+via+the+food+and+water+supply&rlz=
1C1GIGM_enUS535US535&oq=mass+sterilization+progra
ms+conducted+via+the+food+and+water+supply&aqs=chr
ome..69i57&sourceid=chrome&es_sm=93&ie=UTF-8 -
these people must be stopped before they leave the entire
planet barren!!!!!!!!

https://www.google.com/search?q=the+western+world+l
ower+fertility+rates&rlz=1C1GIGM_enUS535US535&oq=t
he+western+world+lower+fertility+rates&aqs=chrome..69i
57.9735j0j8&sourceid=chrome&es_sm=93&ie=UTF-8 - the
wealthiest people invest in these things that lower birth
rates (cause sterility) and increase death rates. Millions are
dying prematurely due to chronic and terminal illnesses
that these people CAUSED!

Our food, air, water, hygiene products, cosmetics,
medications, inoculations, are ALL being tampered with by
persons funding global depopulation agendas! MEANING
THESE WICKED PEOPLE ARE INTENTIONALLY MAKING US
SICK, STERILE, SO THAT WE SUFFER HELLISHLY AND DIE
PREMATURELY AND CANNOT HAVE CHILDREN!!!!!!!!

We must arrest those responsible and reverse
everything they are doing to us! Clean air! Clean water
and food supplies with organic, non-GMO, no herbicides
and pesticides, hygiene products and cosmetics that are
NOT HARMFUL TO US!

STOP LETTING THESE PEOPLE HIDE BEHIND THE "I DIDN'T KNOW" DEFENSE OF FEIGNED IGNORANCE AND STUPIDITY. PEOPLE! THEY WROTE THE LAWS ON THIS CRAP! THEY GOT THE PATENTS! IT IS CHEMICAL AND BIOLOGICAL WARFARE AND THEY ARE USING IT AGAINST YOU! THE TIME OF PEACEFUL PROTEST IS PAST! DO YOU WANT TO WATCH YOUR CHILDREN BEING BORN WITH MORE AND MORE DEFECTS; CONSIGNED TO LIVES OF PROLONGED SUFFERING DUE TO THESE EVIL PEOPLE IN POWER? If the answer is no, you need to TELL EVERYONE, SPREAD THE WORD and unite against the satanic NWO families that have a stranglehold on us all by their control of the world bank! DEPOSE THESE MURDERERS before they succeed in destroying life on planet earth completely!!!!!!!! (God will intervene of course but HOW MANY will suffer and die before you FINALLY take up arms against the few insane lunatics attacking us all?!!!!!!!!) Arrests need to be made! THEY MUST BE FORCEFULLY ACCOSTED AND TOLD IN NO UNCERTAIN TERMS THEY ARE ALL UNDER ARREST FOR THEIR CRIMES AGAINST HUMANITY. WE HAVE TO SHUT DOWN the corrupt corporate plutarchy destroying our nation and the world and we have to shut it down NOW!!!!!!!!

Due to their corruption, we are polluting the world with fossil fuels STILL, when viable solutions of running transit on WATER exist! WITH NO POLLUTION!!!!!!!! Hydro-electric crossover is being held up due to the present corruption. Healthy organic, bio-diverse farming practices, EVERYTHING THAT IS GOOD IS BEING

INTENTIONALLY SUPPRESSED TO MAKE YOUR LIVES ONE OF SLAVERY, SUFFERING AND DEATH BY THE MOST WICKED, DELUSIONAL EGO-MANIACS EVER TO WALK PLANET EARTH!!!!!!!! Tell these people we MUST cross-over to clean and green technologies and STOP LETTING THEM SUPPRESS them for their OWN GREED!

The list is almost endless of 21st century technologies being suppressed by the corrupt, greedy, criminals currently ruining our nation and the world! We could all be living prosperously or virtually all of us!

https://www.blastthetrumpet.org/PublicLetters/AAAUpdatedPublicAlertsMattersofLifeandDeath/Updates053016/Current%20Technologies.pdf - current technologies! better future!

They COULD just be honest and tell people that until we succeed in terraforming the uninhabitable regions on earth, only have 2-3 children; for those that desire them. They COULD just be honest and tell the world that we need to stop clear cutting rain forests immediately and look at the benefits they provide by sustainable care. They COULD be pro-life and pro-quality of life for all. BUT NO! instead, they have been subjecting us all to polices of oppression, destruction and death, pillaging and plundering the earth and hording its resources all to themselves, making the rest of us slave away all our days! BRAINWASHING, DECEPTION, FALSE FLAGS, WARS, CHEMICAL AND BIOLOGICAL WARFARE, ALTERED FOOD, BEVERAGES, EVEN WATER AND AIR!!!!!!!!

PLEASE BECOME INFORMED!!!!!!!! PLEASE READ MY NOTES, WATCH THE DOCUMENTARIES; SPREAD THE WORD!!!!!!!!

https://www.blastthetrumpet.org/PublicLetters/AAAUpdatedPublicAlertsMattersofLifeandDeath/Updates053016/By%20Divine%20Commandment%20I%20Am%20Sounding%20the%20Trumpet%20the%20Alarm%20to%20Prepare%20for%20War.pdf - we have to unite on all fronts and PREACH THE GOSPEL until EVERYONE has heard it worldwide. We have to unite and champion good and moral values that lead to manufacturing items that are HEALTHY! We need to reverse what they are doing to us! Healthy economy begins with ensuring everyone has a right to affordable housing and cost of living! NO MORE CITIZENS MAKING OTHER PEOPLE HOMELESS JUST BY THEIR GREED AS A LANDLORD! There are just too many UNCONSTITUTIONAL PRACTICES still allowed by the wealthy against the poor!   IT'S WRONG!

At the highest levels, it is all just rich people getting together with other rich people and conspiring against the rest of us for their own personal gains; but they have gone INSANE in their arrogance and disdain for the general population on earth!

https://www.youtube.com/watch?v=YoimzqUqm8E - this family of antichrists took over not just the military industrial complex and the Federal Reserve (privately owned central bank finance - a direct act of WAR against what our founders fought to be FREE FROM) in America, but education/indoctrination https://www.youtube.com/watch?v=b7lHva6HAlc, the UN https://www.youtube.com/results?search_query=rockefel ler+funding+the+UN, WHEN PRIVATE INDIVIDUALS CONTROL THE ISSUANCE OF CURRENCY THEY CONTROL EVERYTHING! And so, YOU ARE SUFFERING TODAY UNDER THEIR INSANITY AND UNBRIDLED GREED!!!!!!!!

https://www.youtube.com/watch?v=dOqDM6ypiPk - not just politicians are to blame, it's the money corrupting them! The power behind the visible government, are the ULTRA WEALTHY controlling them!

If these devils remain in power, they will continue to turn children into perverts for their own sick, disgusting, perverse abuse! EVERYTHING THESE PEOPLE REPRESENT IS EVIL!!!!!!!! They all have been commanded by the Lord to REPENT OF THEIR EVIL, PERVERSE and WICKED WAYS!

https://www.blastthetrumpet.org/PublicLetters/AAAUpda tedPublicAlertsMattersofLifeandDeath/Updates053016/Fr eedom.pdf - we must regain our American Christian Heritage and regain freedom thereby!

IF YOU HAVE READ MY CITATIONS AND WATCHED THE DOCUMENTARIES; YOU HAVE JUST SEEN FACTUAL HISTORY UNFOLDING TO THE REALITY WE ARE WITNESSING TODAY WHICH IS THE AGENDA TO ENSLAVE THE MASSES AND DEPOPULATE THE WORLD BY DECEIVING

THEM IN PUBLIC EDUCATION AND MEDIA AND WITH FALSE FLAGS TO DISTRACT THEM FROM THE FACT THAT IN EVERY WALK OF LIFE TODAY THAT THERE ARE BRAINWASHED PERSONS WHO ARE CARRYING OUT THE PLAN TO ENSLAVE AND DEPOPULATE THE WORLD!!!!!!!! MANY SUCH PERSONS WORKING IN big pharma, gmo's, manufacturing, sales, education, healthcare, police and military powers, ARE SERVING VERY EVIL AGENDAS WITHOUT EVEN REALIZING THAT IS WHAT THEY ARE DOING; SOME ACTUALLY THINKING THEY ARE DOING A GOOD THING BECAUSE THE PSY-OPS USED ON THEM ARE THAT EFFECTIVE!!!!!!!!

Now to be sure most everyone working in these areas are to be respected and treated properly as they are only doing what they are given to do, but everyone needs to realize there we all are tempted in various ways and that we all need the Good Lord in our lives by His Holy Spirit to resists the devil and our own selfish tendencies. God helps us all maintain integrity in all walks of life; those who are rebelling against God, are evil so remember His Words on that, because God doesn't lie! (Jn 3:15-21) We need HONORABLE PERSONS in these walks of life (government, police and militant powers, education and media - positions of influence!) or society could crumble and fall.

https://www.google.com/search?q=how+the+government+uses+mass+psy-ops+against+the+public&rlz=1C1GIGM_enUS535US535&o

q=how+the+government+uses+mass+psy-
ops+against+the+public&aqs=chrome..69i57.15743j0j8&s
ourceid=chrome&es_sm=93&ie=UTF-
8#q=how+the+government+uses+mass+psy-
ops+against+the+public&tbm=vid - there are patents for
programming the masses through media.

https://www.google.com/search?q=coining+keywords+in+
media+to+control+public&rlz=1C1GIGM_enUS535US535&
oq=coining+keywords+in+media+to+control+public&aqs=c
hrome..69i57.9655j0j8&sourceid=chrome&es_sm=93&ie=
UTF-8 - media programming the masses.

I am just giving you a few examples, BUT EVERYTHING employed by these people against the masses has been researched SO DO NOT LET THEM GET AWAY WITH FEIGNING IGNORANCE AS AN EXCUSE FOR THEIR CRIMES!!!!!!!! If televisions are in every home and free PROGRAMMING, it is FOR A REASON!!!!!!!! YOUR FOOD, YOUR WATER, YOUR BEVERAGES, YOUR "EDUCATION", YOUR ENTERTAINMENT, YOUR DRUGS, EVEN THE VERY AIR THAT YOU BREATHE HAS ALL BEEN THOROUGHLY RESEARCHED BY THESE PEOPLE THAT WANT TO CONTROL THE WAY YOU THINK FROM THE TIME YOU ARE BORN!!!!!!!!

The only real solution for the world at this point is to UNITE and DEPOSE them and REPLACE them with SANE PERSONS who are for LIFE, YOUR LIFE, HEALTH and PROSPERITY on planet earth, and the only people I know that are even remotely trustworthy in such positions are those who KNOW they will give an account for their deeds to GOD ALMIGHTY HIMSELF!!!!!!!! Which is why I urge ALL souls to come to KNOW the ONE TRUE GOD, as the FIRST STEP in TRUE UNITY, and in the VIRTUES NECESSARY to depose the entrenched evil threatening and attacking us all!!!!!!!! I'm not talking about manmade religions; I'm talking about KNOWING OUR ETERNAL CREATOR PERSONALLY BECAUSE YOU HUMBLY OBEYED HIS COMMANDMENTS! (Matt 28:18-20, Acts 2:38-39, John 14:6-26, Romans 8:8-15)

IN OTHER WORDS, "COME LORD JESUS, COME! WE NEED YOU!" And yet even so it may not look well now, He tells me many will yet repent and believe on Him! God is PATIENT! Not wanting anyone to perish! Let us all hope and pray so many repent before His return that the whole world shouts for His Return!

https://www.blastthetrumpet.org/PublicLetters/AAAUpdatedPublicAlertsMattersofLifeandDeath/Updates053016/JESUS%20SAVES.pdf - Jesus Saves.

https://www.blastthetrumpet.org/PublicLetters/AAAUpdatedPublicAlertsMattersofLifeandDeath/Updates053016/JESUS%20CHRIST%20Sets%20Us%20Free.pdf - Jesus Sets Us Free!

https://www.blastthetrumpet.org/PublicLetters/AAAUpdatedPublicAlertsMattersofLifeandDeath/Updates053016/GAIN%20AND%20RESTORE%20FREEDOM.pdf - Gain and Restore Freedom!

When the Nazis entered our nation shortly after WWII, that's when our nation started replacing Biblical Creation, with the lame theory of evil-u-shun! In just a few generations, coerced indoctrination has brainwashed our nation almost entirely! Darwin's theory of evolution is impossible; it shouldn't be taught anywhere! Not in our schools for sure. READ MY BOOK ON IT! https://www.amazon.com/Theory-Evolution-Impossible-Michael-Israel-ebook/dp/B0D93C76WN/ref=tmm_kin_swatch_0 It is OBVIOUS nonsense! About the only reason anyone believes in it is due to the fact it was drummed into their brain over and over again throughout all their years of education/brainwashing! Lies when told often enough from childhood become believable. SEE YURI BEZMENOV's full interview! That is, if you can still find it anywhere on the Internet.

Hollywood Contributing to the Corruption

In just my short lifetime, I can remember *Father Knows Best, Leave it to Beaver, Andy Griffith, The Donna Reed Show*, and a whole slew full of family values shows. And now? It's rife with murder, sexual immorality, and hardly anything that is of moral, commendable character. Yes, if you search for them, you can still find *When Calls the Heart* on the Hallmark channel, or other commendable shows, but by and large modern media and pop culture have become increasingly corrupted with immoral behavior.

The modern standard isn't moral or ethical, the standard is something detestable. It should be the other way around, where someone has to search for murder and mayhem, immoral behavior, if they are in the mood for violence and the standard fare should be something like *The Chosen* or other Biblically based themes. We have to come back to living righteously and morally, or we will all suffer for choosing to become a wicked and immoral civilization. We must have Biblically minded people in all walks of society or corruption is inevitable. Yes, I know people that even take fault with *The Chosen* but Biblically based programming while none of us are perfect is a FAR BETTER endeavor than the sexually immoral, murderous programming of today.

Violence and filth are what is wrong with our nation. When Hollywood champions those values it cause our society to become more and more corrupt. Corruption is what caused every empire in the world to collapse. Departing from God, in Deuteronomy 28, is what we are suffering from. It's God's way of calling us back to him pronto!

When we view Hollywood, we can see it is becoming more and more global in scope, less and less Godly American Heritage values, we should all be praying that it reverses this trend. The rest of the world needs to get on board with those Godly values that made our nation great, we shouldn't join in the corruption that makes the world so hard and terrible.

A particular note when researching this topic is to glance at how many patents went into TV PROGRAMMING with an eye toward programming you. Full interview with Yuri Bezmenov the four stages of ideological subversion (1984) and Hollywood Red Scare. Once these became prevalent, they have swayed us away from our American Christian Heritage. We should be enrolled against anything our enemies wanted and to do our best to MAINTAIN our AMERICAN CHRISTIAN HERITAGE instead.

While I don't agree with everything Alan Watts says, His take on television programming, designed to program our minds, is interesting. We have to be aware that cultural programming is designed where muslims actually THINK their god, wants them to murder others! That where the rest of us need to draw the lines between religion and OUTRIGHT CRIME, which is what islam teaches in doctrine and practice. READ MY BOOK ON IT! https://www.amazon.com/Save-World-islam-Michael-Israel-ebook/dp/B0D9C5PJ2H/ref=tmm_kin_swatch_0

We have to draw the line between what is TRUTH and what isn't. Jesus Christ plainly said HE IS THE TRUTH! He is the WAY to ETERNAL LIFE and He alone! All of His Instructions are based on loving Him and each other! They are in NO WAY evil! Instead, all FINAL JUDGMENTS are made by Him, He is the One who determines if you ever repented of your evil ways and get to live with Him in Heaven or not! EVERYONE MUST REPENT OF ALL WICKED WAYS, and ALL MUST LIVE GODLY LIVES by the presence of the ONE TRUE GOD, JESUS CHRIST, IN YOUR LIFE BY HIS HOLY SPIRIT! He gives all truly repentant people who get baptized in His Name, HIS HOLY SPIRIT, whereby WE KNOW THE LIVING GOD!

The Holy Bible is Provably and Verifiably Divinely Inspired! Read my book on it! https://www.amazon.com/Bible-Provably-Verifiably-Divinely-Inspired-ebook/dp/B0D9138S7Z/ref=tmm_kin_swatch_0 PROVABLY AND VERIFIABLY DIVINELY INSPIRED means it comes from our Eternal Creator! The literary TRUTH by which all other opinions stand of fall upon past, present and future! NEVER BELIEVE ANYONE OVER THE CONTENTS OF THE HOLY BIBLE! Those are the Words our Eternal Creator has spoken and recorded and made public to all nations. Since He is Eternal, He is alive right now and forever to confirm those are His Words to each of us.

https://www.accordingtothescriptures.org/prophecy/353prophecies.html all these prophecies were given by God before He came in the flesh to tell us about Himself, and proved Himself beyond reasonable doubt! The Septuagint was compiled BEFORE He came in the flesh! THIS MAKES THE IDENTITY OF THE ONE TRUE GOD A MATHEMATIC CERTAINTY! The Holy Bible is PROVABLY DIVINELY INSPIRED! https://biblearchaeology.org/research/new-testament-era/4022-a-brief-history-of-the-septuagint

Since God came in the flesh He told everyone how to know Him and told His Disciples to go and tell everyone else! EVERYONE MUST REPENT AND BELIEVE ON JESUS CHRIST THE ONE TRUE GOD AND GET BAPTIZED IN HIS NAME! Acts 2:38-39 praying to receive His Holy Spirit, Luke 11:13 whereby we KNOW GOD! Jn 14:20-26

This is what OUR PROGRAMMING on television NEEDS TO BE ABOUT until EVERYONE KNOWS HIM and is learning from Him how to face whatever trials and tribulation still exist, because of how many still DO NOT KNOW HIM! Everyone should be witnessing of our Lord Acts 1:8, 4:12, 10:34-43 and praying for His Return! There needs to be all kinds of Programming and Education about God and His Word and how that Christians are still being MARTYRED for the Faith thousands of years later to this very day! muslims are mostly the evil ones doing it because their allah is just another name for the devil! but there are evil dictators also persecuting Christians without any justification. https://www.google.com/search?client=opera&q=how+many+christians+are+persecuted+every+year&sourceid=opera&ie=UTF-8&oe=UTF-8   If they put the real crimes people are facing today instead of all these fantasy films, then maybe just maybe, more people would repent of their wicked ways and so escape the Divine Consequences of the Lake of Fire.

      Ultimately God Almighty has even His Patience tried by deliberately wicked people who refuse to repent and learn to live righteously; that Despite Him showing Himself and telling everyone how to know Him AND His Commandments to REPENT FROM ALL EVIL, there are just some that refuse to do so! Those people will NOT inherit His Forgiveness or the Ability to Live Forever in Heaven, those unrepentant people who die in their sins inherit God's Wrath, the Lake of Fire! Rev 21:8 So, when you hear you need to Repent and Believe on the Lord Jesus Christ and get Baptized in His Name, YOU NEED TO OBEY IT POST HASTE!

China's Failed One Child Policy

I could hardly talk about population management without mentioning China. Population management is taking place all over the world, decreasing birth rates and increasing death rates and the general population is SUFFERING from what these governments, powerful people are doing to us. China is one of the most heavily populated countries so you can see what we're all headed for if we don't get Christian based thinkers in power that know God and people learn to marry as God intends and raise children responsibly so that God will direct you in your life's purpose and you will come up with solutions for each and every generation. Polygamous marriages of muslims, marrying children at just 9 years of age have the islamic population having more children irresponsibly. It's no wonder the government of China cracked down upon riotous muslims who were not adhering to these agendas. I'm not saying China's persecution of religious people in their nation is commendable at all. Especially the Christians in their nation.

But they wanted to prevent over-population with their one child policy, but they let couples choose to abort girls in favor of having a son and now China has a surplus of millions of men! And that has created the problem of trafficking brides into their nation, apparently mostly from North Korea. They should have just mandated, whether it was male or female was born first to each couple, that was their child. So now they have up to three children, apparently. The bottom line is population is maintained naturally so long as everyone acknowledges God and marries only one wife as He commands. God knows how many people to send into the earth, population management by others is not one of their responsibilities especially when it means genocides against us and/or harming our lives, or sterilization!

IF THEY ARGUE THAT OVERPOPULATION is a problem, THEY COULD offer MONETARY INCENTIVES since money is minted by them on demand! That anyone accepting voluntary sterilization, gets something like full tuition and board for their years of college/professional training. They could just be honest that's their position instead of maltreating us all so obviously! We have megalopolises spanning entire nations and in just a few thousand years of history), so those claiming we've been around much longer, like tens of thousands of years, or millions, are absolutely living in fantasy land. God is telling us the absolute truth in the Holy Bible and everyone can know Him and ask Him if those words in the Holy Bible are His Words. They are! And our Eternal Creator doesn't lie!

Instead of leading us to kill each other in wars, and instead of making us all sick, instead of oppressing us with slave wages that aren't enough to live on, they could maintain the population BY OFFERING INCENTIVES for those who decide not to have children and thereby maintain the population so that it doesn't suffer under their views, whether or not people agree! Likewise, they could offer incentives for one parent to stay at home, to raise their children according to the commands of God, so each generation has men and women gifted by God for solutions for their generation. So that there are plenty of jobs for the wage earner of the family.

See any time a nation suffers a decline in the population it means that those living will need to work longer because there are not enough laborers to fill their jobs. So, if there is a serious decline in a nation's population then those living there have to work past their retirement years, or that nation would suffer a lack in goods and services, the nation suffers economically.

But if a nation can maintain or slightly grow their population, then that is ideal. It seems to me that the leaders of the world want to try and maintain that, they just need to work WITH the population IN COMMENDABLE WAYS if that is what they want us to do, rather than working in all these nefarious ways against us! And employ much more people WHO REPLENISH this world and take care of it environmentally as God commands!

The powers that be could offer financial incentives to everyone based on their willingness to have zero, one or two or three children; if they are all concerned about population growth and the ability to feed that population. Perhaps on a sliding scale. It doesn't have to be by OPPRESSION! They COULD JUST BE HONEST about it! And stop making so many people POOR, giving so many a miserable quality of life, and instead offer incentives to all honorable persons working in our civilization; that IS WAGES ENOUGH TO LIVE ON LIFELONG! No more slave wage jobs for anyone! They could offer scholarships to EVERYONE provided they show aptitude and attitude by getting a B average or better in their chosen field of expertise. ANYONE not get a B average, COULD STILL CONTINUE on their career path but it would be at their expense. People should not have to spend YEARS of their life paying back colleges! Instead, everyone should be required to give a minimum investment in their field JUST TO MAKE CERTAIN THEY WANT TO DO IT PROFESSIONALLY and that minimum investment, if a student gets B or better average, is their way of saying they WANT TO DO WHAT THEY'RE LEARNING PROFESSIONALLY! Schools should have a little bit of sway, and salaries also, in needed professions, to steer each and every generation to those fields. DOCTORS AND NURSES are in short supply right now! But it could be different where you're at, or you may not want to go into the healing professions. (Stop making advanced learning so EXPENSIVE, and we would get more doctors and nurses.)

Money should be available for keeping the planet clean and green, clean up the landfills and oceans and rivers! Yes, millions need to be involved in that! It doesn't matter if the recycling of the waste doesn't pay for itself, MONEY IS MINTED BY THOSE IN POWER, so they can dedicate a portion of it to keeping the planet clean and green indefinitely! God gave mankind this world and as His first instruction, He told us essentially to take care of it! Replenish, don't just take and consume, grow, and resupply, don't pollute, don't destroy our "mother earth".

Yes, farm raised species that are mandated by law to be non-GMO, so they can release 10 percent of them back into our oceans for all depleted species to date! Headed by marine biologists, to make certain there is balance in our oceans, instead of just harvesting. All fish operations should be required to restore by law the fish they are harvesting! RESTORE what overfishing has done! She takes care of us; we need to take care of her! Is what God tasked mankind with when He created us! So, take a look at our cities, there is enough money in the world to do whatever good thing mankind can decide on and agree to do! It's just right now alot of money is invested in things that are harming us and the planet! We need to have good visions for the future, beginning with cleaning up all these things we are doing wrong today!

It's when people in government, try to take the place of God, that people under them suffer. Or when they invest in death and destruction instead of life and quality of life for everyone! https://www.barnabasaid.org/us/magazine/why-are-christians-persecuted-in-china/ - like when they want everyone to think like them, dictators.

Our Lord Jesus Christ wants everyone to Love Him and each other. No one should have any objection to that. It just means the world is full of friends, instead of enemies. It's all the would-be rulers of the world offering up their own notions, that throws a wrench in what would be harmonious relationships with everyone, if everyone just listened to GOD, our Eternal Creator!

God, our Lord Jesus Christ, is RULING ALL CREATION, we all need to know Him and learn from Him and He will provide for each generation. It's when nations like China try to take his place that oppression and suffering ensues.

Known Epidemic: The Largest One in the History of the World Diabetes

WE HAVE KNOWN CARCINOGENS, KNOWN DIABETES CAUSING ADDITIVES, AND OTHER MALADIES, IN VIRTUALLY ALL OUR PROCESSED FOODS AND BEVERAGES! As much as seventy percent of food in our markets is genetically modified. Just look at how much high fructose corn syrup is added to so many things. Meanwhile THEY PRETEND to be finding a cure! ALL OF OUR TOXIC SCREENING DONE BY OUR MEDICAL LABS DO NOT SCREEN FOR KNOWN CARCINOGENS OR KNOWN POISONS that are not able to be handled by our organs properly. We DO NOT TRY TO FIND them BECAUSE THEY ARE IN OUR cosmetics, our hygiene products, everything we put on our skin or ingest these days! Manufacturers like Monsanto and Alcoa are to blame! Why are they not being held accountable?!

Virtually NONE of our tests from medical laboratories screen for poisons and they all should! Common poisons we are using prolifically, like round-up, glyphosate and you will see you have been poisoned! Carcinogens should be tested for on the general populace! COMMON INGREDIENTS KNOWN TO CAUSE CANCER SHOULD BE ROUTINELY SCREENED FOR!

PREVENTING CANCER RATHER THAT CURING IT SHOULD BE A CONCERN! PREVENT DIABETES RATHER THAN TREATING IT SHOULD BE A CONCERN! People in the Himalayans that are not part of our industrialized (dead focused, getting people sick so we can profit from them as they die) do not HAVE cancer or diabetes! It is OBVIOUS that our diets, and hygiene products and cosmetics are all to blame! Why are these things this way? WE ARE BEING HANDLED! Social Engineering! Population Management.

You're being killed slowly! And for some its quicker! All of these things are not UNINTENTIONAL CONSEQUENCES from human engineering! THERE ARE JUST TOO MANY OF THEM! Yes, I think doctors and nurses for the most part are just doing the best they can FROM AN INDUSTRY that is corrupt from the highest levels, from toxic pills, to ones so toxic they have lethal side effects! (approved by the FDA, so much for our regulators, so much obvious corruption!)

Look at all the ADDITITIVES for FOOD that are not part of its intrinsic quality. HIGH FRUCTOSE CORN SYRUP, HIGHLY PROCESSED SUGARS, not to mention rice eaters and potato eaters because they are so poor all they can eat are the cheapest staples, ARE CONTRIBUTING TO THIS EPIDEMIC! Diabetes is nothing nice! 80% of them don't make it to sixty! Once you have it your chances of heart attack and cancers and just about everything goes up to make you dead! No wonder the poor die on average 15-20 years sooner than those of means. RICE AND POTATOES in excess contributes to the DIABETES epidemic, it's not like the poor have much of choice, it's eat the poorest things or starve to death! And the poorest processed foods ARE ALL LOADED WITH DIABETES GMO modified HIGH FRUCTOSE CORN SYRUP! Poverty IS a Killer; thanks to those making it so.

PEOPLE! Don't you understand it? Conditions where so many are diabetic or pre-diabetic are DONE DELIBERATELY! This is not suddenly an epidemic of such monumental proportions! This is a result of deliberately altering our food supply with HIGH FRUCTOSE CORN SYRUP and HIGHLY PROCESSED SUGARS, in order to cause us all to be sick! Look at all processed foods and beverages! Virtually ALL of them are designed to make us sick!

When I say the people responsible did it to us intentionally, one has only to look at the statistics AND THE INGREDIENTS.

I'm sorry to reveal to you that they plotted and planned a way to make us all sick and dying and then profit from it, but that's exactly what they did. The "psychiatric industry of death", is the worst perpetrators on the unsuspecting public. Until and unless all these manufacturers get concerned for our health and show it, no more toxins in our foods, beverages, cosmetics and hygiene products, no more toxins in our medicines, then all those are just examples of their maltreatment of us. All the rising cancer rates and rising diabetes, are just the smoking guns on their crimes against humanity!

Until there are cameras linked to off sight servers for all hospital procedures and to firms of attorneys representing the public like the ones representing the hospitals, that's just another area of grave concern for WAY TOO MANY DEATHS AT THE HANDS OF DOCTORS AND NURSES!

Whenever the powers that be, cannot find MILLIONS OF MISSING PERSONS EACH YEAR, we HAVE TO SUSPECT THEM! Who else? Like it or not areas of police powers, doctors and nurses, politicians, all these areas we give the most trust to, are not SUPERVISED with PUBLIC ACCOUNTABLITY and they are the ones that NEED TO BE!

I don't want to go into all the ways people are sowing death and destruction; I just want everyone to change their minds and FOCUS ON LIFE AND QUALITY OF LIFE FOR EVERYONE. To do that I want EVERYONE TO REPENT AND GET BAPTIZED IN THE NAME OF OUR LORD JESUS CHRIST and BE FILLED WITH HIS HOLY SPIRIT! Read His Words in the Holy Bible and ask Him for His Understanding of it and all things! Then apply what you learn! And live righteously now and forever.

What can I say to all persons who are concerned? Have close relatives and friends that are aware of your whereabouts at all times. Make sure cameras are rolling with all interactions with police, and FIGHT FOR CAMERAS for your hospital procedures linked to off-site attorneys that can't be interrupted by anyone in the hospital!

And everyone, make sure you have trusted in our Good Lord Jesus Christ, so that whether you live or die, you are His! You are in His Hands! I have wished that my testimony did not include all these heinous things about our civilization, but someone has to sound the alarm when it's this bad!

You see after doctors and nurses murdered me and then resuscitated me, but then sent me home untreated to suffer and die, I was left so ill that as I laid in bed, I lost my home, my truck, virtually all my possessions. I couldn't believe that I would just be written off like some kind of disposed trash by those who knew me and what had happened to me. My wife left me, and when she did, she pocketed enough from our joint account to make a down payment on a very expensive home, the nicest one she or I ever lived in. When I finally had enough strength to make it into the bank, imagine my surprise when less than one hundred dollars cash was all she left me with. It turns out, she had a private account with another bank and was stealing from me for who knows how long, cashing my checks and putting them into her private account. I would have been tossed out onto the streets to spend my final moments if not for disability insurance in our nation and that it came through just before my foreclosure date.

But to go from an earning person, on his way to becoming a millionaire, down to barely over a thousand a month to try to live on, meant I spent years of my life trying to recover on wages so meager it left me in the cheapest apartment I could find, with mostly only potatoes for nourishment. So I never did recover good health, instead I barely SURVIVED do to my anger about my situation at first, just wanting enough health to rid this world of the murderers who attacked me if no one else would help me arrest them all, and then as my knowledge grew that what had happened to me had caused the deaths of so many others, I wanted to survive to notify the rest of the world to try and stop these kinds of crimes. But as the years passed and how difficult it was, how much I suffered for so long, my health only partially recovered and stabilized as a chronically ill person. So chronically ill that I stayed indoors researching and writing for years, as I was growing even more ill. The diet of mostly potatoes made me obese and gave me diabetes. The lack of exercise due to my chronic fatigue from my poor health also contributed to my ever-worsening health. I suffered so much for so long, I realized I didn't want anyone, not even those who murdered me (they only reason I'm not dead was they resuscitated me afterward due to the presence of others not in on the murder attempts - TWICE!), to suffer that much FOREVER, I chose to forgive them all and pray they all find Salvation in our Lord Jesus Christ, so they don't do to others what they did to me.

It didn't help that investors in real estate were buying and flipping real estate, so my little cheap apartment, went up with every new landlord until at the last I couldn't afford it any longer and was forced to move elsewhere. All over this world wealthy people push poorer people around, just by buying up real estate and raising rents on them. This practice has to end by law. It isn't lawful to oppress and kill people in this manner. It's a crime against humanity to push poor people around until at the last the poorest of us have no place to go but suffer in the streets until we die.

Inflation is hard for everyone but the wealthy people causing it. (just look at the wealth inequality statistics) I had a recent crown in my mouth break below the gum line; it's a lower front tooth. So, the only thing left to do was to extract it and get an implant. After the extraction, I found out to get the tooth replaced was a whopping $4500 dollars! Yes, you read that correctly, four thousand five hundred dollars! And that was the price WITH INSURANCE! So, part of the reason the elderly and disabled are in growing trouble as they age, is that what people are doing intrinsically just trying to stay alive themselves, like buying and flipping real estate, and the goods and services they provide are billed exponentially beyond what those of poor means can afford! Those attempting to live on fixed incomes that are more and more insufficient to pay for basic housing costs, let alone anything else.

I have written my idea of solutions for these problems:

Many Primary Residential Landlords have become Criminals by tossing innocent citizens into the streets to suffer and die merely because they CAN'T pay their greedy demands.

Sometimes I wonder if anyone else perceives our

civilization as I do. It would seem objectively we have aspects that we can commend, but we also most definitely have aspects that deserve criticism. I want to address that dimension of our society referred to as "the cost of living".

The cost of living these days seems to roll off the tongues of commentators as if they were discussing something of minor consequence; rather than that modern civilization has put a price upon an individual's ability to stay alive. In modern civilization, unless each person pays that "cost of living" price, they begin dying and at times rather rapidly. In other words, the moment someone is unable to earn or acquire money for food, clothing, shelter, proper medical care, they begin to suffer and die. So, the "cost of living" isn't some wistful notion for intellectuals to discuss over the airways in an emotionally detached manner, but rather refers to the very real ability to survive or not!

As a nation, we seem to be letting some innocent citizens suffer and die who are not able to procure "the cost of living" necessary to keep them from being homeless, hungry, ill, uncared for and ultimately dead prematurely. When innocent citizens are dying homeless in our streets, how is that not economic genocide?

According to the statistics reported, 40% of the homeless are over 50 years of age. (https://endhomelessness.org/homelessness-in-america/homelessness-statistics/state-of-homelessness-

2020/) Since statistically the homeless die 15-20 years sooner than the housed populace, that means hundreds of thousands of innocent citizens are dying homeless in our streets! In addition, a significant percentage of the homeless (almost 20 percent) are disabled! These truly disabled persons are so obviously disabled that they are considered to be the "chronic homeless", persons that are homeless for many years of their life! WHY ARE THE ELDERLY AND DISABLED DYING HOMELESS IN OUR STREETS?! It's because they are unable to procure the cost of living and don't have the rest of society looking out for them. Since anyone can become injured, chronically ill and disabled, it behooves us all to make certain that none of us are dying homeless!

I've personally investigated various factors for why this is the situation of so many unfortunate souls today. Certainly, there's alcohol and drug abuse involved among a percentage of the homeless population, but such social problems are not confined to the homeless. I wager that almost anyone who finds themselves homeless would be tempted to drown their sorrows with drink, or assuage the deep wounds and aches that made them such, with drugs. So instead of becoming cold and callous in wrongly thinking anyone deserves such a fate as homelessness, I want to address the issues that are beyond the control of these people that are letting them die in the streets.

One of those factors that needs to change immediately is that Social Security is making it too difficult for the elderly and disabled to obtain disability insurance when they need it. Some individuals are so disabled that they cannot advocate for themselves; some of those severely disabled persons don't have anyone to help them complete the paperwork, interviews, etc. in order to properly obtain financial assistance. Some actually do complete the process but are wrongly denied insurance even though they are factually disabled. So, we need to appoint advocates that work with the homeless to get them off the streets and into shelter immediately.

We have to expand social services to hire people to literally hold the hands of the homeless and bring them into safe housing! Once housed, fed, clothed and medically cared for, each formerly homeless person needs a personal advocate appointed that finds out their work history, medical needs, etc. and becomes a limited, temporary guardian of sorts, empowered exclusively to get them social security, social security disability, or supplemental income, any necessary medical care and nutritional sustenance and then project regulated housing that makes certain these people are never again dying in our streets. Their personal advocates need to meet with them at least weekly until they determine what the formerly homeless can or cannot do, by spending sufficient time with them first hand to document the extent of their disabilities and any abilities they might have that can be used to raise the self-esteem of any and all persons so disabled that they end up homeless.

Social Security Disability needs to be granted to the economically disabled. The economically disabled are persons who may appear to have the physical health necessary to perform some kind of work, but have never been able to keep a job during years to decades of their adult life. (They might appear to be able bodied persons, but people who have been constantly fired their entire lives, have what are commonly known as "hidden disabilities".) Hidden disabilities are not just those with mental or psychological disabilities, they are those who need help finding work that is desirable and fulfilling for them. People who have hidden disabilities, often suffer from chronic illnesses, recurring or terminal illnesses, social dysfunction, rebellion against coerced conformity, emotional difficulties and other problems that when all combined leave them economically disabled (poor and needy) lifelong. Drug rehabilitation needs to become a standard part of total recovery programs for any and all drug and alcohol abusers; that aims at keeping people housed and as productive as possible, with the well-being of each individual in mind. I provide other solutions in my notes and videos that addresses the fact that some people, even as adults, actually prefer various levels of supervision/institutionalization. In other words, some people actually prefer having their necessities, room and board, provided for them as part of their daily living. Such people benefit by structured welfare, even down to personal budget managers that help them allocate their earnings and even build savings for themselves (why we have and need social security and programs like it). In other words, not everyone is capable of, or even desires, independent adult living; many prefer communal settings and the safety and security that a more structured environment provides.

Once it's determined by advocates/guardians, legal and medical experts the real extent of disabilities, whether or not an individual is permanently or temporarily disabled or terminally ill, then our civilization needs to construct not just project based housing for the working poor, but retirement housing for all citizens, and disabled communities that have specialists, therapists, etc. help those who have disabilities, whether or not those persons can be healed of them. (I'm not advocating for coerced quarantines or segregation, just the personal freedom for all persons to access necessary proper retirement communities, assisted living, therapies and medical care; regardless of their individual net worth.)

As a civilization we are doing what we can to afford freedom of movement and participation for the disabled, but we are failing when we let anyone die homeless. We need to have healthy people walk through our streets and guide the homeless to safe shelter in every city. I want to encourage investigative journalists to actually walk the homeless down to social security offices and document the process of why these disabled persons are not able to obtain some form of social security; including shelter. I already know it's because government officials are overwhelmed with the need; to the point where they're either being told, or simply have decided, to make it so difficult that innocent people are being denied assistance who in fact shouldn't be. It's also due to the fact that as I stated above, certain people are so disabled they cannot advocate for themselves sufficiently to obtain the help they need.

We need to expand social services to approve the homeless for either social security, disability insurance and/or supplemental income, until such time as they can either earn sufficient wages or become deceased. Regardless, the elderly and disabled need to be provided enough funds to live on (meet the current cost of living) or our civilization is killing them. Right now, Social Security, Disability Insurance, and SSI is NOT meeting the cost of living (mainly because there are insufficient affordable housing units that are perpetually/strictly regulated as such)! Elderly and disabled persons are dying in our streets! This matter should be vitally important to EVERYONE, because EVERYONE grows old and eventually is unable to earn a living for themselves. (virtually everyone who is homeless is struggling with mental and/or physical disabilities/impairments or they wouldn't be homeless). Don't think this doesn't concern you; anyone can become injured, anyone can get chronically ill; EVERYONE who doesn't die prematurely grows old! So, it's past time to stand up to the wealthy rulers of the world and tell them that you want affordable housing as a guaranteed right lifelong! LIVABLE WAGES! and that includes what pittance you receive in your old age or if you become disabled! The wealthy are looking out for themselves fine, but they are not looking out for the vast majority on earth! Shelter from the elements is needed for basic survival; anyone lacking it is in need of immediate assistance until they are safely housed. It's one thing for healthy people to go camping or perhaps choose to travel for awhile to see the world, but it's another when people are dying in the streets.

Another factor that's driving homelessness are landlords and real estate investors. Landlords are factually getting away with extortion and are criminals by definition that are harming innocent citizens by unilaterally raising the cost of living on the working poor, elderly and disabled. I'm not saying ALL landlords are deliberately attacking innocent citizens; I'm sure there are many that are compassionate and reasonable; perhaps even a few that are excessively kind and generous by keeping rents for their tenants at or below what the cost of housing should be with respect to average wages of the working poor, social security and disability insurance (rents at around 300-400/mo.). However, after a lifetime of abuse, far too many landlords are selfishly concerned for their own luxurious living, to the point where they show little to no concern for their oppressed tenants. The temptation for abuse is simply too great to allow the profession of primary residential landlords to exist any longer.

Since the evidence is in that people of their own volition won't control their personal greed; to the point where they are killing innocent fellow citizens in the streets, we have to make that profession universally illegal. Some landlords are factually cruelly attacking innocent citizens; sometimes doubling their cost of living or more at a whim. Let's face the fact that there is a very REAL COST OF LIVING; a very real price people pay to stay alive in modern civilization! One of the most basic factors of which is the cost of housing. So, to allow any citizen to attack the lives of other citizens by raising their cost of living is to encourage crime; very severe and dangerous crimes that are factually driving innocent people into the streets to suffer and die.

Landlords are provably guilty of the crimes of extortion, assault, theft, armed robbery and various forms of homicides from negligent to deliberate. Landlords get away with abusing and maltreating their poor tenants constantly; everything from invasion of privacy to other more serious offenses. Landlords are criminals by definition and practice. Tell me, if you can, how someone who holds you at gun point and demands money from you is acting any different from landlords who call the police to do the exact same thing. Again, jacking rents just as high as you please, is not a fair or equitable exchange for housing; for necessary shelter from the elements; it's EXCESSIVE cost that has been driven so high by ubiquitous personal greed that the cost of housing is starting to exceed what some people earn or are allotted each month to try and survive on!

Some might try to argue the point; so let's get specific:
Virtually all landlords are guilty of extortion at the very least, by legal definitions coast to coast across our nation:

https://dictionary.law.com/Default.aspx?selected=709 -

"extortion
n. obtaining money or property by threat to a victim's property or loved ones, intimidation, or false claim of a right (such as pretending to be an IRS agent). It is a felony in all states, except that a direct threat to harm the victim is usually treated as the crime of robbery. Blackmail is a form of extortion in which the threat is to expose embarrassing, damaging information to family, friends or the public.
See also: blackmail robbery theft "

https://www.yourdictionary.com/extortion -

"The act or an instance of extorting something, as by psychological pressure.

An excessive or exorbitant charge.

The wrongful taking of something of value from another by the threat of force or other coercive measure.

Extortion is defined as the practice of trying to get something through force, threats or blackmail.

When you threaten to release embarrassing pictures of someone unless he gives you $100, this is an example of extortion.

Illegal use of one's official position or powers to obtain property, funds, or patronage.

Something extorted.

The act of extorting, or getting money, etc. by threats, misuse of authority, etc.

The legal offense committed by an official who extorts.

The practice of extorting money or other property by the use of force or threats."

Currently landlords threaten tenants very lives just by their unilateral ability to raise the cost of living to virtually anything they want. My own building was purchased by a citizen who decided to raise rent for one apartment all the way from $675/month to $2000/mo. So, the working poor, elderly and disabled look far and wide to find shelter they can afford, but no sooner than they might obtain it, any citizen can take it from them the very next day; just by purchasing the structure they moved into.

Routinely, leases are short term, if they exist at all,

and as soon as they expire, there is the practice of month-to-month tenancy that offers little to no protection to tenants nationwide. In this particular case, our new landlord deliberately forced the tenant living there to have to move on short notice or face eviction, bad credit reporting, perhaps even armed threats to his life to remove him from his residence, and the loss of some or all of his personal possessions.

TELL THE LANDLORDS AND LAWMAKERS THAT THEY HAVE A WEEK TO THIRTY DAYS TO PACK AND MOVE THEMSELVES (NO HIRED HELP! THE WORKING POOR, ELDERLY AND DISABLED CAN'T AFFORD IT) AND YET THEY IMAGINE THAT'S TOTALLY FINE TO DO TO OTHERS!

It's EXTREMELY difficult to move (I know; I owned a relocation company and personally packed and moved thousands of households and businesses; lifting ten to twenty tons of goods daily for years); let alone when it's unplanned and coerced on short notice.

Forcing the working poor, elderly and disabled to move; whether or not it's during a pandemic, is a very real threat to the lives of those innocent, poor tenants. The working poor can't afford to miss work; many have to work sometimes two or three jobs, while they pack and move themselves. Such coerced moves can cause them to lose perhaps their only means of income for themselves by disrupting their schedules. Sometimes housing rises so high in a region that the poor are forced to move many miles away, sometimes immediately forced to leave behind family and/or friends who are all likewise struggling for survival under these oppressive conditions!

Forcing the elderly and disabled to move on short notice is also a very real threat to their lives as well, because such persons often have little to no savings and simply cannot afford to move and don't have the personal health and strength necessary to pack and move themselves. So for a citizen to intentionally buy a building in which the elderly and disabled are living on fixed incomes; to intentionally, dramatically raise rents on them to such degrees (knowing the poor tenants cannot pay and are deliberately forcing them to move on short notice or become homeless), is factually assault and even attempted homicide on the part of the extremely evil, greedy, cruel and/or apathetic landlords doing so.

Again, legal definitions across our nation say so! When tenants are unable to meet the unilateral, arbitrary sudden demands of landlords attacking their lives by raising the cost of living on them, sometimes so dramatically that it's OBVIOUS their landlord is threatening their ability to survive; like when they increase the cost of living in one month by more than 1 percent.

Any increase at all in the cost of living immediately means a lower quality of life unless it coincides with a greater increase in income. (no citizen should think it's their right or have the ability to raise the cost of living on anyone else! that means we are allowing some citizens to attack others at will!)

It's one thing to let the "free market" regulate prices of luxuries, but necessities like housing have to be regulated; otherwise, greed and extortion, by excessively high housing costs, means people suffer and die! Luxuries are not necessities for life, but shelter from the elements is!

Some landlords increase rent from one month to the next by over 10%; some are so evil they double or triple rent cost from one month to the next. NO ONE but the wealthiest persons on earth can absorb a cost-of-living increase like that! So, landlords are DELIBERATELY attacking the lives of their tenants! And make no mistake, it is an overt attack on their lives! If tenants are unable to store, move or sell their personal possessions in such short time as the law provides for them when so attacked, they suffer the immediate loss of their possessions. This is accomplished by the landlord forcefully evicting them; which entails armed, weaponized strangers, in the form of police powers, who have been duped into acting as criminals by this illegal system of landlord/tenant relations; dragging the innocent poor tenants out of their residence into the streets. Any possessions of the innocent victim(s) of these crimes, then becomes the property of their greedy, criminal landlord, who has successfully committed extortion, theft, assault, armed robbery, manslaughter and even attempted homicide or actual murder by this process. (The same crimes are committed when bankers have their mercenaries drag the elderly and disabled; victims of crime, disasters, aging and/or disease out of their homes by foreclosure.) THE DEFINITIONS OF CRIMES AGAINST INNOCENT PERSONS SAY SO!

Quote

"Assault

Definition

The definition of assault varies by jurisdiction, but is generally defined as intentionally putting another person in reasonable apprehension of an imminent harmful or offensive contact. Physical injury is not required.

Overview

Some jurisdictions label "assault" as "attempted battery." In tort law, assault is considered an intentional tort.

"Apprehension"

In the context of assault, the victim's "apprehension" happens if the victim believes that the tortfeasor's conduct will result in imminent harmful or offensive contact unless it is prevented.

It is not necessary that the victim believes the conduct will be effective in making such contact, only that the victim believes the conduct is capable of making such contact.

Assault and Battery

In an act of physical violence by one person against another, "assault" is usually paired with battery. In an act of physical violence, assault refers to the act which causes the victim to apprehend imminent physical harm, while battery refers to the actual act causing the physical harm.

Aggravated Assault

Aggravated assault refers to an assault with an additional aggravating circumstance. As such, the liability and sentencing for aggravated assault is generally more severe than that for an ordinary assault.

Prima Facie

The prima facie case for "assault" has 3 components:
1. The defendant acts
2. The defendant intends to cause the victim to apprehend imminent harmful contact from the defendant
3. The defendant's action causes the victim to reasonably apprehend such a contact"

https://www.law.cornell.edu/wex/assault

"Murder
First degree murder is the most serious criminal homicide. Typically, first degree murder is both intentional and premeditated. Premeditated can mean anything from a long time plan to kill the victim, to a shorter term plan. The intent of the accused murderer does not need to be focused on the actual victim. If someone planned on killing one victim, but by accident kills someone else, the murder is still intentional and premeditated meaning a first degree murder charge.

When there is a lack of premeditation but the killer intended to kill (for example, in homicides commonly described as occurring "in the heat of passion") the homicide may draw second degree murder charges or perhaps voluntary manslaughter charges, depending on the state.

Manslaughter
Manslaughter generally means an illegal killing that falls short of murder. The lowest form of manslaughter is involuntary manslaughter. This means that the perpetrator didn't intend to kill anyone, but still killed the victim through behavior that was either criminally negligent or reckless. One common example is a DUI accident which kills someone. Someone driving drunk is behaving in a criminally reckless manner, even if they had no intent to kill anyone.

In contrast, voluntary manslaughter usually means that the offender did not have a prior intent to kill such as when the homicide occurs "in the heat of passion" and without forethought. Depending on the state, this crime may fall under a variant of murder charges, instead of manslaughter." End quote
- https://criminal.findlaw.com/criminal-charges/homicide-definition.html

If a stranger shows up at your home, breaks the door down, and you see weapons aimed at your person, you KNOW your life is in imminent danger; so let's stop pretending that when armed mercenaries of the wealthy, known as police, show up to drag poor tenants out of their home, that their life isn't also in danger! The abuse of authority has been documented throughout history; although current governments, including that of the United States, seem unwilling to investigate themselves or admit that such abuses don't occur frequently; even daily. We have to therefore cite citizens that are keeping watch on criminals in uniform.

https://www.hrw.org/legacy/reports98/police/uspo14.htm

https://www.ncjrs.gov/pdffiles1/nij/grants/218583.pdf - while authorities admit holding police powers accountable is important, they also admit that they haven't even been looking at it for most of our history -
"Excessive force. The frequency of police use-of-force events that may be defined as justified or excessive is difficult to estimate [2]. There has been no national database of officer-involved shootings or incidents in which police use excessive force. On January 1, 2019 the FBI launched a national use-of-force data collection." - https://nij.ojp.gov/topics/articles/overview-police-use-force
so we have to cite private organizations, to give us an idea of just how dangerous it is to have armed authorities even show up to anyone's residence:

https://www.vice.com/en/article/595kv3/police-crime-database - just because someone wears the uniform, doesn't mean they're not a criminal. Armed authorities are factually very dangerous!

https://www.facebook.com/notes/michael-swenson/bad-cops/616245898454373/ - in my own research and life experience, citizens can and reasonably should feel extremely concerned for their personal safety, anytime armed strangers are around them; let alone show up at their residence. Since governments are unwilling to give up weapons, EVERYONE should be armed and trained in the use of their personal self-defense weapon(s). When I went to authorities to report homicide attempts on my own life, they actually helped the criminals commit further crimes against me; including the loss of my entire estate. So, police are not just capable of committing individual crimes, but they are capable of committing them with other citizens by negligence of their duties or even by deliberate conspiracy. Thankfully, most police and militant powers are NOT violent criminals or there would be no law and order and civilization would collapse in widespread chaos and ubiquitous violence; survival would demand personal use of force (weapons for survival and self-defense) on a daily basis. Citizens everywhere would need to form their own communes or gangs and be constantly vigilant for their own security.

When landlords can freely commandeer such dangerous use of force, it's EXTREMELY OBVIOUS that they possess more "rights" and powers than their poor tenants.

Forcibly dragging anyone out of their residence into the streets homeless is absolutely an attack on their person. Assault and attempted homicide is being committed in the process:

https://nhchc.org/wp-content/uploads/2019/08/HardColdFacts.pdf - the homeless die on average 20 years sooner than the housed populace. No matter what their age, threats to their personal health and safety, including premature death is increased threefold, just by being homeless.

https://khn.org/news/the-homeless-are-dying-in-record-numbers-on-the-streets-of-l-a/

In addition to the more serious crimes above, landlords routinely are guilty of defamation of character of their innocent tenants. For example, a new landlord feels that jacking rents by 50% is justified even though the working poor, elderly and disabled are unable to pay such short notice increases; virtually no one gets such substantial raises in income; let alone the elderly and disabled. Even IF the poor manage to pay the higher rents, it means a lower quality of life, sometimes even taking away their ability to purchase food! That higher rent demand is provably life threatening and is currently implemented on the mere whim of landlords! The landlord reasons that they can get the higher rent from someone else desperate enough to pay it, so they feel the "free market" justifies their greedy demand and so drives up housing costs just as high as they can.

Currently hundreds of thousands are homeless in the United States alone, millions worldwide, and dying in our streets. How many more must suffer and die likewise before citizens take action to prevent such unbelievable cruelty and apathy?! The existing poor tenants have little to no notice or choice whatsoever over a new landlord purchasing their building and even if they do, they have not the means to pay the inevitable increases that follow; so, they desperately look for less expensive housing which usually means a lower quality of life.

Landlords are not perfect, it's incredible how fast this one threatened to evict me, simply because after months of loud construction, I complained that they were pounding on my floor past 7 pm in the evening! That kind of vindictive retaliation for merely asserting our rights while jacking rents, is a prime example why the profession of being a primary residential landlord must be done away with. Make everyone homeowners by law.

EVERYONE MUST HAVE THE ABSOLUTE RIGHT TO AFFORDABLE HOUSING LIFELONG AND NO CITIZEN CAN BE ABLE TO ATTACK THE LIFE OF ANOTHER CITIZEN BY RAISING THE COST OF LIVING ON THEM! At their personal whim driving up rents just as high as possible and not caring that they are causing homelessness and death by doing so.

Especially as overtly and cruelly as landlords are doing now! Whenever wealthy people look at other cities and nations and think wow, I can make so much MONEY from these poor people. IF THE POOR PEOPLE LIVING THEIR COULD AFFORD YOU IMAGINED EXPENSES FROM YOUR WEALTHY COHORTS LIVING IN WEALTHY PLACES, they wouldn't be living so poorly! Generally, locations that are poor and in need of rebuilding need your generosity; not your greed. If there are any very wealthy persons with real altruism, you should buy all the many apartment complexes in which the poor are now terrified for their lives and immediately, dramatically lower rents nationwide all the way from $1000/mo. on average down to $300 or less! That's what they can afford and still have enough to pay the rest of their bills.

Until such laws are passed or such benefactors arise, the working poor, elderly and disabled are in very real danger. When such poor people are suddenly forced to move against their will, sometimes they are unable to find less expensive housing, so they are in imminent danger of eviction and homelessness. That's an extremely serious threat, but what follows also is a negative credit report, that is wrongly perceived as somehow their fault for being attacked and unable to pay dramatic higher costs of living, at the whim of their existing or new landlord. So, they suffer not only from overt attacks on their lives, but defamation of character that makes it difficult for such poor citizens to obtain future housing for themselves.

Besides defamation of character through credit reporting agencies, landlords routinely dictate to their poor tenants how they can live in their primary residence. Many landlords often think nothing whatsoever of just showing up at their tenant's doors and banging on it to let them in unannounced; to make some kind of demand from them, to let them inspect the property, to take photos or otherwise disrupt their poor tenant's day to day living. They routinely think nothing whatsoever of making their tenants endure loud construction or long renovations etc., depriving their tenants of needed sleep; to the point that if it were done to them, they would have called the police for disturbing the peace. In other words, landlords regularly maltreat their tenants in ways they wouldn't want done to themselves and control their tenants lives in ways they wouldn't desire for themselves.

So, it's extremely clear when anyone looks objectively at what landlords are doing, by raising the cost of living on their tenants, and by routinely abusing and maltreating their tenants, are in fact, LEGALLY DEFINED AS, misdemeanors to very dangerous, seriously life-threatening crimes! Crimes so serious and harmful that they should have criminal and civil consequences, but due to the fact that the wealthy have made these landlord/tenant laws and often have close ties with landlords and real estate investors (other wealthy people), currently such criminals have been getting away with these overt crimes against humanity.

Wealthy persons such as bankers and landlords have obviously created a system and so-called laws, in a vain effort to legitimize their criminal acts, that serve their personal interests; valuing money and possessions above the lives of the vast majority of humanity. Our civilization could and should permanently prohibit evictions and foreclosures; at least against the elderly and disabled! Why would any society choose to abuse those who are already suffering and dying?

Do away with landlords and make affordable housing an absolute right for everyone; so, there is no need for evictions. Bankers would still get paid for their mortgages, just not as fast as tossing injured, elderly, chronically or terminally ill persons out of their homes to do so. Virtually all such persons are relegated below poverty level income, but should we then force them out of their homes for being injured in war, or by crime or disaster, or illness? Should we further attack and add to the suffering of such innocent persons by evictions and foreclosures?

SHOULD WE BE SENTENCING INNOCENT CITIZENS TO DEATH BY HOMELESSNESS WHO BECOME DISABLED AND UNABLE TO CONTINUE TO EARN A LIVING FOR THEMSELVES THROUGH NO FAULT OF THEIR OWN?!

NO! the bankers can get their money by adjusting the mortgage for such innocent citizens such that the payments are no more than 30% of the pittance of disability insurance they're given to try and survive on until the poor homeowner either recovers and can pay more or until they are deceased; at that time the bankers can collect their money through the estate sale, but stop letting them attack already injured and disabled persons through foreclosures! (perhaps then the bankers might lobby congress to make certain social security is keeping up with the cost of living) STOP LYING TO PEOPLE! There is enough money in this world to build your skyscrapers, palaces and mansions, there's enough to house the homeless!

It's one thing to foreclose on people who are able to pay back their loans, but refuse to do so; but quite another to toss injured, chronically or terminally ill, disabled persons out of their homes to further suffer and die homeless!

Both landlords and bankers have been evicting and foreclosing on innocent citizens during this pandemic. It looks like bankers have not just been compassionless but actually have been exploiting citizens with high credit rates during a time when many were asked or forced to stop working and were in need of credit and loans as a result just to survive. It's past time for citizens to realize that their lives can be just as seriously under attack financially as by outright violence. So, I'm encouraging all citizens everywhere to unite and stand up for yourselves! Tell your lawmakers and governing officials that you want affordable housing declared an absolute right for all persons! (and to make laws against charging anyone excessive usury like pay day loans, etc.) Tell them that they either pass such laws, or face arrest for enabling and perpetuating these crimes against you!

GET THIS STRAIGHT! THE COST OF LIVING IS CALLED SUCH BECAUSE IT IS THE VERY REAL PRICE PEOPLE PAY IN MODERN CIVILIZATION TO STAY ALIVE! ANYONE, ANYWHERE RAISING THAT COST IS FACTUALLY ATTACKING THE LIVES OF THOSE INNOCENT CITIZENS! LANDLORDS ARE BY FAR THE WORST ABUSERS OF INNOCENT PEOPLE TODAY! Never, ever allow any individual or group of people to so obviously get away with attacking the lives of others!

We have a real problem in America and all over this world! The wealthy have made laws that seemingly allow them to commit open and obvious crimes against the general population; one of the most common and pervasive of which is allowing the existence of primary residential landlords.

Landlords are statistically more of a threat to the lives of the working poor, elderly and disabled than anyone else. At any moment, a landlord, on their whim, can attack their tenants and seemingly get away with it. Landlords must immediately be recognized for what they are - VERY DANGEROUS CRIMINALS! Primary Residential Landlords must immediately cease to exist.

I'm not saying put landlords on death row for their obvious crimes; I'm saying recognize that landlords commit them, to a greater or lesser extent just by being one, and therefore, make that so called profession expressly illegal! Face it, landlords are just people, and everyone has emotions, and the cases of landlord abuses are countless. A landlord can evict someone out of their residence, just because they feel like it, just because they might not like that person or group of people. Sure, we have laws against discrimination, but the poor are so poor they often cannot find legal representation, and even if they can, proving a landlord has violated laws isn't always that easy. But it is extremely easy for them to raise rents and to make someone homeless.

Civilization needs to take the temptation away from people to abuse others, excessively; giving any citizen power over another citizen to make them homeless on short notice, is excessive power and excessive temptation for someone to be deliberately or negligently cruel to the point where many thousands have already died homeless in recent history. A homeowner can choose to house guests at no charge on their property or provide room and board to people that work for them, but the practice of residential landlords who can kick people out of their primary residence/shelter from the elements has to come to an immediate end.

BY LAW, MAKE AFFORDABLE HOUSING AN

ABSOLUTE RIGHT FOR ALL CITIZENS SUCH THAT THE COST OF LIVING IS ALWAYS AFFORDABLE OR YOU ARE ALLOWING THE WEALTHY TO OPPRESS, ENSLAVE AND MURDER THE POOR AT WILL, SIMPLY BY RAISING THE COST OF LIVING BEYOND THEIR MEANS.

Housing is "affordable" in modern civilization when it doesn't cost more than thirty(30) percent of an individual's net income each month. So, I'm not advocating for FREE housing, I'm advocating for AFFORDABLE housing, so that no one can forcibly be made homeless! Everyone is entitled by law to AFFORDABLE housing lifelong.

If I were president, this is how I would make the transition. I would announce that lawmakers have properly recognized that any and all landlord/tenant laws are collectively unconstitutional and inhumane. I would prove, as I have above, that landlords daily commit crimes against innocent citizens by having the power to raise the cost of living on them and therefore the practice of being a residential landlord is no longer allowed to continue. I would give landlords the choice of selling all tenant held structures to their tenants or face arrest on the charges of the crimes they are committing above. In other words, landlords would become "for sale by owners" to their tenants (purchased at a rate of not more than 30 percent of their tenant's net monthly income and not be allowed to charge them excessive usury in the process).

It's one thing for someone trying a business model

to be able to rent commercial space for their new business, but it's another when shelter from the elements as a primary residence, necessary to sustain life, is subject to the whim of citizens who have acquired more money than others. EVERYONE would immediately be entitled, by a declaration of national emergency and by law, to AFFORDABLE housing! (to cost no more than 30 percent of their net income each month until their residence is paid for in full) AFFORDABLE housing is not a PALACE or a MANSION, but basic shelter from the elements! It's also not so meager that it's not much better than a dog kennel. Some kind of minimum standard of square footage and modern amenities needs to be specified or people might construct cages like in Hong Kong. I find such low standards of living completely unacceptable. That kind of mentality engenders criminal activity and mental and emotional illnesses. Mankind needs to create civilization that is civil and treats other people humanely.

Innocent citizens are not to be caged like animals! It's one thing to imprison criminals, but quite another to make the lives of innocent citizens so stressful and miserable that they die prematurely.

Any able-bodied person refusing to do work of any kind, would still have access to a residence, but it would be the most humble of dwellings modern civilization affords. (Again, a minimum standard needs to be established as humane and ethical based on current technologies available for that region) (Remember that just because someone might appear to be able-bodied, doesn't necessarily mean that they are. Some people might be disabled and yet not recognized as such ("new" diseases, rare conditions, etc. are still being discovered); so, it's wrong to toss even those citizens who appear able-bodied out into the streets to suffer and die). Real estate could still be bought and sold as it is presently, BUT NO ONE COULD BE MADE HOMELESS through those transactions! Anyone selling their existing primary affordable residence must be acquiring a different one in the process. In this way, homelessness and the threat to innocent lives, by arbitrary and unilateral raising of the cost of living on them, would be ended.

Once the existing landlords had sold all tenant held properties, they could purchase other real estate if they chose, BUT NOT FOR ACTING AS A PRIMARY RESIDENTIAL LANDLORD EVER AGAIN. It's one thing to offer room and board at a personal ranch or residence for those who work there, it's another to own multiple, multi-family apartment complexes, or houses in which more and more innocent citizens are being crushed to death by uncontrolled rising housing and residential leasing costs. If someone wants to invest in real estate for the purpose of providing secondary shelter to other citizens, it needs to be in the form of commercial real estate such as hotels, motels, resorts, etc.; in which those who reside there have their own primary residence elsewhere. NO MORE HOMELESSNESS! HOMELESSNESS IS A PROVEN DANGER TO LIVES AND IS INHUMANE! Having a homeless population is an indictment against the government and citizens of that nation!

It's fine for someone to want to travel about, but they must have an affordable primary residence they can retreat to any time they want or need shelter from the elements!

The average cost of housing in America is three to four times higher than it should be due to landlords and real estate investors "buying and flipping" real estate.

1) Average small apartments for rent across America are at or over $1000/mo.

2) Average income for the working poor, elderly and disabled on fixed incomes are between $1000-1500/mo.

3) Every time someone purchases real estate in which there are poor tenants, the investor/new landlord expects to make a profit and so immediately raises rents on everyone living there.

This routine has extorted money, by threat of homelessness and unplanned coerced relocations, from the working poor, elderly and disabled who are in understandable fear for their lives; to the point where everyone involved in it are currently getting away with very terrible crimes against humanity; economic genocide.

It's commendable to run charities that give shelter for little to no charge to those desiring it; it's quite another to be charging so much for shelter that the working poor, elderly and disabled are begging for food and terrified of being driven into the streets to suffer and die from the cruel, selfish, greedy criminals attacking their lives. If there really isn't enough affordable housing, then our governing officials need to expand HUD to construct units nationwide until there are no more homeless and no more landlords attacking their fellow citizens!

So instead of allowing the wealthy to continue to oppress, maltreat and enslave the poor, as it is today through bankers and landlords; we just need to give all citizens the right to life; which, in modern civilization, means the right to affordable housing, nutritional food, clean air, clean water and jobs that pay livable wages lifelong. (This can be accomplished by telling the ultra-wealthy that either they make certain the wages they are paying are keeping up with the cost of living or they will be arrested for enslaving people and their assets will be liquidated to compensate their victims!) Again, simply regulating affordable housing will solve so many problems in that regard! We need to improve social services to properly recognize that disabilities come in many forms; most of which are not readily visible to the naked eye and make certain no one is turned away that has them (anyone dying in our streets is obviously disabled!)

Under a moral society that has properly established affordable housing as a right for everyone lifelong; as a matter of routine, children graduating from secondary education would either go into some form of higher education with the option of boarding there, staying with their parents or beginning to pay for their own affordable primary residence, or they would join the military with either boarding there or likewise begin paying for their own primary residence, or they would seek employment and begin paying for their own primary residence at no more than 30 percent of their net earnings each month. Some people choose to live in extended families or communally, but all persons still need to have the absolute right by law to their own primary residence; so, no one is homeless against their will. Homeless orphans will either be adopted or appointed legal guardians and housed accordingly until they are adults themselves. Once any citizen becomes an adult, they can choose to remain with their parents as long as they wish; even if it means inheriting that residence upon the passing of their parents. In other words, such laws enacted to ensure that everyone has the right to affordable housing lifelong must be worded to also ensure personal freedoms; while protecting individual lives and not used as a method of social control or social engineering.

I encourage everyone to unite and make the world a better place for us all, instead of just a few of the most selfish and greedy, viceful persons on earth as it is today. Almost every landlord I've ever encountered are intelligent, talented people, WHO COULD MAKE THEIR WEALTH BY HONORABLE MEANS, but instead are choosing to enslave, oppress and kill their fellow brothers and sisters on earth; because it's currently allowed by law and seems easier to them. Making landlords expressly illegal therefore solves more than just premature suffering and death by homelessness and undue stress on the working poor, elderly and disabled, but it improves civilization by making the intelligent, talented persons in it make their wealth by honorable methods: such as, starting businesses and employing people with livable wages; such as, loaning money without charging excessive usury; such as, funding or creating innovations and inventions; such as, starting non-profit charities, and such as, focusing on life and quality of life for everyone, instead of just themselves.

Ultimately, wealth inequality is to blame for why so many suffer so much in this world. (https://youtu.be/QPKKQnijnsM and https://www.youtube.com/watch?v=uWSxzjyMNpU) but I want it understood that I am not arguing for socialism (in which the government/wealthy persons own everything) but rather I am arguing for capitalism in which EVERYONE is a primary home owner! And laws prevent inflating housing costs, by preventing people from buying up all the real estate and making everyone else either buy it back at inflated cost or rent from them (as it is today). The free market is regulated through competition, which is why EVERYONE must own their own residence, or housing becomes inflated automatically by the greed of the wealthiest people on earth. It's one thing for a homeowner to sell for a reasonable recovery of their own investment plus the cost of any improvements they made during the time they owned their home, but another when wealthy realtors and investors snap up all affordable housing in an area before anyone else even sees it and then inflate the cost having done nothing whatsoever other than deplete a region of any and all affordable real estate.

"12In everything, then, do to others as you would have them do to you. For this is the essence of the Law and the Prophets. " Matthew 7: 12 - the words of our Eternal Creator, Lord and Savior Jesus Christ; the Judge of all souls.

Rents in this region have virtually doubled in a very short time. Perhaps the pandemic drove some people out of cities into more rural areas; thereby inflating housing costs and displacing the poor people already living there. That kind of rapid housing cost increase/cost of living increase is well beyond what the working poor, elderly and disabled can afford and if landlords were on the receiving end of such obvious attacks on people's lives, they would understand why I've written this plea to all mankind. We must make affordable housing an absolute right and protect citizens from the ubiquitous evil of primary residential landlords, bankers and real estate investors who have become so greedy, they're killing millions of innocent citizens worldwide. Please stop crushing the poor, elderly and disabled to death in the streets, by homelessness, slave wages, excessive housing costs and by other methods and vices; instead, right these wrongs now.

For more details listen to this presentation:
https://youtu.be/uU4kgJqFhX8
Thank you.

Landlord tenant relationships and laws across the United States CLEARLY violate the Equal Protection Clause of our Constitution.

Tenants are NOT safe and secure in their domiciles, at least anywhere near the same degree homeowners and landlords are.

Look at lease agreements across the nation. Landlords are dictating to tenants how to live in their own domiciles WELL BEYOND the LAWS that govern all of us. Homeowners and landlords are not subject to massive increases in the cost of living regarding their own domiciles. They are not told how to live within the confines of their homes apart from the laws that govern us all. If they have a mortgage on their home, they are typically long term with FIXED costs over a period of twenty, thirty or even more years! In order for tenants to have the same rights and treatment, their leases would have to be as long with affordable costs to their own dwellings. They wouldn't be able to be evicted into the streets short term or told they cannot do this and that including having no pets within their own primary residence!

Homeowners and landlords are not subject to other citizens raising the cost of living on them, on a whim, or being kicked out of their homes by other citizens for so many reasons as tenants. Face it, NO ONE renting is being treated equally or afforded the same rights and protection landlords and homeowners are in America, or for that matter anywhere worldwide. Rich people are maltreating and bullying poor people and in the worst-case scenarios driving them homeless to suffer and die prematurely. NO ONE IN AMERICA IS TO BE DEPRIVED OF LIFE OR LIBERTY WITHOUT DUE PROCESS OF LAW AND YET THE POOR ARE ROUTINELY. (economic genocides)

Due to my lifelong experience with renting, I dread it. Every time a property changes hands, the new owners understandably want to make as much money as they can in the transaction. As you can see from national statistics, everyone who is participating in the buy it and flip it practice is factually driving housing costs nationwide beyond the means of the poor, elderly and disabled to keep up. As such, this practice is the leading cause of homelessness and premature deaths due to exposure to the elements.

It has become so bad in recent years, that if I were in empowered by the people, there would be no more landlords; no one allowed to own more than their primary residence until there were no more homeless people and no one begging for food or unable to pay their bills because of overpriced housing. It is overpriced rentals that are taking the vast majority of the wages of the overtly oppressed poor working masses, elderly and disabled citizens on fixed income.

People can increase their wealth without attacking those so much worse off than themselves. They can increase their wealth by actually solving problems, like founding businesses or charities; employing people. But instead, the whole world (especially the poorest) suffers under excessive usury and exorbitant rents.

I've personally suffered so intensely lifelong due to such practices that if I were president, I would declare a state of national emergency and force landlords to offer all their tenants ownership with affordable terms of their apartments or homes and if they didn't, arrest them for assault and attempted homicide. In the event that was unacceptable, I would fund HUD to buy so many homes and multi-family units that landlords who refused to participate would have no tenants because they would leave and move into all the available affordable housing. Any complainers would be told they should be grateful that I don't arrest them for obvious crimes against their fellow innocent poor citizens. SHAME ON PEOPLE BEING THAT GREEDY, as to drive elderly and disabled citizens on fixed income into the streets to suffer and die!

Far too many landlords have bullied and oppressed the poor incessantly, forcing them into a lower and lower quality of life until they're begging or dying in the streets. It's so obviously evil, that I can't believe it hasn't been outlawed already. We can enact laws that ensure affordable housing as a right for everyone lifelong, if we stop allowing the wealthy to own everything and the poor to own nothing. HUD should be working with the poor to move them into long term fixed mortgages instead of supplementing rentals, because it's obvious that landlords are encouraged to raise housing costs, which are depleting HUD funds from helping the vast multitude in dire need of affordable housing. Because instead they are funding the GREED of the landlords! Such practices only increase this trend of wealth inequality and all the suffering of oppression and death that it results in. To solve the problem STOP MAKING THE GREEDY LANDLORDS EVEN MORE WEALTHY by supplementing rents and instead help the poor to become home-owners! People who own their apartments and homes instead of renting from anyone ever again!

I don't believe landlords really understand what they're doing to their tenants, because I don't believe the vast majority of them are deliberately that cruel. I imagine most landlords just think of it as an honorable way to increase their net worth, without giving much thought as to the overall impact of looking at rentals merely as an investment; rather than the homes people are living in. Most all hope that the cost of living remains affordable; especially poor tenants; because when it isn't, it means suffering and/or death.

When I say that those who are forced to rent their primary residence are suffering. Let me expound on the details. Every month, many of those renting, are literally praying for things like a raise or a lower cost of living or that their current landlord won't raise their rent, or worse sell the home or apartment complex they're living in. They pray their health and strength holds up under the financial stress. Their housing costs are ALREADY higher than they can afford and as such they either have to work additional jobs or beg friends, family, charities and government programs for their additional needs. Most who are renting have little to no savings, they're struggling just to survive under a lower and lower quality of life as wages and benefits are not keeping up with the cost of living/rent increases. If a person is injured either through crime, accidents or war, they're not guaranteed legal representation, compensation or restitution and as such can find themselves immediately reduced to below poverty subsistence on disability insurance (what happened to me). The elderly, disabled and poor working masses suffer the dread of housing increases that FORCE them out of their homes, into a lower and lower quality of life, longer commutes, smaller spaces, no land, no pets, driven into the slums, higher crime regions and even homelessness by those enjoying a much better quality of life. Due to housing costs, I had to sell my own vehicle, which has had the effect of placing me on home arrest. I am too ill to hike miles, and so even on good days, when I would love to go smell the wild flowers or take pictures of the wilderness or use my fishing license, I can't. I have to sit at home because I have no means to travel, since landlords have taken even that from me. Some imagine the poor have friends and family to help them maintain some quality of life, but they forget that those in poverty are often surrounded by people who are just as financially challenged. So, everyone they know is either working two and three jobs and has no time for recreation, or are so impoverished they too have no vehicle or means to travel. Those who are struggling just to survive often are in the lowest priced housing in any area, so when ANYONE buys those buildings and RAISES rent, they have fewer and fewer or NO PLACE LEFT TO GO! So, what's happening is an all-out assault on the working poor, elderly and disabled on fixed incomes.

Often, landlords that raise rents think that the rents are so cheap (because their own homes are that much better/more expensive; or where they moved from had an overall higher cost of living), but to those living in those dwellings, it's often already as much as they can afford. People moving inland from coastal metropolises need to realize that their higher cost of living is only sustained by all the better paying careers; so, regions inland aren't cheap to those living there on lower wages. In other words, such people need to stop imagining those living in less expensive regions can pay the same as those coastal cities with higher wages.

Average social security pays only 1500/mo and average disability only 1200/mo, but average rents nationwide for the smallest units are now at 1000/mo; making the cost of living impossible for millions of innocent people. These facts indicate housing, the lack of affordable housing, is the number one factor in the cost of living being too high today for too many; leading to homelessness, suffering and premature deaths.

Lawmakers who respond with "social security was never meant to live on"; need to ask themselves, why is that the all make sure their pensions, and disability insurance is more than enough to live on, when they know that millions of Americans, don't have the means to invest in their own retirements, and so only have social security and disability insurance. It seems lawmakers are representing themselves quite well, but not the American people they are elected to represent. One set of laws and policies for the wealthy and another for the poor.

Many are in terror of what is taking place in our nation now, it seems that people are allowing the elderly and disabled to be driven into the streets or forcing them to commit suicide before they die homeless. I personally have been forced to move by landlords raising rents my whole life.

When people who own multiple properties move, it's usually planned, and they hire professionals to pack up their household goods and deliver them often to an improved living situation, but when renters are forced to move, they look desperately in their region for anything available that they can afford and when there's nothing available, they're FORCED to look FURTHER and FURTHER and FURTHER away from even the places they were born and raised. FORCED to leave family, friends, into unknown regions; often where crime rates are higher due to extreme poverty. EVERY TIME a poor person moves, they have little to no savings and if they're elderly and disabled they have not the physical strength to move their possessions. So, for such persons it means having to sell some to everything of what they own just to come up with moving costs, security deposits and such in their lower quality rental. Eventually, the poor, elderly and disabled have nothing left to sell and no more reserves; this is why in the cities where affordable housing has run out, they're dying in the streets. So, they're not just driven from their homes, but wealthy persons by comparison are robbing them even of their personal possessions in the process; while separating them from pets, families and friends; crushing them to death in a most cruel manner. Lower rents, are more often than not, lower quality of life, no pets, no companions, and the dread of someone snatching up that building also, imagining they can extract blood money from those not wanting to die in the streets. It appears that most landlords have never suffered as a tenant, because if they had, they wouldn't be raising rents, they'd be lowering them by at least half nationwide. I don't believe landlords are deliberately cruel, I think that they imagine the tenants who can't afford rents have SOMEWHERE they can go, but sadly, rents are being raised at an alarming rate nationwide and causing hundreds of thousands of the working poor, elderly and disabled to become homeless. Such persons die prematurely under such hardship more often than not. Statistically these persons die on average 20 years sooner as a result of such duress lifelong. Whether landlords intend it or not, they are factually assaulting, robbing and killing the poor, elderly and disabled under these conditions.

If you're one of these people who like to blame victims of crimes rather than the criminals, then leave your cushy abode and try surviving homeless for at least a year. In other words, if you suffered like so many of them, and were dying of poverty and exposure, you might try to soothe yourself with alcohol or drugs too; so, don't judge any homeless person who is self-medicating; you have no idea what hell they went through to put them in that condition. If you have a job that pays the bills, keeps a roof over your head, etc. realize that not everyone does. Many are working two and three jobs and still don't earn enough to pay their bills due to excessive housing costs primarily. Some have power bills that are more than they earn all week! So wealthy people are in fact the ones who own the companies that offer such pitiful wages and yet are also the ones driving the cost of living ever higher. Yes, poor people, like most everyone make some decisions in life that can hurt them, but overall it isn't the poor jacking rents and paying such low wages that mass millions are destitute and upwards of 2 million or more go homeless in America each year.

Rent control might work if those in charge of the regulations couldn't be bribed, but there are examples where even rent controlled housing was changed simply by corrupt officials accepting bribes from landlords. I think landlords should ask themselves how would they feel, if people jacked their own housing cost beyond their means and kept forcing them to move lifelong. How would they feel if tragic circumstances left them poor and disabled only to have people kick them out of whatever home they could find for themselves. Even if they could afford to move, moving is one of the most stressful things people go through; so just the act of FORCING people out of their primary residences is by definition a form of assault and when it forces the elderly and disabled into homelessness to suffer and die from exposure, it is by definition, manslaughter, if unintended; or homicide, if they knew there was no affordable housing left for those tenants.

Jacking rents from one month to the next is an outright attack on everyone living there. I dare say no one can endure that kind of sudden increase in their housing costs. Virtually, no one gets that kind of drastic increase in their income, so why do landlords think this kind of treatment is acceptable. Rent increases instantly reduce the quality of life for their tenants; sometimes to the point of homelessness. I mention this, because you might know investors who think this buy and flip it thing is just great. From where I sit, such practices are cruel and at times murderous. If people want the hope of meeting our Maker in a good way, then all participating in this buy and flip it nightmare against the poor, elderly and disabled need to desist immediately. (Mt. 25:31-46) People are factually suffering and dying because of it. The American dream has become further and further away for growing numbers of American citizens.

The problem is easily rectified by making affordable housing a right for all citizens lifelong. People say then some people might not work, but no one saying these things has gone through the government red tape that makes sure people receiving social security or disability, actually qualify. In other words, people can't just decide to never work and qualify for benefits that would authorize them to receive such assistance. So, the law would protect the WORKING poor, (those who work on minimum wage or low wage jobs are still honorable people, they don't deserve to be driven homeless or forfeit most to all of their entire earnings to landlords), and the elderly and disabled. Lazy, healthy persons, might still end up begging, especially when there are little to no decent jobs with adequate wages, but many people are suffering due to ailments that doctors are unwilling to diagnose or unable to even recognize, so it would be very few that would face homelessness under such laws protecting citizens from maltreatment by other citizens; such as landlord tenant laws currently allow.

Sadly, arbitrarily raising rents on the poor and suffering population, is still legal and so according to the law, landlords have no complicity in what happens to all of us. I really think landlords are not thinking much about their tenants at all, only their own wealth and how to grow it; so, I don't believe the vast majority of them are sadistic and cruel; just lacking knowledge as to what the circumstances are really like for those who are renting.

I'm weary of contending with evil in this world, but greed is definitely the worst of it. People who are enjoying a quality of life so much better than their poor tenants, extract just as much as they can from them, until at the last the oppressed die on average twenty years sooner than they do. How can such people hope to enter into Paradise? (Luke 16)

Perhaps some haven't been involved in the buy and flip it practice for an extended period, but it's most definitely one of the most sinister evils of our day. Money can be made and increased in so many honorable ways, but raising the cost of living on people who can't even afford to own a small apartment is horrible.

If I were wealthy enough, I would try to start foundations and ministries to increase affordable housing to such a degree that it would drive rents down instead of higher. People renting are caught between homelessness and hunger just to try in vain to keep up with housing costs. Some blow their heads off. How can a poor tenant ever escape under such circumstances? Lifelong, I've been forced to move by wealthy landlords shoving me ever further into whatever poor sections of our nation still remained and now it's gotten to the point where desperate people nationwide have given up and are dying in the streets. It isn't due to a lack of housing, it's due to a lack of AFFORDABLE housing; because investors are buying it all for themselves and leaving nothing for the working poor, elderly and disabled. We would have plenty of housing instantly, if owning more than your primary residence was illegal. That would tend to force investors to find other ways to grow their wealth, perhaps some of them might actually contribute to life instead of death as a result.

It's obvious to me that the poor have little to no representation in our nation, otherwise landlords wouldn't be able to get away with oppressing them. The poor, elderly and disabled are not just subject to rents they can't afford, but in worst case examples landlords are driving them to homelessness and premature horrible deaths. (we show more compassion to serial-killers putting them down humanely, than to innocent people who suffer and die homeless.)

A simple way to make money is to offer an alternative to lenders that are cutting the throats of people with 6000% pay day loans. People who have enough can act as an alternative lender that still charges higher interest than the banks, but yet helps the poor to own a small patch of dirt somewhere, or buy a mobile home in a rent-controlled park. That way a person can make money while helping the poor instead of victimizing them. People needing tax write-offs can work with HUD to build affordable housing across the nation, and yet they STILL make plenty in the process. Another huge need is AFFORDABLE RETIREMENT communities; the NEED is so

GREAT that volume makes up for cost per unit in profits! What I'm driving at, is there are almost endless ways to make lots of money without driving the poor, elderly and disabled into the streets to die prematurely! Investors COULD buy complexes and offer terms to their tenants for unit ownership and make a bundle just like banks do on mortgages; but in a way that helps the poor instead of making their lives worse.

Our Lord Jesus Christ/Yeshua Ha Mashiach is so good, He's willing to forgive anyone and everyone of any and all sins and offenses whether known or unknown (except blasphemy against His Holy Spirit – Mt 12:31-32), if they're truly sorry for them and unwilling to go on committing them. He commands us all to repent and be baptized in His Name (Mark 16:15 and Acts 2:38,39) and if we are wise, we obey His Commandment. Such persons then will know the One True God and then also know that they will enter Paradise when they take their last breath. I don't blame landlords exclusively for the sad and terrible plight of the poorest among us, but to imagine they have nothing to do with overpriced housing is delusional.

The wealthiest people on earth have depopulation agendas which is one of the reasons they have been pushing the buy it and flip it practice on television. They KNOW it's killing people. They have access to the census and other statistics proving it.

Being bullied lifelong by people who have a quality of life so much better than myself has made me think that perhaps if the wealthy do know they're killing the poor, maybe some of them might at least have a conscience enough to offer us sedative palliative end of life options rather than driving us into homelessness and horrible deaths. If they really want to kill people so badly, it seems to me that they could at least show some mercy and euthanize the poor, elderly and disabled with sedatives; rather than dying of exposure homeless, miserable and hungry. If I'm wrong about thinking most landlords don't realize what they're doing to their poor tenants and this really is a form of deliberate assault on the elderly and disabled, then seriously, if the world has become so evil, cold and callous, that's what I would choose. Death by sedation is much preferred to a slow and painful death by exposure/homelessness. At least that way society doesn't have to endure the stench of rotting corpses in the streets.

I tell you these things with the intent that perhaps you might ask other people not to continue this practice of "buy it and flip it" any longer. I know it would be a miracle if landlords all agreed to halve rents, but that is how far they are above what they should be for the working poor, elderly and disabled now; in some regions they're four times or more what those people can reasonably afford. What I'm hoping for is legislation to be passed that protects everyone from being maltreated in this way. Just imagine if the wealthiest people on earth treated landlords the way they're treating their tenants. Forcing everyone to rent at their demands by buying up all the real estate. Then it would be obvious to the people of the world that just having landlords is a peril to those who cannot afford to own real property. EVERYONE should have the RIGHT to affordable housing lifelong. If I had my way, as soon as someone turned 18, they would have the RIGHT to OWN their first residence, even if it was only a studio apartment. A home of their own that NO ONE could raise the cost of beyond their means LIFELONG!

I'm not trying to make anyone feel bad, I really don't hold landlords any hard feelings. Most are just trying to improve their own finances and really haven't given serious thought to the impact of their methods.

Everyone knows it's a crime to demand money from people under threat: muggings, robbery, armed robbery etc.; they even make movies about organized crime demanding "protection" fees with demands that might have a time limit attached; like, "you got one month to come up with the dough, or else..." And yet, landlord tenant relationships are just as confronting and assaultive, if not worse. You have one month to pay my demands or leave your home! Rent hikes are made under extreme threats and duress against innocent poor people all the time; which are identical to definitions of CRIMES! I just think that most of them don't realize that things have become this dire due to this nationwide practice, but they have.

Many cities have over a ten-year waiting list for affordable housing now. Rents might self-correct in a free market, but only when the poorest have suffered and died in sufficient numbers that vacancies force them down.

Since there are so many honorable ways to grow wealth, I'm most definitely wanting landlords to be a thing of the past. Or at least make it something that CANNOT drive ANYONE into homelessness, by making sure EVERYONE owns their own primary residence that other citizens can't take from them or arbitrarily raise the cost of living on them, as it is presently. Rentals could exist as long as EVERYONE has a safe and secure dwelling of their own.

People get injured or become chronically or terminally ill and so are reduced to below poverty level income through no fault of their own and then are subject to being driven homeless by other citizens living a quality of life so much better. Just the very nature of landlord tenant relationships and laws is attempting to legalize what would otherwise be considered outright felony offenses. Anywhere from trespassing, to robbery, assault, and manslaughter to premeditated homicides!

How are landlords committing these crimes against poor, innocent citizens? They simply raise the rent beyond their means to pay, then evict them on short notice. In the process, the poor tenant has little to NO PROTECTION nationwide from this unbelievably evil practice! Often, they cannot scrape together funds fast enough to move, come up with security deposits, etc. And so are either forced to sell their personal possessions or just be thrown out, where the landlords then sell or keep what factually belongs to their poor tenants. When landlords employ police officers to do their dirty work, it would otherwise be called armed robbery. (In other words, if groups of citizens got together and demanded money from homeowners and landlords that were unable or unwilling to pay, and then raided their home and tossed them out and took all their personal possessions, it would be considered SERIOUS FELONIES!)

So, face it, the very nature of landlord tenant relationships are NOT LEGAL, NOT ETHICAL, NOT MORAL; NOT RIGHT BY ANY STRETCH OF THE IMAGINATION! AGAIN, secondary housing can be subjected to the free market, but primary housing, shelter from the elements, must be regulated to be absolutely affordable or we are killing the poor economically.

What needs to be done, is the implementation affordable housing laws for people LIFELONG, rich and poor alike; NO ONE can toss anyone else out of their homes! (Unless they are in fact committing arrest-able offenses under the laws that govern us all.) And NO ONE can just jack the cost of living on another citizen on a whim! In my own complex, the new landlord raised rent on one tenant all the way from less than 700/mo. to $2,000 USD from one month to the next! that is OUTRAGEOUS maltreatment! pure evil! No excuses! I hear wealthy people saying things like tenants know what they're entering into when they sign leases, etc. Suppose homeowners were given only the options tenants have?

would you still be trying in vain to defend such obvious evil? In other words, there are little to no long-term leases or renewable leases from year to year that do not include the option of landlords to raise rents just as high as they please on a whim! So, any time for any reason a landlord just decides to attack existing tenants they can and do! It's obvious that tenants are not being afforded equal rights and protections in America to other US citizens that own real property.

Everyone please lobby congress to immediately make laws that ensure Affordable Housing is a Right for all citizens lifelong. And what remains in the industry of motels, hotels and rentals should be under laws that dictate things like:

Any and all tenants are under the protection of these laws:

1) the SAME rights afforded all citizens, even their landlords to be safe and secure in their own dwelling.

2) landlords may not raise rents more than 30% of the percentage of increase to minimum wage or social security cost of living increase, on their respective poor working tenants or the elderly and disabled on fixed income! In other words, if minimum wage is increased from 10$ to 11$ that was a ten percent hike; then and only then could their housing cost be increased by a maximum of 3%. Their current rent or cost to own could not be more than 30% of their net monthly pay and as such rent or cost to own would be an affordable increase. For example, if someone earns 1000$/mo. or is allotted that in disability insurance

then the most their housing could cost them is $300/mo. and if their annual increase in cost of living was 12% then their housing cost could only be raised .3% each month 12%/12 = 1% increase monthly of which housing can only be 30% of that. So, their rent could only be increased MAXIMALLY to $309/mo.

That is STILL worse treatment than landlords and homeowners are under. People say, who will pay for this affordable housing? who will maintain it? IF all citizens had the RIGHT to affordable housing, it only means that what they PAY each month to live in their primary residence is commensurate to their earnings, or retirement income or disability insurance, until their home is paid for completely by them. It just means EVERY adult citizen qualifies for up to a lifelong mortgage that is AFFORDABLE. Maintenance and improvements to such properties are still the responsibility of homeowners, but in the cases of the poor, elderly and disabled (people who might not be able to afford necessary repairs and maintenance or be too disabled to do the work themselves) can be under the same regulations that currently govern HUD in which property managers that are able bodied citizens look after such matters for them. REMEMBER THERE IS ENOUGH MONEY IN THIS WORLD TO DO WHATEVER GOOD THING THE PEOPLE DECIDE TO DO!

IF YOU, ANY OF YOU, become injured, chronically or terminally ill, do you want other citizens taking what little you have as you fight for a return to good health or at least try to enjoy what little time is left you? Do you want other citizens to be able to drive you out of your residence into the streets homeless to suffer and die of exposure? If not, then we need affordable housing as a RIGHT for ALL citizens lifelong to be implemented IMMEDIATELY!

https://www.facebook.com/photo.php?fbid=2854249944653946&set=a.115635768515391&type=3&theater - indifference, apathy or maltreatment of the poor brings curses upon those doing so; whereas helping the poor bring blessings.

https://www.facebook.com/photo.php?fbid=1898732813539002&set=a.115635768515391&type=3&theater - INNOCENT POOR PEOPLE, EVEN THE ELDERLY AND DISABLED ARE BEING DRIVEN INTO THE STREETS TO SUFFER AND DIE PREMATURELY. THESE ARE MOST DEFINITELY CRIMES AGAINST HUMANITY!

https://www.apartmentlist.com/rentonomics/national-rent-data/ - this is the problem: RENTS across America for just a 1BR **average** around $1000.

"The **average** Social Security benefit was $1,503 per month in January 2020. " - https://money.usnews.com/money/retirement/social-security/articles/how-much-you-will-get-from-social-security

https://www.facebook.com/groups/220827085367015/pe

rmalink/696088404507545/?notif_id=1584220422120932&notif_t=group_post_mention - help for those seeking affordable housing

"The estimated average Social Security disability benefit amount for a disabled worker receiving Social Security Disability Insurance (SSDI) as of Nov. 2019 is $1,237 per month." - https://www.investopedia.com/ask/answers/082015/what-are-maximum-social-security-disability-benefits.asp

The elderly and disabled are increasingly unable to afford housing.

https://www.youtube.com/watch?v=JmjL_WD3DZo

https://backpackbed.org/us/facts-about-homelessness

https://www.nationalhomeless.org/publications/facts/elderly.html

https://endhomelessness.org/homelessness-in-america/homelessness-statistics/state-of-homelessness-report/

https://www.justiceinaging.org/wp-content/uploads/2016/04/Homelessness-Older-Adults.pdf

https://www.ncbi.nlm.nih.gov/books/NBK218239/

https://www.americanprogress.org/issues/poverty/news/2018/11/20/461294/lack-housing-mental-health-disabilities-exacerbate-one-another/ - ANYONE who goes through the circumstances that puts people on the street might not present all that well or could be classified by others who have not walked in their shoes as "mentally ill". When you listen to their stories that put some people on the streets, some just simply disbelieve those people and so wrongly label them. Just because someone goes through tragedies you haven't is no reason to look down upon them or think they deserve to suffer and die homeless.

I'm writing this letter not with hatred toward landlords, but compassionately; as a defense for the working poor, elderly and disabled; hoping to find what I believe to be true. I believe the vast majority of landlords are decent people with compassion; people who would show mercy on those who are already suffering under poverty, instead of apathy or cruelty. I think they really don't understand what it's like now to be one of their poor tenants or they would be joining programs like HUD to radically increase affordable housing for people lifelong. I really do hope you don't take my personal aggravation as an affront. I'm just trying to avoid discouragement and a premature demise myself and needed to vent to people I think have a heart that cares. Please spread the word, everyone needs to be safe and secure in their own homes and the best way I can think of to do that is to make affordable housing a right for everyone lifelong.

You would have thought with my clear-cut case of medical malpractice, I would have received some kind of compensation, after all the attorneys who advertised to represent people who suffered medical malpractice. But in my own efforts, it seemed those doing so only represent known threats like drugs that injure or kill people. But to find ones willing to represent me, an indigent, asking that they get paid if they win, who was alleging attempted homicides, was impossible for me to find anyone though I must have contacted over a thousand firms of attorneys from across our nation. So, I filed a complaint in behalf of everyone who had been injured or killed in these United States. When I realized that it was perhaps millions of innocent citizens, I made the class action suit in the amount of ten-trillion dollars. Not surprisingly, the courts dismissed it illegally.

https://www.blastthetrumpet.org/iTestifytheTRUTH/USGovEuthanizingUSCitizens.pdf - When NO ONE in our nation would help me arrest the mass murdering doctors and nurses, the government became complicit through either their intentional negligence or by their deliberate attempt to leave doctors and nurses in hospitals for the purpose of murdering citizens. Based on my research, deaths of citizens have been going on in our nation(s) through all manner of malpractice against us for decades!

Earlier this year I suffered a stroke; I just want my story told before I die or am unable to tell it any longer. I'm scheduled for an angioplasty this week. I can't tell if I'm suffering due to a failing heart, or diabetes or just the medication I've been prescribed treating both. You see due to my diabetes, the Ozempic once weekly injection was prescribed, and it made my bowel movements so sluggish that I bloated up with around thirty pounds of water weight, that led to my stroke. It could have been coincidence, or it could have been the medication, regardless it looks like I'm on stool softeners now indefinitely. But trying to get doctors to admit that you suffered due to prescriptions they gave you, isn't easy. So more often than not, we get injured with no legal recourse in the courts. The poor just suffer due to all these things, we are suffering and dying.

Whether or not population management is deliberately killing people or not, these things about our civilization are seriously life threatening. I wanted to tell you things that God taught me, instead of just the things that are not great about our civilization. I have much more things I wish to tell citizens about God and about our world, to hopefully change it for the better.

I'm for a rapid return to the foundational principles this country was established on. The ultimate reasons our quality of life is suffering is due to the religious worldviews of those ruling/ruining the planet and all life on it. The theory of evolution and resulting atheism are factually linked to eugenic fascism, abortion, etc. https://www.youtube.com/watch?v=qMWGgY6wT30&list=PL7F9B57EBDCCEECF8 and it is these worldviews that are allowing people, in the minds of the so called "ruling elite", to become so greedy, blood thirsty and cruel that all the rest of us are losing our freedoms, rights, and our lives.

http://www.facebook.com/notes/michael-swenson/treatise-on-greed-and-corruption/517410181671279

THE BILL OF RIGHTS

1) First Amendment issues – Congress shall make no law respecting the establishment or prohibition of religion

   a) It is therefore the absolute right of every citizen to practice the religion of their choice, to hold their beliefs, to speak their mind on any and all topics so long as practicing their religion is not murdering other people or otherwise raping, pillaging and plundering crimes of violence to persons or property (criminal organizations disguising themselves as lawful religions, like islam or satanic cults, if your religion openly advocates crimes against humanity, like murder, that is not lawful to practice that religion)

   b) In the educational setting it is the right of all persons, students and teachers to practice their faith openly without embarrassment or harassment; so long as the course curriculum and educational standard is not interrupted thereby for undue periods beyond a reminder to all present that it is a constitutionally protected right

c) In government or the work place, it is the absolute right of all persons, political or otherwise to practice their faith openly without shame or repercussions (again only lawful religions)

d) In the residence or workplace, if such a location is inherently of one religious belief that specifically tells them to have no fellowship with persons committing acts such as adultery, fornication, homosexuality, it is the absolute right of that location to fire or prohibit such persons from seeking employment in that location. GET IT STRAIGHT PEOPLE, WHO YOU HAVE SEX WITH IS A CHOICE, AN ACT, not a protected attribute of existence, people have the right to "discriminate" against offensive actions to their faith if the inherent organization is all about that faith! COMMON SENSE PEOPLE, the Boy Scouts has the absolute RIGHT and DUTY NOT to hire pedophiles and homosexuals! Frankly, if we held the wicked judges accountable for going against such common sense in protecting children from openly professing predators; by making any of them ruling in such a way that allows such predation to occur to be held accountable by conspiracy charges for the crimes perpetrated by such homosexuals and pedophiles against innocent children that they encouraged to enter into such godly establishments; I do not think there would be such perversions of justice and improper conduct occurring from their benches any longer; despite what bribes were thrown their way to destroy this nation and it's godly heritage.

e) Any all-male organizations of a Judeo-Christian foundation, has the absolute right to excommunicate, ban from employment by churches, persons such as openly practice and profess a lifestyle CLEARLY PROHIBITED by their religion- THIS MOST DEFINITELY INCLUDES HOMOSEXUALITY! (Lev 19; Rom 1:26-32) While I'm for everyone's right to life, this trend of FORCING people to accept what our Eternal Creator calls UNACCEPTABLE must cease. Suing people just because they refuse you to bake your wedding cake as a homosexual, is not how our nation was founded and not what it should become. Christian bakers that believe in one man and one-woman marriages, should not be forced to advocate/bake for homosexuals. Holy Matrimony is a Divine Institution! Frankly, until sodomy laws are all removed from the books (even though most have or been modified; my point is that if they had actually been enforced, our nation would not have degenerated to the degree it has today threatening the lives of everyone coast to coast for the present depravity), all openly practicing homosexuals were/are breaking such laws and as such can be arrested at will; so this point would be moot under those once existing laws (and in some places still exist) in America. (just like the "don't ask don't tell" military policy which is ignoring its own United Code of Military Justice laws strictly prohibiting sodomy) Bottom line, if you are headed for the wrath of God, you need to hear from society that you are; in the form of not tolerating your perversities at all. Yes, we allow you to live, but no we do not condone your crimes against God and man. Sodomy is one of those crimes.

f) Because sodomites are bringing the wrath of God upon themselves and the nation that embraces such behavior http://www.pinkoski.com/sodom-a-gomorrah.html, https://www.youtube.com/watch?v=If9yzHwOeUc ; I propose marriage be legally defined and recognized as strictly between a man and woman, that no state recognizes "same sex unions", which is morally reprehensible behavior and a shame to any society. It is unbelievably SAD that this even needs to be addressed!

g) The right to bear arms!

i) ALL citizens have the absolute right to bear arms! ALL means ALL!

ii) I encourage the open ability to bear on your person at all times the weapon of your choosing either in plain view or concealed.

iii) I would like to see mandated (with an opt out parental consent) as part of course curriculum as soon as children are strong enough to wield a weapon without injuring themselves, trained in the proper use; so that by the time they are 18, they can openly possess a weapon of their choosing and be proficient in its use.

iv) The greatest crimes against humanity have always been governments that possess too much power over the people and the only way to keep this in check is to tell citizens openly they have the absolute right to defend themselves and their loved ones with lethal force if necessary. I would make it publicly known "make my day" laws are clearly enforceable; that each citizen can defend their person and their family; especially in their homes from home invasions by anyone INCLUDING government! (NO MORE IRS MOB-LIKE BREAKING AND ENTERING YOUR HOME AND RESIDENCE WITH WEAPONS FOR NOT PAYING THE CRIMINALS IN CHARGE (CORRUPT GOVERNMENT, DRUNK WITH EXCESSIVE POWER) "PROTECTION", "TRIBUTE", "TAXES"! The government like all the rest of us should have to obtain a judgment for any and all money they claim is due and AT MOST have the ability to garnish wages IF AND ONLY IF, what remains is sufficient to live on! FRANKLY, ALL taxes upon citizens (not tariffs or trade taxation of foreigners or foreign made products) but ALL taxes by elected officials upon the electorate (resident citizens they SUPPOSEDLY represent) is a form of oppression and tyranny! In the United States and around the world COMPLETELY UNNECESSARY!

(1)   i.   My proposal – make all taxes permanently ILLEGAL! NEVER AGAIN TO BE PLACED UPON THE SHOULDERS OF CITIZENS!

(2)   ii.   NEVER ALLOW THE GOVERNMENT TO SELL TREASURY BILLS OR BORROW MONEY FROM ANYONE OR ANY ENTITY BECAUSE IT IS COMPLETELY UNNECESSARY! (and, as far as I'm concerned, TREASONOUS)

(3)   iii.   Make the Federal Reserve and all associated mints once again directly controlled by the US government in behalf of the people and restore the right to mint currency as necessary for the nation's solvency

(4)   iv.   Inher
ent national natural resources "pay" for
quality education, healthcare, firefighters,
police powers, military, disability insurance,
"welfare", retirement pensions and other
agreed social services!

(5)   v.   The
IRS employees instead of being charged
with monitoring the public would be in
charge of monitoring government spending
and giving the public accountability of our
elected officials! (They would process the
revenues of the natural resources and
allocate funds to the various social services
of government and NEVER again be
breaking your doors down threatening your
lives and that of your loved ones and to
steal your home or business out from under
you)! That is absolutely identical to criminal
mob-like behavior and is NOT to be
tolerated by any civilized and sane society!

(6) RE-ESTABLISH AMERICA AS IT WAS
FOUNDED TO BE!

(a) Do away with Wallstreet, publicly
traded stocks and options!

(i)   i.
Multi-national entities have

become so large and influential as to corrupt political officials to the suffering of billions of souls on the planet

(ii)   ii.

No way to hold the multi-nationals accountable behind armies of attorneys and personal anonymity

(iii)   iii.

No more price setting and fluctuation of commodities that form the foundation of economies like food and transportation costs (oil)

(iv)   iv.

In order to make money citizens have to provide products or services; keeping the public employed locally and nationally! Wallstreet allows the rich to simply loan money to multinationals taking jobs overseas and paying slave wages making living conditions worse for the vast majority of humanity but small businesses with conspicuous owners and managers are more easily held accountable civilly and criminally and morally to providing the people that work for them LIVING WAGES! (Doing away with the excessive greed of CEOs making billions and tens of millions while they lay off employees)

2) Create consumer watch advocacy entities, like the FTC should be, only this would be a conglomerate of attorneys of all kinds of specializations that represent the poor and oppressed to fight the wealthy entities until there is once again a balance between consumers and manufacturers or service providers. SPECIFICALLY, to fight corruption in:

a)   i.   Medical malpractice and especially hospital homicides

b)   ii.   Insurance frauds where insurers deny claims of the chronically or terminally ill because they know the person will be dead or is too sick to fight them

c)   iii.   Insurance frauds (life insurance) that don't seek out beneficiaries of policies but make it the responsibility of claimants when the policy was paid for already

d)   iv.   Billing frauds like Verizon's and other phone companies' mystery charges, duplicate billing, duplicate collections etc.

they've been busted for ONLY instead of paying government fines, they have to PAY the victims (consumers)

e)   v.   Collections frauds where a consumer disputes a debt only to have another collection agency tack on more fees and continue as if it wasn't disputed in the first place would be held criminally and civilly liable

f)   vi.   I would like to make it mandatory that no credit reporting agency can report a derogatory claim without verifying with the consumer FIRST, and any disputed CLAIM forced into immediate arbitration provided as part of this social service to protect consumers from the wealthy oppressors of today. (James 2:1-**6-9**)

g) DEPROGRAMMING

     i)   It is necessary for all souls to realize; whether they like it or not, the GOD of the HOLY BIBLE is in fact the Eternal Creator and Ruler of all Creation. He has given us CLEAR INSTRUCTIONS for all aspects of life!

         (1)   i.   As such, when you are suffering, you must be honest with yourself and ask if your nation and the people all around you and perhaps even yourself have departed from following

those instructions to your own detriment (Deut 28). If so, then REPENT and RETURN to GOD and following His Instructions and you will return to a state of blessedness. ALWAYS BE THANKFUL! DO NOT FORGET AND BECOME IDOLOTERS!

(2)   ii.   If you and the general populace are honest, willing to work, following God's Instructions and you are suffering then it is definitely because greedy and corrupt persons are in places of public trust and are wickedly oppressing you either in their incompetence, ignorance and negligence or by evil intent. GET RID OF CORRUPT AUTHORITIES AND MAKE SURE ONLY PERSONS FULL OF THE HOLY GHOST ARE IN POSITIONS OF MANIFEST PUBLIC TRUST, POWER AND AUTHORITY!

3) NEVER AGAIN ALLOW YOURSELF TO BE BRAINWASHED INTO A SLAVE MENTALITY!

a)   i.   Paying taxes is a form of tribute to greedy, elite oppressors; anyone asking you to pay them tribute is saying you are subject to them; they are superior to and rule over rather than serve you

b)   ii.   If as a society you ELECT as a whole to PAY for public services, then YOU should have a say so in how that money is SPENT! But as I've mentioned taxes to provide social services to run a country are completely unnecessary and are only a means to subjugate, control and brainwash the populace.

c)   iii.   NEVER again allow "king of the hill" personalities to tell all the rest of humanity that they own all the oil, coal, water, food, sunlight and other natural resources God has provided for us all to steward and benefit from!

d)   iv.   Wild animals and birds and insects build or find homes for themselves, they eat, drink, mate, and live without having to pay tribute to anyone or anything other than that everything that lives owes its' existence to Almighty GOD. (POINT IS, wild animals are FREE, but most of humanity has been turned into slaves!)

e)   v.   When anyone tells you that YOU have to PAY for what they SPEND or BUY, that is INSANITY and outright OPPRESSION, so NEVER again let propaganda or corrupt politicians tell you that YOU have a "national debt", if those corrupt officials borrowed or spent money WHEN THEY OWN THE MINTS AND WERE EMPOWERED FUNDAMENTALLY TO PROVIDE

CURRENCY AS NECESSARY FOR THE NATION'S SOLVENCY, then tell those persons who spent that money, THEY have to pay; not you and your children for their lunatic borrowing and spending when they didn't have to!

f)   vi.   Our government has violated the First Amendment in establishing the religion of the metaphysical concept of origin being a "big bang" and "evolutionary" without one shred of scientific support to date. It is a religion fundamentally of a belief system adhered to despite scientific evidence to the contrary. The only theory of origin supported by the sciences is that of Biblical Creationism and since that is the fact and truth of the Universe in which we exist; it is NOT a violation of the Bill of Rights to teach it. Telling lies to little kids that they came from monkeys and pond scum IS! NEVER AGAIN ALLOW YOUR CHILDREN TO BE BRAINWASHED BY INSANE LUNATICS WHO CHOOSE TO BELIEVE A COMPLETE LOAD OF CRAP OVER FUNDAMENTAL SCIENTIFIC TRUTH! If you do, then you all deserve to be rounded up like the animals you've been successfully brainwashed to believe you are and put in cages until you come into your right minds.

g)   vii.   NEVER again allow the rulers to set prices of commodities!

These days the reason so many are suffering is that GREED at the highest levels has created MONOPOLIES causing suppliers to set prices rather than consumers and so by this corruption and greed we are no longer a free-market society and is why the greedy elite bailed out their buddies while leaving mass millions of us to be driven out of our homes; losing our entire life's savings in the process. Make it fundamental law that the poorest among you set the prices of basic dietary staples and the factors that affect overall costs of goods (such as transportation – oil)!

i) Conversely, this means elected, intelligent officials must show proof that the poorest citizens are NOT starving homeless in the streets, NOT being euthanized, NOT being imprisoned, BUT

ii) ALL citizens that are able to work, willing to work have enough of a LIVING WAGE to provide food, clothes and shelter for themselves!

iii) Medical disabilities might not be TOTAL disabilities; as such more proactive assistance for such citizens needs to be implemented so those who still want to contribute and be productive are allowed to

iv) the poor and demographics of a region should produce commensurate developments, improvements, when the poor are driven off like chaff before the wind to make way for the wealthy we have left off being a sane, representative society into caste oppression, enslavement, and human rights violations leading to outright oppression and eventually euthanization of any members of society perceived as having little or no worth by such persons as think such is acceptable behavior being adopted more and more worldwide. This mentality is fundamentally flawed as ANYONE can become ill, disabled, and reduced to poverty EASILY, so just because the sun is shining on you today doesn't mean you won't have a storm tomorrow; IN OTHER WORDS, HUMAN WORTH IS FUNDAMENTALLY EQUAL! The moment any individual is considered less valuable than another in thinking and practice, we are headed to VERY DANGEROUS and even LIFE-THREATENING trends! Therefore, NO MORE RULERS (except GOD), only PUBLIC SERVANTS! Accountable to the public and treating even the poorest citizens with absolute respect as an equal human being!

v)   viii.   We must make equal opportunity education for ALL citizens by making it a right and public service of the nation to obtain at least an employable trade school degree. Higher education is the right of all citizens that show the aptitude (grades) and attitude (desire); thus, we get passionate (and competent) persons pursuing higher degrees for more technical and responsible positions (such as doctors) rather than just those who can afford it! (In my opinion, all med students should be REQUIRED to obtain only B grades or above, any C should result in review as to why and possible dismissal! (Doctors are dealing with lives!) Incompetence can result in lifelong torture or death! They should be held to the highest standards; NOT becoming such just to become rich! And NOT going to med school just because mommy and daddy are wealthy enough to send them. In addition, our current system engenders corruption, nepotism and such in politics and law, by making law school excessively expensive and thereby omitting such persons as would have a natural inclination to sympathize with the poor and oppressed, the enslaved and imprisoned citizens of our society. Thus, the greedy elite employ armies of attorneys further strengthening their oppression upon consumers, citizens causing rampant fraudulent billing, slanderous and libelous credit reporting, increasing impoverished citizens which are losing their rights and voice and even admittance to courts by these measures.

vi)   ix.   Little to no adequate paying jobs – FIRE government officials! The only reason there are no jobs is by willful intent! (in connection with all the aforementioned) However, REGARDLESS, of greed, corruption, multinational enslavement of impoverished citizens worldwide, Wallstreet (people thinking it's okay to make money by laying off other people, reducing their wages, reducing their benefits, so they can make higher dividends without a conscience; rather than providing a product or service which is the fundamental foundation of a strong, working economy), yes, REGARDLESS of these major contributing factors, when there are no jobs offering living wages IT IS THE ABSOLUTE FAULT OF POLITICIANS! All of history shows that politicians can create MORE THAN ENOUGH JOBS to employ the whole world! ONLY when authorities turn corrupt and selfish, caring about their personal bank accounts more than others, do such conditions occur! I list dozens of jobs that need doing around the world that could employ every able soul thrice over worldwide! Just the infrastructure needs in America could employ all persons now unemployed; so, if there are no jobs, it is for the reasons people don't want to face:

(1) Population management- proven fact birth rates go down and death rates go up during economic crises

(2) Economic crises (depressions and recessions are INTENTIONALLY CAUSED) – this is extremely simple to do; those who own the mints and control banking processes like the feds, cause depressions/recessions just like they did repeatedly as often as desired by loose lending followed by a hangman's noose:

(a) Step one – inflate real property values by giving 100-110% LTV (loan to value) to individual homeowners

(b) Step two – provide plastic the same way casinos give people chips; so, they detach from the concept that they are spending real money

(c) Step three – provide legal ways to charge loan shark values like 35$ fees for a 1$ over draft or increasing the compounded interest rates after seducing a victim and entrapping them with a low introduction rate

(d) Step four – inundate society with shows, advertisements, and other materialistic values to drive consumer spending above their means

(e) Step five- AFTER giving plastic cards (inherently worthless), loose loans (100-110%LTV; again inherently worthless), loose paper money (again inherently worthless), they then get together with their rich buddies, laugh it up as they reduce wages, lay off jobs, withdraw loans, increase interest rates on all the worthless credit they gave to all the suckers that were created by the above steps, and after the poor, slave, "suckers", poured their entire life's energy and savings into their homes, drive them off with foreclosures and thus the wealthy elite increase their REAL VALUE NET WORTH by getting YOUR REAL PROPERTY when all they actually provided was WORTHLESS credit of NO INTRINSIC VALUE WHATSOEVER! That all the manipulated masses spent on their advertised products and services and thus were completely scammed out of their houses and years of their hard work by these controlled and obvious measures, tried and proven historically AND currently.

(f) In this manner, recessions and depressions, are used to control population rates, kill off the poor, sick, elderly and oppressed, and increase the ruling elite's real property holdings and net worth at the expense of the masses that they have so easily manipulated by these measures

(g) Practice money management the way GOD tells you to and don't borrow from others; save instead for all you wish to purchase, if you borrow; you are choosing to be a slave. (Prov 22:7) What choice do people have when the wealthy raise the cost of living so high that the poor can't afford it? So economic slavery, ending in economic genocides are facts taking place in front of our eyes.

(i) If you are a Christian or of the Jewish faith you know it is against God's commandments to loan with usury to anyone of the faith, but many are doing just that by participating in Wallstreet, note buying, and even direct hard money loans (Ex 22:5, Lev 25:36,37; Deut 23:19, 20)

(ii) Christian landlords COULD show compassion to your tenants under such oppressive circumstances that exist at present and reduce your rents thereby potentially alleviating brothers and sisters in the faith and having mercy upon the poor and needy

(iii) If you DON'T give generously to those in need when you have abundance it is most certain that one day you will be in need and yet no one will help you! (Gal 6:7) conversely, Christ promises great blessings to the cheerful giver (Lk 6:35-38)

(iv) Some ministries' methods of taking "pledges" are setting up something almost as solemn as a vow; rather than just accepting contributions, they use a "pledge" method to make a person feel guilty if they are unwilling or unable to continue contributing to such ministries; using this method which borders on Christ's warnings not to make promises, or swear, or talk of the future as if it is certain without mentioning God's will. (Jas 4:13-17; Mt 5:34-36) It's acceptable to accept offerings and tithes, it is not acceptable to falsely accuse benefactors, contributors or partners of making a pledge in the process. (I mention this because it is linked to the problem of Christianity adopting too much materialism and greedy practices of the worldly persons cleverly manipulating citizens) It's not as bad as citizens being defrauded by our government out of billions through the illegal income tax (16th amendment never ratified), but all attempts to enslave and obligate another person into indefinite donations is practicing distasteful manipulation rather than honest charity. POINT- Christians need to transform the world for the better; not be transformed by the world for the worse!

(v) Jobs can be created incessantly by national projects and vision of proper stewardship of the earth; by public servants (government) auctioning publicly on local, state and national levels whatever tasks that need doing (like the dozens I list on blastthetrumpet.org). (unfortunately, now due to political corruption, often government contracts are not made public at all but sold to their rich, corrupt, greedy buddies in business (of profiteering at the expense of all the rest of us). The criminals in politics and business partnerships that now exist simply embezzle all the funds such as the massive missing funds annually in the Pentagon, military/industrial complex, Halliburton so called rebuilding of IRAQ that was clearly just blown on luxurious partying by many corrupt persons all well documented but NO ONE is holding all these criminals accountable! Citizens MUST unite and realize the true POWER is in sheer numbers of unified protests by MILLIONS nationwide; not a few thousand here and there)! That way government down sizes from being a direct employer and funds the free competitive market. Where does the money come from?

(aforementioned, natural resources, national products and services, people (elected officials/public servants) mint currency as necessary for national solvency/productivity – YES! IT REALLY IS THAT SIMPLE!)

(vi) RECAP –to avoid suffering and be blessed

1. Teach all children the truth that they were created by God with careful thought and intent (1Pet5:7; Is 44:2; Jer 1:5; Jer 29:11-13)

2. Teach all children the instructions for life as found in the Holy Bible (Deut 4:1-14; 6:1-7)

3. Then you will have enlightened citizens in all walks of life (including politics, law enforcement and healthcare)

4. When suffering read Deut 28 publicly and objectively observe to see if you are cursed or blessed thereby; if you and your nation has strayed from the One True GOD and His Instructions

for life REPENT! Before you all suffer even more or perish!

5. If you and the general populace is living as GOD instructs and you are being persecuted by corrupt authorities; then you either have NOT repented but are practicing sins behind closed doors OR you are not praying for your leaders as instructed OR you have not ENOUGH honorable citizens to arrest criminals WHEREVER they may be (even politicians, judges, war criminals, treasonous officials, etc.)

6. Teach your children (and all citizens everywhere) to LOVE AND OBEY GOD! And the rest of these problems we face will vanish!

7. http://www.godempowersyou.com/documentation/Ideas.pdf

8. http://www.biblegateway.com/passage/?search=Matthew+22%3A37-40&version=NIV

http://www.godempowersyou.com/documentation/WhatTODOimmediately.pdf

Polluting and poisoning the planet has become a crisis threatening mass extinctions; including our own. However, the overworked populace habitually has shown that they have not the energy to unite until they realize their own lives are in peril if they don't. For some reason, people are getting sick and dying and yet still do not perceive this peril. All who are still healthy need to take a good look at how many are getting sick from diseases that never existed in our past and realize that you are indeed in grave peril if you do not unite and effect changes for the better immediately. I suggest that people tend to rebel against all kinds of legal mandates; however, tend to respond positively if rewarded for their actions. I suggest governments implement monetary (significant) rewards for all who compost their organic waste; for all who separate their inorganic waste.

Waste management needs to be internationally focused on because like it or not the waste of nations affects all of us globally (all that we think, say and do affects one another globally to greater or lesser extents). As such, technology for waste sorting into recyclables needs to be implemented and until then massive hiring of individuals to do the task. Any material not recyclable needs to be incinerated in waste disposal refineries. I would like to see such refineries be solar incinerators constructed of giant magnification lenses that concentrate enough heat to melt even metals almost instantaneously. The heat from these refineries run steam powered turbines for electricity. http://www.greenfudge.org/2010/04/14/danish-incinerators-are-shining-examples-of-clean-energy-and-waste-disposal/

These need to be modified and improved until there are zero toxic emissions in the refining process and all that remains are recyclables. I would like to see restaurants given monetary incentives for using all organic waste for composting in nearby agricultural endeavors. (Urban tiered farms using composted organic waste.)

I would like to see free heirloom seeds provided to all citizens to combat this new attack on ecosystems and our lives through the ignorance of genetic modification and giant monoculture farms. All citizens who plant and maintain fruit and nut trees on their property and annual gardens rewarded monetarily. If I hear one more person ask where does money come from; I'm tempted to slap 'em because they are NOT using the brain GOD gave them. Money is paper and ink, or electronic credits these days. There is enough money to do whatever people agree to do on planet earth; the only reason you think there isn't is that the mints that print the money have been commandeered by very evil, selfish, greedy people who horde it all to themselves to live in luxury and enslave all the rest of us.

Ideas

I. Solutions – see www.blastthetrumpet.com and https://www.youtube.com/@TheLightofGod for more

A. Economies

1. Premises

    a) Global is dependent upon strong national GNPs

    b) National is dependent upon strong state/provincial GNPs

    c) State or Provincial is dependent upon strong Local GNPs

    d) Local is dependent upon strong business entities and individuals

        (1) All economies are based on providing needed or perceived necessary products and services

        (2) Proverbs 8:12 Individual innovations leads to continued supply of needed products and services

        (3) All economies are dependent upon Wisdom; Wisdom comes from GOD (James 1:5,17) therefore strong economies on all levels are based on individuals KNOWING GOD and praying for WISDOM!

2. Remedies

    a) Know GOD! (Jer 31:31-34; 29:11-13; Acts 2:38,39; Jn 14:26; 1Jn 2:27)

    b) Pray for Wisdom (James 1:5, 17; Proverbs 8:12)

    c) Provide a needed or desired product or service!

    d) Do away with all taxation!

        (1) Taxation always has been and always will be oppressive and unnecessary!

        (2) Citizens should demand of their governing officials to print currency as

necessary for the nation's solvency and governing operations without demanding tribute from them at all!

(3) The IRS should exist in the future as an accounting service to the public for all revenues brought in by the natural resources, energy providers and utilities owned by the people, managing the operating costs of all public servants in all aspects of government, all branches, all levels, all public service entities giving posted annual accounting of all revenues and expenditures, providing true and accurate profit and loss statements to the public for all governing operations; clearly itemized and available publicly in printable format via the Internet.

(4) No more taxes including real property taxes! Never again should citizens lose their home and lands to extortionist governing corrupt officials! All revenue for governments on all levels come from the natural resources provided by GOD for all mankind and those services such as energy and utilities that should be owned and managed by the people! (All citizens working in those fields become regulated public servants)

(5) No more taxes mean no more estate taxes! Intestate situations should be eliminated altogether by mandating all adults have last will and testaments; and real properties should fall by law to the

beneficiaries so declared by legal mandate and sealed by the same encryption methods that secure legal tender internationally. Public servants in the form of legal executors that are authorized by the people to open such sealed records upon the demise of the benefactors such that it is impossible any longer for insurance companies to avoid paying on policies needs to be implemented immediately. (Sealed Wills, Testaments, and Life Insurance Policies will save some benefactors from being murdered by perspective beneficiaries as no one will know if they are a beneficiary with this method unless the benefactor trusts them enough to tell them personally.) The public servant executors would only be authorized to open such sealed legal documents in the presence (physically or virtually, by video conference and permission of the beneficiaries) of the beneficiaries listed on the first document opened. (In other words the first page of such legal declarations would simply list the beneficiaries who would then be notified by law to appear for the opening of the rest of the declarations and policies) Only by confirming identities of the beneficiaries such as by registered finger print scan, or retinal, or voice or whatever standard becomes the secure standard of practice in the 21st century and beyond; could the rest of the documents be opened; such that beneficiaries know that no tampering of the deceased' declarations occurred. For noncompliant citizens that still die intestate; possessions and properties should fall to charitable organizations designated by the people or the proceeds from such government sales clearly declared by the annual accounting statements by the future services of the IRS who monitors all aspects of government and governing officials; NOT the people! Public servants must be virtually incorruptible; otherwise, the masses inevitably SUFFER and die!

e) Citizens should demand all natural resources are to benefit all citizens equally! (Fund all agreed social services like education, police powers, correctional facilities, fire prevention, water, sewage, healthcare, etc.) Taxes are unnecessary! Funding for all social services is the prerogative of the people empowering citizens from among themselves to govern them and provide these services by minting currency as necessary to maintain all such agreed operations!

f) Free your thinking from brainwashed, slave mentalities! Governments do NOT exist to rule over, oppress or dictate to the masses; but to SERVE them! You tell them how you want your quality of life to be! NOT the other way around!

(1) Elected Officials salaries must be approved by the people by popular vote! At the highest levels; to attract the most qualified citizens the pay should be commensurate; but the elected officials

should NOT be able to grant themselves raises without public approval and any public officials taking bribes of any kind (monetary, services, sex or anything at all) should be permanently barred from holding public office; have their assets liquidated to benefit common services after paying any respective victims, and find themselves working as an indentured servant to the public who are the ones that are inevitably ripped off by political and plutocratic corruption.

(2) Absolutely no bribes, kickbacks, or incentives to pass laws favoring wealthy contributors which always comes at the expense of oppressing the poor masses! (Increase the penalties until corrupt politicians and the bribers are either all in prison, working as indentured servants to the public or if that fails to correct the problem increase the penalty to capital punishment because their oppression leads to the death and destruction of many)!

(3) No public service is to be extracted from the working masses in the form of taxation or any other tribute to elected PUBLIC SERVANTS! Instead, those persons elected to govern or working in the fields of agreed social services have their salaries approved by the rest of the citizenry by regular annual public votes with the cost of living clearly known in the process! (This would give the public regular chances to address minimum wage; for if your politicians didn't grant the

public a livable wage, then citizens could mandate they have to work for the sorry slave wages they think others deserve!) All funding for all social services is provided by minting currency as necessary for all such operations and the natural resources sold to manufacture products and services in behalf of the masses! (Thus, the billions being pocketed by a few greedy individuals claiming ownership of all the oil, all the coal, all the trees, etc. would be profiting all citizens equally in the form of high quality of life as everyone would have the RIGHT to all publicly agreed social services!

(4) Even quality education and health care could be paid by the proceeds of natural resources and by the will of the people to mint currency as necessary to pay all associated expenses! People just have to agree to make it so! All of society benefits because as long as people show the aptitude and attitude they could choose the profession of their Divine calling; no longer dependent on personal or familial resources to pay exorbitant private education fees; only dependent upon each individual maintaining the standards set by society to pursue education for that particular trade or profession! (In my opinion all healthcare providers should be required to maintain at least a 3.5 GPA (out of a 4.0) in their fields of specialization and at least 120 hours annually of current education; as people's lives are at stake and

individual errors result in lifelong tragedies, agonies, and even death of their patients!)

g) Citizens must unite for their common welfare to change the world in which they exist for the better. (Universal Unions with firms of attorneys representing workers' rights against employers publicly funded through the proceeds of natural resources, energy and utilities and the empowerment of minting currency as necessary to cover citizens public rights; including legal representation against the greedy megalomaniacs of today that have amassed so much wealth the poor no longer have a legal voice in civil or criminal arenas.)

h) Citizens must make sure all other citizens are obedient to God's Instructions or they will be cursed according to Deuteronomy 28 and 1Tim 1:8,9; this includes becoming impoverished!

i) Citizens should demand that there be no public trading on commodities! (and in my opinion the entire stock market should be done away with)

(1) Investors speculate on grain prices driving it higher and higher until the poor are literally starving to death; the masses should demand of their governments that a portion of land belong to the masses to grow affordable staples sufficient to provide daily nourishment for the entire population! Subsidize the farmers as necessary to keep staples affordable for the poorest members of society so no one is starving and yet the farmers working for the people are receiving commensurate income with the private sector.

(2) Investors speculate on oil which is a resource that currently drives the price on virtually all other products and services for all developed nations.

> *(a) Oil (and all natural resources) must become essentially owned by the people and social workers in behalf of the people harvest it, refine it, at salaries set by the people just like salaries set for politicians, law enforcement, firefighters, teachers and in my opinion should become for healthcare workers and persons dealing with the harvesting and refining of all natural resources (I know people working in these professions dread such an idea; but how many in these professions today don't get paid in a so called "free market" and do you really think the public will underpay persons responsible for their health, safety, welfare and their very lives? Have faith in the innate human desire to live and live well! None of these professions would suffer by socialization and the public making sure quality professionals are rewarded with incentives for providing quality services and products!)*
>
> *(b) Prices are then set by annual vote of the public and with respect to the poorest members of society; not by a*

*few wealthy individuals' literally
driving people out of their homes
to starve to death in their unbridled
greed! The poor uninsured
masses are turned out in the street
to die; even insured persons
are told what treatments are
covered and which are not;
whether or not it is in their best
interest. Socialized medicine
as a right of all citizens would ensure
that quality healthcare
workers remain in practice while
those who are not would be
fired! (Because the system would
include annual public review
of all public servants and the
compilation of citizen surveys for
all serviced by each public servant
made public in a database
for easy viewing on the Internet.
That is, the public should have
the absolute right to know the
quality of service being provided
by their public servants (especially
healthcare workers that
citizens have to trust with their very
lives) based on mandatory
reviews of all citizens coming into
direct contact with those
public servants) In addition, no one
would be left to suffer and
die and all could choose the
treatment of their choice by*

mandating the creation of an international database of all known ailments; diagnostics, treatments and the success rate of recovery for each together with the absolute right of all citizens to choose the treatment of their own personal desire based on those statistical facts and all such treatments are covered without exception! (Even those considered "alternative medicine") (see www.blastthetrumpet.org for more details)

(c) Trade only such commodities as are unable to be produced locally; avoid shipping costs as much as possible by planned demographic development that mandates all future residential structures are as self-sufficient as possible; and by creating urban tiered farming and ranching (reduce petrol needs until solar; hydroelectric conversion of all transit occurs)

(3) Doing away with publicly traded stocks and huge multinationals has the following benefits

(a) Currently investors often throw money at entities expecting profitable returns without conscience reflection as to how those profits are generated; history

*now proves this results in slave
wages; poor working conditions; lay-
offs; excessive work hours; unpaid
hours; lack of benefits; and
destroys economies making a few
wealthy people very wealthy
by consolidating profits in this
manner while the masses
become impoverished slaves; in
addition, many entities are so
large they place or bribe corrupt
politicians that enable them
to charge ever higher fees to the
oppressed masses and break
ever more laws without consequence
often causing lifelong illnesses and
death as they cut costs such as
adhering to environmental
regulations
(b) Where there is no accountability
there is crime! Publicly traded stocks
enable personal profits without
personal accountability; it
fundamentally leads to criminal
behavior; exploitation of every kind;
and brings out the worst in human
nature – pure greed even though it
means the suffering and
deaths of millions if not billions of
citizens worldwide as a result
(c) If the only way to increase one's
wealth was to continue
to provide products and services; it
would force wealthy persons to*

continuously innovate and employ people.

(d) If huge multinationals are done away with and all business must have conspicuous persons posted responsible for all operations and working closely with all employees as these owners and upper management officials would be criminally and civilly liable for all actions of entity owned then it forces once again the connection between the common laborer and the white-collar owners and managers and thus better pay and quality of life results. When ownership is some detached investor; it is easy to pay slave wages; but when owners and upper management are personally and conspicuously liable for all products and services of the entity and actually see the employees at work it is not so easy to treat them like slaves. Furthermore, when profits are dependent upon producing high quality products and services; as opposed to cutting corners at the expense of the workers, all society benefits. Individual entities, small business, and conspicuous accountability is a

must! Laws should mandate all owners/CEOs have to personally meet with all their employees at least annually face to face and spend at least 4 hours in every position annually (as long as their health allows) the entity working as their employees do. If the entity becomes so large that this becomes impossible then it has become too large. Frankly, the business model I prefer over all others is employee ownership.

(e) When only a few enormous entities exist; it enables corrupt political ties more easily. Monopolies owned by a few ultra-wealthy individuals can be coerced by corrupt politicians to do things such as spy on citizens, ignoring the 4th and 14th amendments of the US Constitution (as has already occurred with certain telecoms and the illegal executive orders created primarily during the terms of George W. Bush) Government controlled propaganda is also the result; causing an ignorant and brainwashed society as has occurred in virtually all nations; including the United States as so much of what we see

on the networks is censured. (Like the news stories of the
millions of Americans that have died in hospital caused deaths, treating chronic and terminal conditions with more toxic medications (causing the pharmaceuticals to make
billions in profits due to this willfully created public ignorance); and even such simple stories as the disabled cruise ship which was caused by an EMP missile attack that the
public was kept in complete ignorance of; or the oil drilling disaster in the gulf which was also an attack by foreign powers
the US public was kept in ignorance of; or the 911 treasonous
and murderous act of US officials against US citizens that the
public has been intentionally lied to by the corrupt politicians controlling the media (over 98% of all media is now owned
and controlled by only 6 entities in the United States); etc. etc.
etc.). Diversification; competition and redistribution of wealth
and independent media rights; ensures more people have more of an opportunity to resist coercion, bribes and alert the public

to dangerous political corruption! (www.blastthetrumpet.org for more news worthy stories that have been censured by corrupt US government and controlled major media.)

j) All government contracts MUST be OPEN to bids from the private sectors of the public at large and Correctional Industries consisting of prison labor should be regulated only to such associated tasks as the private sector is unwilling to do (such as cleaning litter from highways) but printing government brochures, constructing public park benches, fashioning license plates or any other service the private sector of the public is willing and able to do must again become bid to citizens not being punished for bad behavior. Correctional Industries has become a multibillion-dollar enterprise and a few crafty businessmen and corrupt politicians have gotten wealthy off robbing the private sector of these contracts and employing the modern slave population of the huge penal colonies in the United States now. What would be a better use of prison labor is working with charitable organizations like the red cross; or disaster relief efforts; some noted examples are the refitting of discarded wheel chairs, crutches, other medical equipment, manufacturing blankets, emergency supplies, which will become more necessary if nations continue to depart from GOD and His Instructions in the Holy Bible; as more and more "natural disasters" will result. Prisoners that

have reached trustee status should continue to assist in wildfire and other disaster relief efforts to alleviate costs of such needed social services in times of crises that the private sector does not have enough workers to handle.

k) Stop brainwashing innocent little children with the metaphysical, fictional concept of evolution. Teaching little kids that they came from pond scum and monkeys instead of the Truth of the Creator of the Universe, who are carefully and thoughtfully designed by Him in His Image, is causing massive ignorance, degradation of character, degradation of quality of services and products universally and is destroying the economy thereby.

(1) Fossilized footprints of dinosaurs and homo-sapiens have been found literally embedded in each other; so, dinosaurs and man existed simultaneously and the theory that they became extinct millions, tens of millions, hundreds of millions of years ago is factually; scientifically disproven by this evidence set in stone

(2) Living dinosaurs have been found that were thought to have been extinct for hundreds of millions of years like the coelacanth and strong evidence exists that Plesiosaurs or similar creatures have also been found living in the 20th century.

(3) Artifacts and newspapers exist showing many varieties of dinosaurs existing simultaneously with modern man in recent history.

(4) Living animals fit the description of dinosaurs in all respects; but because they are living, they are not given such fancy scientific names by the religious extremists; ludicrous acolytes of the theory of evolution; such as alligators, crocodiles, rhinos, horseshoe crabs, and an almost endless list of species that if they were extinct would be considered as one of many on the fictional "evolutionary tree" as dinosaurs, pre-historic, Cambrian, pre-Cambrian, etc. incorrectly labeled, classified, dated and documented species. Of course, when you can brainwash someone by showing them animations of how they came from an explosion of something that came from nothing, of inorganic chemicals that spontaneously generated into a life form with all necessary aspects to live, reproduce, and then spontaneously mutated into more of the same again with all such necessities to sustain life and reproduce even that singular mutation; and then to suddenly mutate from single celled life forms to multi-celled; with all the necessities to sustain that mutation and reproduce (together with the inherent knowledge to do so) and so on until they show a cartoon of pond scum, turning into a tadpole; turning into a four-legged land animal; turning into a monkey; and finally, "presto-boomo" little, pond scum for brains beings; just like them! With that

kind of monumental brainwashing it's no wonder we have a decline of quality of character, sound knowledge, wisdom and understanding, a decline in sanity, a decline in happiness and wellness, a decline in stable marriages and families and society as a whole; and a decline in products and services across the board. Yup when you can get an innocent little kid to believe that mountainous load of crap; you destroy their ability to think critically altogether and even innovation ceases. The standards of education in America have gone ever lower trying to keep up with the ignorance that has resulted from teaching little kids that completely fictional; scientifically disproven load of crap called "the theory of evolution"! If America is to regain its glory and pre-eminence in products and services (again have a populace of happy, stable marriages and families and people who take pride in their work) then public education should return to the Christian Church; not the state and the Primary Text Book needs to once again be the Holy Bible! Yes; we need to return to GOD and return to our public education system as it was founded to be in this country mandating that all citizens should know what the Word of God contained in the Holy Bible states as its primary purpose! The Holy Bible was the primary text book in our public education in this country for more than a century and when it was; together with reading the literary classic of "Pilgrim's Progress"; our nation excelled and became blessed above all nations on earth! But now that we're brainwashing little kids by telling them they came from pond scum and monkeys; that came from the something that exploded; coming from nothing; we have fallen behind virtually all developed nations in educational standards and achievement tests! All fields of true and sound science; practiced by rational, intelligent, reasonable, sane persons; support Intelligent Design by an Intelligent Creator! When you study Creation scientifically it will always lead to the Creator because that is in fact the TRUTH; and the Reality in which we all exist! (the theory of evolution is NOT scientific and has not one single shred of scientific evidence to this date to support it; it never has and never will because it is factually complete fiction!)

So, if you want a strong economy stop turning innocent little minds into mush by lying to them and **tell them the Truth: that they are a complex being Created lovingly, carefully and thoughtfully by GOD, the Creator of** the Universe; that they each have been given gifts, talents, skills and abilities to accomplish their Divine Purpose! read my book https://www.amazon.com/Theory-Evolution-Impossible-Michael-Israel-ebook/dp/B0D93C76WN/ref=tmm_ki n_swatch_0

The Theory of Evolution is Impossible.

l) Citizens should take over not only the minting of national currencies, but demand one national bank that handles all financial transactions. A One Bank Solution regulated directly by the people would solve much of the exploitation of the poor and oppressed by the wealthy of today. (www.pinkoski.com)

m) Nations should come out from under the existing control of the IMF and privatized control of national monetary systems altogether. Never again allow a few wealthy persons to control national currencies and exchange rates. No nation needs to borrow money from private persons or entities and never let a few people lend to the many by this means of universal oppression and tyranny.

n) Recent NAFTA "free trade" and other influences by such persons as the WTO and Bilderberger group favor only a few ultra-wealthy elites at the exploitation of the masses; turning the vast majority of citizens worldwide into an expendable slave workforce without rights and devoid of livable wages. Citizens worldwide need to form unions powerful enough to employ and retain attorneys and maintain political influence to make sure this trend toward enslavement of the masses is reversed and a redistribution of wealth occurs such that many more citizens have decent opportunities at a fair quality of life. The concentration of the world's wealth in the hands of a few persons is highly dangerous as these persons have demonstrated eugenic philosophies in their greedy and corrupt practices of controlling nations by controlling their respective currencies. "Bankers" should therefore become public servants regulated by the commonwealth. National currencies must be controlled by individual governments that are under constant scrutiny of the public they represent and exchange rates must be dependent on whether or not nations are providing desired products or services to other nations; not set and controlled by a handful of elitists as it is this day that have openly stated they are establishing a "New World Order". (In which these wealthy eugenicists are the lords and ladies; and the expendable masses are completely controlled by biochip implants linked to credits at the banks these elitists control to shut off access to by anyone they label a "terrorist", dissident, etc.) They have stated and intend to brand all citizens globally as their slaves with the RFID biochip ("mark of the beast" forewarned of in the Holy Bible) and will take over all agricultural commodities and potable water sources. In a cashless global economy; no one will be able to buy or sell (including your food and water) that does not submit to their "New World Order" agenda; which is enslavement and complete control of the masses via the RFID biochip implants linked to Internationally Regulated (IMF, Bilderberger Group) universal banking system.

o) Support nationalism. All nations need to be responsible for ensuring your citizens have the basic necessities for life; working with other nations in that regard! Make sure you have sufficient staples and potable water such that your people cannot be reduced to this NWO takeover!

> (1) This is possible if nations will now concentrate on desalination units that border oceans and large precipitators that are landlocked. With potable water available; then concentrate on agriculture by mandating composting of all organic wastes and developing bio-diversity appropriate for your region and growing seasons.
>
> (2) Nations that are wise enough to have leadership that makes the laws of GOD found in the Holy Bible their laws; will be shown by GOD where undiscovered natural resources are and the citizens will be given Wisdom that will cause that nation and its inhabitants to prosper; no matter how small and/or impoverished it is today.

Governments under GOD; our Living LORD JESUS CHRIST, have the Old Testament laws to convict of crimes and designate criminal and civil justice. All convicts are to be given the opportunity of Mercy under the New Testament. If the convict elects Mercy they are to be discipled by Holy Ghost filled elders who teach the convicts the wisdom of living righteously instead of wickedly. Until that individual also is filled with the Holy Spirit of our Lord Jesus Christ, they are to be under close discipleship. Anyone rejecting Mercy; is to be disciplined EXACTLY as GOD states in the Old Testament. Any nation that makes laws and consequences contrary to GOD's Clear Instructions in the Holy Bible is in rebellion against GOD and our Lord Jesus Christ. All such nations will now be receiving judgments of all the curses written in Deuteronomy Ch. 28 ("natural disasters", diseases, death and destruction) increasing in severity and rapidity until you either Repent and Receive the LORD JESUS CHRIST and follow His Instructions contained in the Holy Bible or perish in your willful rebellion against the Instructions for Life; the Lord our GOD, our Creator has given us all, in the Holy Bible.

(3) Any nation murdering, oppressing, invading other nations strictly for selfish greed and control of natural resources is

demonstrating to the world their leaders; controlling their military, are under the influence of the spirit of anti-Christ. All other nations should unite against such aggressive, imperialistic, destructive greed and universally cease any trade or other agreements that benefit such a nation until its people are able to again have honorable persons in their positions of public service; government.

(4) Any nation persecuting Christians, or desirous to murder Christians and Jews are demonstrating to the world their leaders are under the influence of the spirit of anti-Christ. All other nations should unite against such a nation(s), seek to correct peacefully, if possible, by encouraging citizens worldwide to have only persons filled with the Holy Spirit in positions of public trust, power and authority!

(5) Any nation embracing the abominations listed in the Holy Bible (the Torah, Leviticus 18, (Numbers 5:11-31 needs to be implemented to stop all the whoredoms and adulteries)); such as nations that are now legalizing homosexual unions; while simultaneously making criminal laws against "hate speech" to include even reading the text contained in the Holy Bible is demonstrating willful and open rebellion against GOD, the LORD JESUS CHRIST, and its people and entire nation are on the verge of complete destruction such as the ashen ruins of Sodom and Gomorrah that

exist to this very day as a warning to us all not to become as wicked, perverse and corrupt; such that you punish Christians while embracing every form of sexual perversion! All nations should beware of becoming this corrupt such that you insanely bring about your own decimations! The Holy Bible records "there is a way that SEEMS right to man, but the end thereof are the ways of death." And nations equivocating homosexuality or any other choice of who or what you choose to sexually engage with; or any choice of action with inherent genetic traits of race, or other choice-less facts of life such as when a person is born (age), or where they are born (nation) are falling into this category! It may SEEM right to embrace sexual perversion; especially in a culture where pleasure has become everything; but it will only result in your utter ruin! Anti-discriminatory laws violating the First Amendment or any laws in the US that have been created that are unconstitutional are unenforceable. The US and all nations have to ask themselves do you want to be blessed or cursed? Do you want to live or die? When a nation makes laws so contrary to God's such that they embrace crimes worthy of capital punishment; then that nation is ripe for destruction; judgments will now be increasing upon the United States and all nations that wickedly depart from Almighty God and His Instructions for

Life! If you do not repent and place only leaders full of the Holy Ghost and return to teaching your children the Instructions for Life contained in the Holy Bible; judgments will increase in severity and rapidity until you do. If you still rebel as a nation; increasing weapons for the purpose of oppressing the masses, invading nations, greedily consuming, making laws embracing abominations, making movies violating all the instructions for life and celebrating all that is expressly forbidden (Torah, Leviticus 18) in unbridled greed and sexual immorality, then judgments will be poured out upon you with Vengeance! If you punish God's Messengers (Christians (body of Christ), Israelites, Jews (body of Moses); (Many descendants of Ishmael are in the Islamic religion; thus, many Arabs represent the body of Ishmael); all Israelites and Jews practicing the Torah devoid of Faith in the One and Only Messiah, YAHOSHUAH, represent the body of Mosiah (Moses) it is time they ALL found freedom in the Faith of the common father, Abraham such that Israel and Ishmael are reconciled and unite against the spirit of anti-christ that seeks to destroy you both; cease to embrace leaders who are at enmity with Christianity and the Israelites; all such persons are under the influence of the spirit of anti-christ regardless of what religion, philosophy or traditional worldview they claim for themselves)) for telling you the Truth; not just judgments but Divine Vengeance will come upon you in the sight of the whole world!

(6) Nationalism until the return of the Lord Jesus Christ is essential for maintaining "checks and balances" which ultimately is between the Spirit of Christ and the spirit of anti-christ. Just as the solution for a strong economy is the competition of an honorable free market that motivates constant innovations and improvements in products and services; so also do nations refine and improve each other in this manner. The NWO seeks to unite through control of each citizen through the RFID bio-chip implant linked to the NWO cashless monetary system. This move of centralization by these ultra-wealthy eugenicists is the clear and overtly prophesied rise of the anti-christ and should be resisted on all levels by all persons loving freedom and GOD! Christians need to stop fantasizing of floating off the planet and realize they are here on earth during a time of open warfare and persecution by these wicked and greedy persons under the influence of the spirit of anti-christ. Christians in the USA and all who love freedom must NEVER give up the right to bear arms until Christ returns and establishes His Glorious Kingdom on earth! Not just your lives depend on receiving Jesus Christ and resisting the anti-christ and his perverse, depraved and degenerate

followers; but your welfare and that of your children! Satanists, satanism, cannibalism, vampirism exists in the USA and being practiced by members of the United States government; including child molestation and sacrifice, Molech worshipping and other such demonic activity that if not arrested and stopped could cause torture and murder of Jews and Christians in this nation, and the enslavement of all other citizens through the RFID bio-chip implants. This activity must be addressed and arrested NOW in this nation! Shine the light in all the dark places out of public sight! (Pentagon, CIA, FBI, military, Bohemian Grove, Orion, MK-Ultra, prisons, mental wards, graveyards of such as die in these places need to have remains examed which will prove these atrocities are going on; there are real "Hannibal Lectors" loose in hospitals now that are taking human flesh off murdered victims in addition to all the illegal organ harvesting going on in the process. These types of atrocities are being actively covered up by organized satanism; as there are now members in various levels of government, agencies and police departments and controlling the media, from shining the light exposing these dreadful atrocities occurring in our nation now and must be stopped if the United States is to remain unto the coming of our Lord and Savior Jesus Christ from being annihilated and incinerated and if Christians don't want their homes invaded by satanic maniacs that want to harm you and your families. NEVER give up the right to bear arms until Christ returns and stop pretending these things of which I write are not occurring by choosing to remain willfully ignorant!

(a) Join me now in placing pressure on the media to shine the light on all the "secret" places in our nation and any place off limits to the media must be told to the public; there is no greater threat to an economy, the health and welfare of people and the nation than these types of excessive evil practices

(b) Join me all Holy Ghost filled persons in active spiritual warfare!

(i) In the Name of JESUS CHRIST (YAHOSHUAH THE MESSIAH), address every xxx store, every satanic church, every structure that houses foul and unclean spirits. Face these structures and say, "In the Name of JESUS CHRIST (YAHOHSUAH THE MESSIAH), I tear down this stronghold of darkness and evil and let a meeting place for Holy Ghost filled citizens be erected in its place!"

(ii) In the Name of JESUS CHRIST, Let the Spirit of Repentance come upon the citizens of the United States and the whole world now; followed immediately by the Holy Ghost; let the lies and deceptions of the antichrist cease now and forever; let Truth prevail and expose all the acts of darkness and those who are doing atrocities such as satanism, cannibalism, vampirism, (and ARREST these evil doers immediately). Let the darkness be exposed by the Light everywhere and let all practicing wickedness, either repent now or be arrested spiritually and physically; immediately!

(iii) In the Name of JESUS CHRIST (YAHOSHUAH THE MESSIAH), I command every foul and unclean spirit to come out of our nation's leaders and to be silent! All you devils are not allowed to move upon anyone or anything to do evil of any kind! I bind you all and cast you out of the heavens once and for all! You

*are not allowed to touch,
harm, move upon anyone or
anything to do harm or evil
to the Children of GOD! I
cast out the spirit of
antichrist out of this nation!
It was founded upon the
Gospel of JESUS Christ, sound
Wisdom, Knowledge and
Understanding; so, let the
people return of one accord
to the One True GOD and
Creator of the Universe now!
And Let the United States
remain a haven for freedom!
For justice! For
Righteousness! For God's
people! For the distribution
of the Gospel of Jesus Christ
and Holy Bibles throughout
the nation and the world! Let
all citizens see the evil of
the RFID biochip implants
and refuse and reject the
mark of the beast! Let the
"New World Order" fail and
fall in its conception and
practice! And instead; Let the
Kingdom of GOD come in all
its Glory upon the earth;
the world entire!!!!!!!!!!!!!
(iv) In the Name of JESUS
CHRIST (YAHOSHUAH*

HA MASHIACH), I bind all powers and principalities of darkness and command them to depart from the United States and whole world now and forever!!!! Let the darkness be forever bound in the Abyss and no longer loose in the heavens or earth! Let all such concepts of wickedness forever depart from the hearts, minds and souls of mankind and instead only imaginations of righteousness, honor and praiseworthy notions of every kind abide forever!

(v) In the Name of and to the Glory of the LORD JESUS CHRIST (YAHOSHUAH HA MASHIACH), Let all the nations, all the people of the whole world shout of one accord, "COME, LORD JESUS, COME!" until He Returns to earth in all His Glory! Amen and Amen!!!!

(vi) In the Name of YAHOSHUAH HA MASHIACH, let all who Love GOD; join me now in shouting, "The LORD rebuke you, satan!" for concerning the body of

Moses (those thinking salvation comes through adherence to the Instructions (Torah) given to Moses by GOD); it is time they all recognized the One True Messiah, YAHOSHUAH HA MASHIACH (commonly known in English as the LORD JESUS CHRIST)! And let all who Love the LORD join me in shouting yet again, "The LORD rebuke you, satan!!" for concerning the body of Ishmael; those in bondage in the Islamic faith thinking they can earn their way into Paradise through works of the flesh and carnal will-worship. For I repeat what has been shouted by the True Messengers of the Most High GOD; saying unto the body of Moses and the body of Ishmael and to all souls everywhere; if SALVATION could come by any other person, method or means, than the ONLY HOLY INCARNATE MAN, BLAMELESS IN ALL RESPECTS, WOULD NOT HAVE NEEDED TO BE SACRIFICED ON THE ALTAR OF THIS

EARTH FOR US ALL! Born of the Virgin; Fulfillment of the Law and Prophets, YAHOSHUAH THE MESSIAH, the Incarnate Holy One prophesied to take away the sins of the world; was ALONE found worthy to take our death penalty for breaking GOD's Commandments! GOD has stated ALL have sinned and fallen short of His GLORY! (ALL but ONE) Therefore let us no longer rebel in foolishness; neglecting so great SALVATION; for there is but ONE GOD, ONE LORD and RULER OF ALL! EVERY KNEE WILL BOW AND EVERY TONGUE CONFESS THAT YAHOSHUAH THE MESSIAH (JESUS CHRIST) IS LORD! Let every man, woman and child on the planet now do so to your everlasting JOY! There is SALVATION in none other! Acs 4:12, 10:34-43 None other demonstrated and yet demonstrates to this day; that He and He alone is fulfillment of the Law and the Prophets; none other incarnated in flesh and blood; tempted in all ways such as we and yet without sin; none other was blameless before GOD and worthy to die in our place for our personal crimes against the Almighty! What is this SALVATION? It is to save your soul from present and lasting ignorance, apathy, evil imaginations and deeds, torment within and without; it is to save your soul from the frustration of meaningless, purposeless existence in confusion, depravity, degenerate chaos, it is to save you here and now from the darkness of insanity of self and others, from insatiable desires that destroy you in every way, and from the flames of hellfire and the lake that burns forever! It is to save you from your endless search for personal happiness and fulfillment and to bring you even NOW into the Holy Presence of the Living GOD and Creator of the Universe! To save you from the sins that separate you from communing with Him in holy fellowship Divine here and NOW and forever! It is SALVATION so GREAT that it sets you in every way RIGHT before ALMIGHTY GOD and enables you to learn directly from the Creator of the Universe! It enables you to KNOW and EMBRACE the LIVING GOD as your own HEAVENLY FATHER! It is SALVATION so AWESOME that you actually become one of GOD's TRUE SONS or DAUGHTERS and communicate with Him (and He with you) here and now and forever! It is SALVATION so incredible as to lift you out of the abyss of darkness, suffering and torment you are already in and set you in Heavenly Places to see the Universe clearly as it really is; to supernaturally behold angels and demons; yet to fear such devils never again having Divine Authority over them all! It is SALVATION so ineffable as to restore to you true Adamic Dominion granting you the ability to speak with animals and all manner of creatures and to understand them as well; the barrier of darkness lifted such that all creation is filled with the Light of True Understanding! It is SALVATION beyond any words to describe as you spend NOW and forever with the Eternal GOD; the Source of all Virtues, all Wonders, all that is Praiseworthy Good and Commendable and as you mature begin to demonstrate the Creative Power supernaturally imbued upon and within all who KNOW the ONE TRUE GOD by simply repenting of all your sins; receiving YAHOSHUAH THE MESSIAH (JESUS CHRIST) as your personal LORD and SAVIOR and becoming filled with the HOLY SPIRIT OF GOD, THE HOLY GHOST! When that occurs; you will in fact be a new creation; no longer of darkness, confusion, apathy and ignorance, whose vile passions will only torment and destroy you in every way; but you will become a Radiant Son or Daughter of the Most High GOD here and now! You won't believe only and struggle only with your own strength ever seeking for Truth; but you will KNOW the POWER OF GOD within and upon you; aiding you and transforming your very thoughts into righteousness! You will come to know, understand and demonstrate that ALL things are possible for you who KNOW and LOVE the LORD, the One True GOD, the One and Only SAVIOR, of all mankind! (1John 5:20) Let every incarnate soul now OBEY with ACTION what is commanded in Acts 2:38,39 and Pray until you KNOW, beyond all doubt, you have received the Holy Ghost of GOD's Promise! (John 14-17; Acts 1:8) Then KNOWING your Divine Purpose; fulfill it! Do it! JOYFULLY here and now and to your everlasting Joy when you rest from the journey of your incarnation and are

*ascended with all confidence
in the Grace and Love and
SALVATION of our Living
LORD, YAHOSHUAH HA
MASHIACH (JESUS CHRIST).
Yes, all who KNOW and LOVE
the LORD are no longer
fearful of "death" for
they know by the Spirit in
and upon them; that when
their journey of incarnation is
over; they will ascend
into Paradise and so will they
ever be with the LORD;
seeing Him face to face
clearly in all His Glory! There
is no Greater SALVATION and
indeed no SALVATION in
any other! Acts 4:12 (In the
Holy and Omnipotent Name
of YAHOSHUAH THE
MESSIAH, JESUS CHRIST, I
command every devil; every
foul and unclean spirit to
come out of; depart from and
never return to torment
anyone reading these words!
You are not allowed to move
upon anyone or anything to
distract the reader from this
moment and from this Prayer
of SALVATION! In the Holy
and Omnipotent Name of*

*YAHOSHUAH THE MESSIAH,
every foul and unclean spirit
everywhere in all the world
BE SILENT! And prevent
not any soul who would
come to know the LORD
know the Truth, Know GOD
from reading and fulfilling
these words! Amen. And
Amen!!!!!!!!!!!!!!!!!!!!!!!!!!!!)
Won't all who possess at
least the instinct of self-
preservation; bow the knee
with me now wherever you
are and call out from your
heart, mind and soul with all
your strength; "SAVE ME
LORD YAHOSHUAH (JESUS)!
Thank YOU for dying for me,
LORD! Raise me up LORD!
Empower me to live a life
that pleases YOU, LORD; to
show my gratitude for
SAVING me in every way!
Remove from me every sinful
and wicked way! Cleanse
me from all sin and
unrighteousness! Fill me with
the Holy Ghost and let me
KNOW YOU Now and
Forever!" Then renew your
mind, grow and mature
spiritually by reading God's
Words recorded in the Holy*

Bible daily and following His Instructions and Personal Guidance for the rest of the journey of your incarnation! And, if you are willing, continue in prayer with me, "FATHER IN HEAVEN; LORD YAHOSHUAH (JESUS), cause me to hunger and thirst after righteousness! Inspire my prayers, thoughts and actions to be pleasing in Your Sight! Move upon my tongue and lips to speak boldly Your Words and let not the accursed thing depart from my mouth or well within my soul! Let not any vile way have place in my thoughts, words or deeds! Instead fill me to overflowing with Your Divine Holy Will for Your Creation! Let Life and Light, Truth and Wisdom; together with all the Virtues, well within my soul like a gushing spring flowing into all creation! Let Your Saving and Healing Power be so present with me that everywhere I go souls come out of darkness and are healed of every ailment, injury, malady, birth defect and are made whole in every way to Your Glory, LORD!!!! Change me into Your Glorious and Holy Image and transform me so wonderfully that You are Pleased to Show Yourself in my life always! Have Mercy Upon Your Creation O LORD and Let Your Glory flood my soul, the heavens and the earth! Drive away the darkness forever LORD! And let the words written by Jeremiah the Prophet in 31:31-34 be fulfilled; such that everyone from the least to the greatest and greatest to the least KNOWS You LORD! Let me not love in word only; but fill me with the LOVE that You demonstrate for my own soul to motivate me and Faith to work supernaturally all my days. Cause me to LOVE what You LOVE, and HATE what You HATE with the same Intensity as YOU, O' LORD! Grant me and all Your Children; Miracle working Faith, Inexhaustible LOVE, and the Wisdom, Knowledge and Understanding to

apply Your Good Works to
Your Glory; here and now
and Forever! Establish me,
and all who agree with this
prayer before You forever
and never let us stray from
You, the Path of Life and
Righteousness; but keep us
always as Your Beloved; so
will we Give You Thanks
and Praise Now and
Forever!!!! We know it is
Your Grace and Mercy alone
that Saves and Keeps us,
LORD, and Your Creative
Power that transforms us
and empowers us; so let us
never be desirous of vain
glory or become prideful or
arrogant as if we ourselves
did such wonderful things;
but let us soberly and
truthfully, Remember Always
Your Work on the Cross; we
SAVED BY GRACE; and, as the
elders, cast our crowns
at Your Feet; for YOU alone
are Worthy of ALL the
Power, ALL the Honor, ALL
the Virtues, ALL the Praise,
ALL the Thanksgiving, ALL the
Worship, ALL the Treasures,
ALL the Strength, ALL the
Blessings and ALL the GLORY;

Now and Forever and Ever!!!!!!!!Amen; HALLELUJAH; Amen!!!!!!!!!!!!!!!!!!!!!!!!! (Now all of you who have called upon the Living LORD JESUS CHRIST; show forth your first act of willingness to do GOD's will; and go and be baptized according to the commandment! (Acts 2:38,39) When you do, pray that the LORD Himself would baptize you with the Holy Ghost according to the Promise! And may the truly repentant and truly desirous to KNOW GOD; knowing they will apply themselves to becoming a mature disciple of Christ; be so filled with the Holy Ghost that the presence of GOD is seen within their lives in Power and Authority now and forever! (Jn 14:11-26; through Jn 17; 1Jn 2:27) Amen and Amen!!!!!!!!!!!!)

B. Healthcare

1. Make Wellness a Universal Right of all citizens
2. Healthcare and wellness need to be an integral part of education
3. Create an international database of all known signs and symptoms, ailments, respective diagnostics and treatments with the statistical

facts posted with each treatment for percentage of successful recovery from the ailment via that treatment. Mandate its use in all healthcare professions from general practice to specializations.

4. Optional bracelets, necklaces, rings caring medical information can be worn alerting medical practitioners to personal living wills; or conditions that might not be so obvious; such as antibodies against the – Rh factor; (no O negative blood) or genetic traits that can cause complications with various treatments.

5. Medical care along with all agreed Universal Rights can be funded by public control of renewable energy revenues, natural resources and utilities.

C. Education

1. Make Education a Universal Right of all citizens

2. Use "My Baby Can Read" method to teach all children to be fluent in at least three languages (of their choosing recommend most influential and widespread culturally). In a global society of global trade; people need to be fluid and multi-skilled to keep up with change in demands and needs with all the change caused by innovations.

3. Identify learning styles of children and preferences through increased diversification during primary and secondary years; such that by the time students are 18 years old they can choose with guidance counselors; professional, technical trade schools; two-year colleges with professional hands-on training; or 4 year or higher education. Regardless, of higher

education choices; only students showing aptitude and attitude can continue. Otherwise, they are working in fields commensurate with their training; entry level general laborers; etc. Much as it is today; but the difference is no longer will students become indentured servants to wealthy persons; just to get an education; nor will families lose their homes just to put their children through college.

4. Make it mandatory that for a full year one hour class (seniors) is spent personally interviewing at least one neighborhood of retired individuals, rest home, hospice, care facility and documenting in an international database the Wisdom of Elders; with standardized questions (optional for all citizens to choose whether or not they wish to respond); such as What is the most important thought/idea/concept you would like to pass on to the world? What is your greatest regret? What do you consider to be the most important products and services today? What product or service has vanished that you wish was still present? What would you like to see invented? What is your religion? Why do you adhere to this worldview? What was your profession(s)? What did you enjoy most about working in your profession(s)? What would you like to see done about _____ (waste management, energy, food, water, sewage, air quality, environmental standards, space exploration, space colonization, creation of living wages for all, etc. (any and all matters of significant importance at that time and the near future)?

5. Increase teacher salaries to attract the best and brightest in fields and include regular visits from inventors, innovators, entrepreneurs, and large variety of professions; with a one year, one hour class, that exposes high school seniors to as large a variety of qualified professionals as possible; together with each student spending one semester in two-week long internships in the field(s) they are most interested before designating their choice of professional, technical, trade schools or 4-year colleges of higher education. Minors should not be allowed to "dropout". If conventional class schedules are not working out for some reason; then secondary professional; trade school and life management classes need to be an alternative for teen parents, etc. For youngsters set on being rebellious juvenile delinquents; the "scared straight" program might be necessary or disciplinary measures such as military schooling. (Even so; I would like to see it mandatory that all citizens be fluent and literate in their national language and that the Holy Bible remains the primary text book in all educational settings). I would hope that each class setting begins with prayer to the One True GOD (1Jn 5:20) by choice of the people, students and instructors or facilitators.

6. Knowledge is increasing at such a rate as to necessitate lifelong continued education in virtually all fields. Skilled Professionals after 20 or more years should be required to share knowledge as instructors during mandatory continued education in their respective fields. Any

innovations/inventions resulting during these annual continued education meetings; should give residual percentages to the originator(s) of all gross sales following.

II. Counsel to nations

A. Egypt

1. You are choking your own life in the physical realm by developing the delta of the Nile. In the physical world, the Nile is the life's blood of your nation; your people. If you want your nation and your people to live:

a) Stop poisoning the Nile with your refuse!

(1) Remove all developed structures within a linear mile of the banks of the Nile and the entire delta region! You heard me! Level and remove entire cities! Relocate into the desertified regions by:

(a) Building huge water precipitators on a scale capable of creating rivers in the desert

(b) Mandating by law composting of all animal and human excrements by your sewage treatment facilities

(c) Mandating by law composting of all food wastes by all food processing plants and restaurants and asking citizens to do the same by a national training policy and conspicuous

composting turbines within easy walking distance spaced throughout all residential developments

(d) Recapturing the fertile delta and banks of the Nile for agricultural purposes; encouraging the next generation to keep it that way by implementing agricultural training, gardening, harvesting within your public education by giving each child a small patch for their personal garden each year of their primary and secondary education and grading them on the results. (Teach your children to speak unto the plants in faith saying; grow, become strong and fruitful; let your roots find water and nourishment and let no weeds or pest choke your life; etc. Teach them to not only care about the physical realm with the physical necessities; but with the spiritual faith of proper stewardship of the earth that makes for life!

(e) Take the composting material and start

Terraforming as far into the desertified regions as temperatures will allow for agriculture. (Remember silver and gold will do you and your people no good whatsoever if there is no food or potable water to be had and so a nation's true wealth is not the black gold of oil; or the shiny bits of metal; but whether or not it has food and water enough to sustain the lives of its citizens!

(f) In relocating cities and developments determine which structures are worth salvaging; otherwise demolish; remove and recycle building materials; large structures can be moved with specialized systems these days; seek structural relocation specialists if you do not know how to do this

(2) Build not only huge precipitators but individual ones for homes and apartments and even atop commercial structures for as much potable water as possible from the air

(3) Build desalination units along your sea fronts and aqueducts inland from the sea for additional desalination units and sea salt processing

(4) Employ as public servants agricultural specialists to maintain the delta and Nile bank regions along with fresh and salt water fisheries respectively in the Nile and coastal regions

(5) Encourage your people in these regions to keep the Nile protected for the life of your nation and future generations by opening walking regions through herbal, medicinal, botanical gardens interspersed along the walkways of groves of regional fruit and nut varieties and agricultural crops for your staples

(6) Become completely independent of any other nation for your food and water (all nations need to do this or you will be at the mercy of megalo-maniacs so greedy they will turn you all into complete slaves or laughingly watch you and your children die; as starvation and dehydration set in and people are dying all around!)

(7) Encourage the development of tiered farming for all urban

residential developers. (Mandate by law that developers building apartment superstructures need to provide within the structure composting shoots for all food wastes, recycling shoots for all recyclables, and provide a tiered farming structure that uses solar collectors and solar tubes to bring the growing season into each level. Include honey bee hives; sufficient to pollinate each tier intrinsically in the process.)

(8) Learn the 21st century processes of waste incineration for energy leaving virtually no toxins in the process or physical waste. You are in a region where solar collectors easily generate enough heat to melt even metals! Make advancements therefore in solar collectors/concentrators and photo-electric power cells to lead the way in renewable energies and waste matter/energy converters!

b) The sand itself is a natural resource for the construction of solar collectors and solar farms; attract innovators with whatever incentives entice them to help your nation out! (Get knowledge, wisdom and understanding in the spiritual and physical realms; keep it always a priority!) The Middle Eastern and North African regions stand to become

the world leaders of solar power and so
even a small percentage of gross
revenue would amount to enough to
attract investors/contractors in this
wise endeavor.

2. It is not enough to address only the physical self-destructive path you have been on; but spiritually I call you to the Light of Truth that you may live at peace and be Blessed! Your people were blessed when Pharaoh received Joseph and God's counsel thereby and it is time to receive the Messengers of God again if your people would be blessed! BE AT PEACE WITH ISRAEL AND THE GOSPEL OF JESUS CHRIST! If you war against God's Message of Salvation; then you war against GOD! And if you do that; no matter what physical measures you take; your people will not be Blessed.

B. Israel

1. Woe unto the nation that puts its trust in man, in weapons, in anything at all and forgets the LORD their GOD!

> *a) Your salvation does not lie in alliances with any other nation or nations on earth!*
> *b) Your salvation is not dependent on nuclear bombs or any other weapons of any kind!*
> *c) If your people would live and not die; be Blessed and not Cursed:*
>> (1) Reject the RFID bio-chip implants you have already started to use! Stop branding citizens! These implants are the manifestation of

the mark of the beast and no matter
how deceptive the lies of the
spirit of anti-christ (i.e. it's for your
safety and security, it will make
it easier for you to identify yourself;
all your medical records will be
available if you are unconscious; you
will be able to shop without
ever having to carry a wallet, purse,
money; thus, also safer from
robbery and mugging; identity theft,
etc.) It ultimately will enslave
each citizen and their very lives will
depend upon submitting to the
will of the anti-christ as their credits
will be linked to the RFID
implant and shut off at will (not able
to purchase even food and
water). The snake slithers in
apparently harmlessly until it
strikes!
(2) Your people; young people
especially need to return to
YAHOVAH by finally recognizing your
MESSIAH! YAHOHSUAH HA
MASHIACH! As the fulfillment of the
Torah and Prophets! Only the ONE
TRUE GOD can fulfill ALL His Words
to us in the Holy Bible, because only
He understands the true intent and
meanings of His Words and is why
we all must receive Him and learn to
Love Him and each other. Our
Eternal Creator teaches us and

empowers each of us to fulfill our Divine Purpose and live at peace with Him forever in His Perfected Creation. (Paradise/New Heavens and earth Rev 21 and 22)

(3) By the spirit of anti-christ; nations will be moved by greed and spiritual hatred against you; even ones that pretend they are your friends and allies are NOT to be trusted! (Stop sharing innovations; especially military weapon's advancements!)

d) If you remember nothing else; THE LORD YOUR GOD IS YOUR SALVATION, YOUR HOPE, YOUR LIFE! No one and nothing else! In the time of trouble; He will provide food and water when there is none to be had! He will provide strategies of warfare to defeat modern battalions and fleets with earth, wind, fire and the seas themselves! GOD gives your people Wisdom above the nations round about as long as you are FAITHFUL to Him! You cannot be defeated in battle as long as your people; especially your warriors are not sinning! GOD AND GOD ALONE IS YOUR REFUGE! YOUR MOUNTAIN OF STRENGTH! YOUR FORTRESS! YOUR PROVIDER! YOUR LIFE! YOUR HEALER! RECOGNIZE! HE AND HE ALONE IS YOUR SALVATION! GIVE HIM THANKS AND PRAISE NOW AND FOREVER!

YAHOSHUAH! YAHOSHUAH! YAHOSHUAH! YAHOSHUAH HA MASHIACH! Is 42:11; Acts 4:12 NOW AND FOREVER!!!!!!!! He raises from the dead! Keeps your soul from Sheol, hell, the Abyss, outer darkness and the Lake that burns with unquenchable fire. Gives hope to the downtrodden and oppressed! Nourishment to the starving! Comfort to the brokenhearted! Heals every disease; ailment; malady; deformity and injury and makes whole in all respects every wounded soul! Makes even the fearful so bold as to face a whole world of enemies! Feeds the hungry; gives drink to the thirsty and lifts into Paradise all who Love Him! There is NO GOD LIKE OUR GOD!!!!!!!!!!! Let your people KNOW and LOVE the LORD by finally of one accord receiving their one and only True Messiah! YAHOSHUAH! YAHOSHUAH! YAHOSHUAH! YAHOSHUAH HA MASHIACH!! NOW AND FOREVER!!!! GOD AND GOD ALONE IS YOUR ALL IN ALL!!!!!!!! YOUR EVERYTHING!!!!!!!!!!!! ALL YOU'LL EVER NEED!!!!!!!! AND YAHOSHUAH IS YOUR ONE AND ONLY SALVATION NOW AND FOREVER!!!!!!!!!!!!!!!!!!!!!!!!!! Amen and Amen!!!!!!!!!!!!!!!!!!!!!!! HALLELUJAH!!!!!!!!!!!!!!!!!!!!!!!!!!AMEN!!!!!!! !!!!!!!!!!!!!!!!

TRULY, THERE IS NO GOD LIKE THE GOD OF ISRAEL!!!!!!!!!!!!!!!!!!!!!!!! MAY ISRAEL AND ISHMAEL FIND PEACE IN THEIR COMMON FATHER, ABRAHAM,

NOW AND FOREVER!!!!!!!! ABRAHAM BY FAITH RECEIVED FROM YAHOVAH THE BLESSINGS THAT HAVE MADE YOUR DESCENDENTS GREAT TO THIS VERY DAY. LET THEREFORE, THESE BROTHERS CEASE TO WAR WITH EACH OTHER; FOR A COMMON ENEMY ARISES TO GREEDILY DESTROY YOU BOTH! LET ALL WHO LOVE GOD JOIN TOGETHER AGAINST THE SPIRIT OF ANTI-CHRIST NOW RISING IN PERSONS SO WICKED, GREEDY AND SELFISH THEY WOULD ENSLAVE THE WORLD AND DESTROY ANY PEOPLE AND NATION THAT GETS IN THEIR WAY! LET ALL WHO LOVE FREEDOM REJECT THE "NEW WORLD ORDER", THE RFID BIO-CHIP (MARK OF THE BEAST), AND THE WICKEDNESS OF GREED AND CORRUPTION IN ACCEPTING BRIBES FROM THEM AND THEIR LIES TELLING YOU WILL GET A POSITON OF POWER IN THE NEW WORLD ORDER IF YOU ONLY ACQUIESCE TO THEM AND THEIR INSANE DESIRE TO RULE THE WORLD! LET ALL OF THE FAITH FACE THIS WICKEDNESS TOGETHER OF PERSONS SO DELUSIONAL THEY WANT TO TAKE THE PLACE OF GOD ON EARTH AND ENSLAVE YOU ALL!!!!!!!! BE NOT DECEIVED! BOWING TO THE WILL OF THE PERSONS OF THE "NEW WORLD ORDER" WILL BE SUBJUGATING YOU AND YOUR CHILDREN TO COMPLETE SLAVERY TO THEIR WHIMS! IT WILL NOT BE FOR YOUR SAFETY AND WELFARE BUT FOR YOUR LIVES! ALREADY THEY ARE TURNING YOUR SONS INTO GIGALOS AND YOUR DAUGHTERS INTO PROSTITUTES; NO GOOD THING WILL COME OF RECEIVING THE MARK OF THE BEAST (RFID IMPLANTS); OR THE PERSONS NOW FORMING THE "NEW WORLD ORDER"! LET EVERYONE, EVERYWHERE, NOW COME TO KNOW THE ONE TRUE GOD AND CREATOR OF THE UNIVERSE!!!!!!!!!!!!!!!!!!!!!!!! YAHOSHUAH! YAHOSHUAH!!! YAHOSHUAH!!!! YAHOSHUAH HA MASHIACH!!!!!!!!!!!!!!!!!!!!!!!!! FOR GOD

AND GOD ALONE IS FIT TO RULE HEAVEN AND EARTH; THE UNIVERSE ENTIRE!!!!!!!!!!!!!!!!!!!!!!!!!!!

C. Japan

    1. You have the resources, technology, and self-disciplined, motivated people to construct the first successful prototypes of wave generators set at a distance to trigger tsunami retainers and wave bafflers in emergencies; that will save lives and billions of dollars in damages to infrastructure

    2. Wave and wind generators can be improved to a standard that replaces all nuclear generators and any other biohazardous method of generating energy; lead the way in these improvements, by leading your already disciplined society to the One True GOD and away from religious traditions that cannot save! The Creator of the Universe will then give you knowledge of innovations in these areas and more!

    3. Lead the way in wave baffling technologies, artificial reef creations in the process; use naturally growing sea forests as much as possible

    4. With limited land mass; consider expansion via carbon nano-tubes into a portion of the population that resides and manages the manmade reefs, baffles, sea farms, hatcheries and fisheries that should be massively underway now and into the 21st century addressing global hunger.

D. United States of America

    1. Return to your Christian Heritage Proudly

    2. Investigate and hold the treasonous and murderous public officials of 911 accountable.

    3. Apologize to the world for selfish greed motivating wars for oil; the slaughtered innocent

civilians; rebuild those nations; give them the right to govern themselves and their own natural resources

4. Stop policing other nations until your own internal corruption in all levels of government and law enforcement has been dealt with.

5. Christians in America; take the Gospel to each house; every town or city that rejects the Gospel of Jesus Christ; leave from; shake the dust off your feet!

6. "Christians" in America, will also be receiving the Divine Judgments coming upon the ungodly as long as you continue to compromise your life in ungodly practices; sinful ways as Romans 1:21-32 speaks so clearly of. Until God's people stop playing with pornography, committing adultery, sinning in every way like unbelievers, greedy, covetous, ambitious, and in all ways no different in practice of their way of life from heathen, the people will continue to suffer judgments in continued increase in severity and rapidity; upon your nation, including those claiming to be "Christians" but in no way acting like such. Only when God's people fulfill what is written in 2Chronicles 7:14 will the USA again rise up blessed in all respects.

7. Restore public education with the original intent to make sure every citizen knows what GOD states as the Instructions for Life contained in the Holy Bible! THAT IS THE TRUTH!

8. When all citizens know the word of God then your politicians and law enforcement will not be so corrupt that they commit false flag operations like 911; accept bribes to allow rapists, robbers,

murderers, pedophiles, drug dealers etc. to get away with their crimes at the expense of innocent victim's lives! They will not be so deceitful that they lie to the whole world in order to invade nations and rob those people of natural resources for their own personal greed and ambitions to rule the world!

9. As long as you as citizens are remaining willfully ignorant of these crimes and oppressive, imperialistic measures, don't whine to GOD when judgments come upon you all to humble you for your greedy, selfish, bloodthirsty ways!

10. Stop shedding innocent blood! Military bases in the majority of nations on earth! Using weapons of mass destruction on others while publicly disdaining their use for political purposes, slaughtering infants and even funding the murderous institutions ripping babes, limb from limb, making millions to suffer and die if you want their oil or anything of value from them; (instead of peaceful coexistence and trade negotiations), inciting wars and riots in nations that don't favor your imperialistic agenda, spending trillions of dollars on weapons and distribution of such worldwide, leaving chemical toxins, biohazards, radioactive materials, mines, to cause loss of life, birth defects and unimaginable human suffering as your footprint of death and destruction for decades now upon the planet, embracing the murderous rich and wealthy, blaming the poor and innocent, enslaving the masses and in all ways turning what was once a great nation founded by the Wisdom,

Knowledge and Understanding of GOD and true Christians, into a filthy stench in the presence of GOD and the whole world in your degenerate debauchery and GREED!

11. May the true Christians now within your borders be strengthened and empowered mightily to do supernaturally the will of GOD so gloriously, that this trend in America towards perverse evils and greed of every kind is stopped immediately and America ends far more glorious than she began instead of falling into ruin and corruption (due to individual sin and depravity of the masses) like all other empires that have ever existed on earth!

12. It is amazing how Americans trumpet their generosity worldwide that really have not contributed to the altruistic outreaches themselves! Most all charitable organizations that have existed in America were Christian based and due to the benevolence of these Christian organizations many Americans are thought well of despite the atrocities aforementioned. These same people all too willing to take a bow nationally and internationally and benefit from these charitable acts are the very ones cursing Christians and opposing the Gospel of Jesus Christ in our nation!

13. Stop comparing yourselves to other nations that have never heard the Gospel of Jesus Christ or had Bibles available for every citizen; for before GOD you are not justified by the even worse behavior of others! You have known the Truth and are rejecting it for lies! Teaching innocent

little kids that they are descendants of monkeys! (Such ignorance is not to be tolerated by a sane civilization)

14. Repent! Turn from your wicked, greedy ways or great will your fall be in the sight of the nations of the whole world!

15. Americans (and every nation) are suffering due to Greed at the highest levels; the Stock Market; all a wealthy person has to do to become wealthier is lend money (buy stocks) and expect returns (usury; whether or not you call it dividends), all this does is concentrate wealth without providing products or services and enslaves the masses in ever lower wages while actually driving higher and higher the cost of living (expecting ever larger profits) and ever worse working conditions. This results in exactly what we see today more than 60% of the world's wealth controlled by less than 2% of the population and an increasing percentage of impoverished citizens worldwide. Make no mistake people are starving to death; dying homeless because of this incredible unrestrained GREED! Why not be the first nation to do away with publicly traded stocks and commodities? Make people with money have to provide a product or service to get more wealth (employ people that provide a quality product or service)! One national bank regulated by the people to set usury rates commensurate to the lowest demographics so all have a chance at home/flat ownership again. Boycott or put such high tariffs on corporations that relocate manufacturing jobs to other nations that it's no

longer profitable for them to do so; such that manufacturing jobs remain in America. Again place quality control measures such that made in America means the best you can buy anywhere! Only when children are taught properly that they came from GOD will you again be able to find honest, competent employees who take pride in their work rather than people who work harder at hardly working; expecting top dollar for less than mediocre labor.

16. Concentrate on 21st century innovations, sharing of renewable energy innovations in exchange for usage rates set by the beneficiaries of the energy that now contribute to the innovations and construction globally of renewable energies. Hydrocarbons, fossil fuels need to be utilized for materials; not wasteful and unnecessary burning!

17. In addition to focusing on rebuilding America's infrastructure via transcontinental subsystem as an underground backbone for all infrastructures (electrical, black and white water, high-speed transit, smart truck superhighways, information network, communications network), focus on 21st century superstructure models, that free up green space, and are virtually self-sufficient.

18. Coordinate with nations making such innovations already and champion this cause by mandating all autos be refitted with hydroelectric motors and/or solar boosted by the year 2025.

19. Mandate by law to shut down all coal, nuclear, fossil fuel power plants worldwide by the year 2050 and improve the existing wind turbines by

refitting them with the turbo systems similar to jet aircraft; create instantaneous step-up transformers within the turbines by placing wind generators within windings such that a smaller generator is the rotor of the next size and so on. Wave generators need to be radically improved think of buoy/pendulum/gyro models as opposed to the snakelike compression models currently.

20. Cooperate and support the African equatorial regions and start building cities in the desert of state-of-the-art solar collectors and generators, with water precipitators and create international agreements based on contribution to such an endeavor of knowledge, materials and labor to build a worldwide virtually inexhaustible solar farm along those nations for electrical energy globally. (This does not mean nations should not continue improving their own wind, wave and solar renewable energy sources and innovations; just an alternative to destroying the planet and killing all life by continued poisoning through fossil fuel harvesting, refining, and burning and pretending that due to "shortages" is the reason people are starving to death and dying of all the associated ailments.)

21. Chemical toxins are NOT medication for health and wellness! It is time the pharmaceutical companies made available health remedies in the natural form that God created; unaltered genetically or in any way! All nations should concentrate on bio-nano technology of creating programmable "cells" of bio-assimilated

substances that have NO harmful side effects and can be programmed to remove all cell abnormalities, viral, bacterial, coccidial or parasitic infections. That can even be programmed to replicate healthy cells the body may be in short supply of. Already tissues and organs have been biologically generated and now it is time to address all ailments on a cellular level in this manner!

E. Australia

1. Work on building one of the largest desalination processes in the world as your central region that sits below sea level (America can do this with "death valley") Create an aqueduct system that takes in sea water into this low region and using high grade translucent plastics or glass (or the newer semi-osmosis materials becoming available) take advantage of all the natural evaporation processes along the way and the natural condensation set to funnel into freshwater man-made aquifers. You and I both know fresh water holds much of your continent back from agricultural and demographic expansion.

2. Stop considering uranium for sale to other nations at this time; the global political climate is far too unstable. Instead, lead the way in solar collectors and generators and wave and wind renewable energy sources. Until mankind can come up with a way to have no radioactive waste with fusion reactors that consume all usable energy until the material is virtually completely stable; radioactive materials should be prohibited from use globally.

3. The LORD sends rain upon the faithful and gives increase to the generous! Practice His Instructions for Life contained in the Holy Bible and droughts will cease and your land will yield bountifully!

4. The amount of sunshine you receive is also ideal for building solar powered waste incinerators/refiners. Using solar collectors and concentrators enough heat can be generated to melt even metals and then refining processes already available can be utilized to separate the waste into usable recyclables.

5. Champion national and global mandates to build easily accessible automatic composting centers for all food wastes. (Or a choice between slopping the pigs and composting for all food wastes) And/or integrate composting as part of universal proper waste management.

6. Champion salt water farms, hatcheries and fisheries and chefs to prepare gourmet meals as part of a global effort of sustaining populations with adequate and tasty nutrition.

F. Indonesian Region, Fiji, portions of New Zealand

1. Beware of the very darkness that once had cannibals roaming your lands! This dark power must be constantly spoken against in the Name of Yahoshuah the Messiah (JESUS CHRIST), and forbidden from having any place in any of your citizens. If anyone is found committing cannibalism, execute them immediately and send their dark spirit to the Abyss (or the will of the Lord Jesus Christ) to remain bound until the final judgment of all souls! (You control unclean, foul, dark spirits by commanding them in the Name of

JESUS CHRIST (YAHOSHUAH HA MASHIACH)); but you also must be filled with the Holy Ghost or your words will have not the Power of GOD behind them (Acts19:13-16).

2. Continued idolatry brings continued judgments upon your people and lands; only by embracing the Gospel of JESUS CHRIST will your people and lands be healed.

G. Haiti; Gulf regions, Philippines, Island nations, into Central America

1. Hurricane Alley – Hurricanes the size of continents and more powerful than ever will sweep through these regions if people fail to Repent of their many sinful ways, idolatries, sexual immoralities, murders, child abuse, slave trades, you cannot serve both God and idols! Repent of voodoo; get your shamans to Repent; stop playing with devils and foul and unclean spirits; or judgments stand ready to sweep you all away and purge the lands of blood guiltiness and idolatries.

2. Stop the hidden ways of darkness while claiming to be Christians or you'll be reproved by GOD in the Light of Day! Until the people truly repent and truly receive the Living LORD JESUS CHRIST; all the curses of the Torah remain; destroying you in the sight of the whole world. Only true Repentance will bring your nations and people into a state of healing and Blessedness and the hostile winds will blow warm and friendly once again.

3. All island nations must learn to properly steward (increase desalination units, sea farms, hatcheries and fisheries enough to support all

citizens without trade from other nations) the surrounding waters that will sustain the people; or overpopulation will result in mass starvation.

H. Denmark, Holland and other northern European countries

    1. Well done in mandating hydroelectric autos; share the method with political systems analysts and show how you succeeded in this endeavor.

    2. Wind farms; tell the world of the pros and cons thus far as you've expanded this renewable energy more than other nations.

    3. Higher sea levels, dike systems, aqueducts, etc. what automation advancements have you made; please share with the world as flooding will become more of a problem until the nations return to GOD and His Instructions for life. In addition, mankind should be creating rivers to renew dwindling spawning populations of certain species of fish.

I. Norway

    1. You have made advancements in proper sewage to white water, and irrigation procedures; please share your innovations with the nations.

    2. Your natural resources benefit social services in a commendable manner; please share the pros and cons (if any) you have experienced by this most sane culture concerning natural resource management.

    3. Beware of islamic immigration, don't accept criminal organizations into your midst.

J. China

    1. You are in an economic boom as your hard-working populace is manufacturing much of the world's goods currently. As such you are in an

ideal place to model demographic development of self-sustaining superstructures that marry both residential and professional services in one building.

2. Consider mandating smart cars powered by renewable energies and prohibiting fossil fuel burning engines.

3. Consider innovating HPVs and modeling a whole town or city primarily around HPVs. Maybe giving economic incentives or cultural incentives to citizens choosing HPVs as primary transit.

4. Monitor closely the melting ice caps on the Himalayans; once gone; rivers will dry up if you have not adequately prepared water precipitators and desalination plants to provide potable water for your people.

5. It would be commendable to champion universal health care and make certain eastern practices are included in treatment options globally.

K. Iceland, Polynesian Islands, Volcanic activities globally

1. Geothermal energy may seem like a renewable energy source and can be weighed against cost of structures, management and improvement based on life of the plant; but solar, wind, wave technologies are more cost effective. Geothermal activity is unstable by comparison and especially as the world continues to depart from God will become more unstable; destroyed geothermal plants will be the least of your problems compared to major eruptions though. So, make sure your people KNOW and LOVE GOD the Creator of the Universe! Our Creator provides solutions to all people who know Him, just ask!

And when God gives you answers PRAISE AND THANK HIM!

2. All islands need to train marine biologists that work with the fishermen; find out which populations have declined where and start immediate construction on sea farms (vegetations for human consumption), hatcheries and fisheries; enough that if trade ceases for any reason your people can live off your own efforts. Desalination units around your land base for adequate fresh water supplies need to be constructed and maintained until the Glorious Return of our Lord and Savior, JESUS CHRIST.

L. Russia

1. You have a large reserve of gems and some unique to your region; advertising is key to retailing and liquidating.

2. Concentrate on bringing your infrastructure current with the information age; Wireless transponders and repeaters are less expensive than hardwire Infrastructure.

3. Overcome western disdain by embracing more capitalism and freedom of religion in some fields while maintaining high standards of socialism in other areas. Agreed socialism for social services for your people, mixed in with just enough capitalism to provide incentives for your people, to advance in industry and services innovations and inventions, makes for a healthy stabilized government and nation as a whole. BEWARE OF GREED which enslaves everyone.

4. You have plenty of fresh water and oil reserves; one of your less capitalized resources is raising animal populations for quality furs. The same

animals that produce quality furs can be used for food; hire chefs to prepare tasty dishes so the raised animals aren't wasted. Many societies have become hypocritical in this regard; as they lounge on leather furniture, leather car seats, where leather jackets, and at the same time snub furs. Luxury furs and gems aforementioned are only lacking wise advertising to increase your GNP.

5. Northern seas contain some of the least polluted species of fish in the world. Building hatcheries and fisheries in these climates will have high yields of those species; keep your ice breakers in good repair. Just release ten percent of what you raise back into the depleted seas from overfishing.

6. Embrace the Gospel of JESUS CHRIST; and innovations and prosperity will be upon you; but attack Israel or Christians in your nation or neighbors and Divine Consequences will come upon you.

7. God has much more to say to you and your people; only embrace the Gospel of JESUS CHRIST and Wisdom will inspire your citizens to achieve great advances.

M. India

1. False religions will lead to starvation of the masses; the worship of creatures must cease; instead turn to the One Creator (false notions of reincarnation into another person or animal is untrue dogmas that keep people in bondage imagining that one day those who are imperfect can make themselves perfect instead of realizing that only our Eternal Creator who is Perfect can perfect us, His Creation and that each person will

be in their own bodies when He judges each and every soul. Jn 5:22, 2Tim 4:1, Acts 10:42; 17:31

2. While feeding your children is commendable; neglect not spiritual enlightenment which is achieved by knowing the One True GOD! (Jeremiah 29:11-13; 31:31-34; 1Jn 5:20; Acts 2:38,39; Jn 14:6-26)

3. Tsunamis; floods; and other "natural disasters" will continue as judgments as long as idolatries are adhered to by your people; only true Repentance will bring relief from judgments coming in increased severity and rapidity.

4. Outdated productions and services may sustain briefly; but innovations cause you to prosper. Embrace biodiversity and small farms; reject monopolies that will place you and your people in strangleholds.

5. Just taking over dental paste production can result in billions of dollars of revenue. Replace the highly toxic fluoride products with Neem and other natural healthy herbals, botanicals and medicinals. A portion of cosmetics and perfumes that also are not toxic chemicals can be a large source of revenue for your GNP.

6. Maintain your naturally unaltered grain stores such as millets that grow in drought regions; these naturally occurring grains; not genetically modified can mean the difference of starvation or life in harsh climatic regions of the world. Reject genetically modified foods and cheap grain supplies (In my opinion, if even bugs with microscopic brains won't eat it; it can't be healthy). It is a capitalistic method to put out of business competitors in the short term; so, they

monopolize in the future for long term gains by creating a stranglehold on what matters most (food and water). Free your people from this threat of global enslavement and encourage your small farmers; if necessary, by boycotting imports of cheap staples and subsidizing your farmers with grants and education to bring back local produce diversity and competition. Just like citizens don't have a legal voice against the armies of attorneys representing multinational entities; individual farmers can't compete against corporate conglomerate agricultural giants; without aide from the people and political powers. In America we see superstore giants like Wal-Mart drive small retailers out of business; only to raise their prices when all the competition is gone. This is the danger of monopolies. (Cheap today and costs you your lives tomorrow).

7. Ayurvedic remedies and other eastern practices should also be included in treatment options of universal healthcare for all citizens.

N. Nations near world super powers

1. Greed and pride moves upon megalomaniacs to desire more and more endlessly. If you do not have people willing to fight to the death for your freedoms and independence; careful negotiations with nearby superpowers are in your interest.

2. Certain nations possessing natural resources or in the path of natural resources (oil today, food and water for the unprepared future) are being targeted under international façades. It is therefore in your interests to sell such resources to powers nearby and form alliances thereby;

until you and your people are strong and willing enough to fight for independence and freedom. Keep the resources at affordable rates or history and current events show invasion and militant conquest is virtually inevitable.

3. Such nations should make sure all citizens significantly benefit from such trade negotiations or caste instability will create years of corruption, warlords, riots and revolutions as all history shows clearly. If you want to be a nation of free, peaceful and happy families; citizens must unite to demand equal benefit from existing natural resources. True personal and national security is in knowing the One True GOD! And even bullies learn to respect their victims if only punched hard enough. Sadly, freedom in all of history has been purchased by souls willing to fight to the death by whatever means available to them and until Christ returns in Glory; that is the way it is; so, one of the first things all citizens in smaller nations should demand is the right to bear arms; and to receive competent training in their use!

O. Arabia, Middle Eastern; Oil-Rich Nations

1. Have no fear, oil will continue to be a necessary resource for materials such as plastics; so, your economic status is not threatened by a shift to renewable energies.

2. However, you have the wealth and the days of sunlight to fund solar power farms and make innovations to make generators even more productive than at present. By crossing over into building solar generators and water precipitators,

regions once thought uninhabitable or hostile will become veritable oases!

3. You house some geographic holy sites (such as the fenced off Mt. Sinai); opening these up to the world will increase knowledge, tourism, and benefit your people thereby through good will of the visitors.

4. Share more of the national wealth with your citizens (by employing them all with living wages toward construction of the solar generators, water precipitators, desalination plants and new cities in the desert thereby); a happy and prosperous people makes for a strong and stable government; which in turns improves global relations.

5. Telling your people, that islam is wrong, and essentially a criminal organization in doctrine and practice will enable your people to survive and thrive as you recognize Jesus Christ properly as the One True God and Savior of mankind that He is. If you don't KNOW the Savior, you're NOT saved! You are still in your sins! Dead to our Eternal Creator because you are not recognizing who He is and so you haven't obeyed His Commandments! Heb 6:1-2, 1Jn 5:20, Acts 4:12 Do so if you want to live and be Blessed instead of under His Wrath! Jn 3:15-22; 2Th 1:8-9, Rev 21:8

P. South American nations

1. The Rain Forest has the largest variety and most potent forms of naturally occurring medicinals in the world; stop burning and leveling acreage of the rain forest throwing out billions and billions of dollars of revenue in the process by properly maintaining the forest and harvesting all

the remedies!

2. Fresh water fisheries throughout the Amazonian region could supply the world's population with the largest variety of fresh water species anywhere!

3. The Andes steppe regions (large concentration of microclimates) are ideal for identifying climatic and elevation limitations for a large variety of agricultural commodities. (In the process of creating more tolerant varieties of fruits, nuts, grains, vegetables, legumes and tubers.)

4. Certain species of fish migrate to the waters off Chile, Argentina, Peruvian coasts to spawn; these giant varieties should be protected species and added to those regions' hatcheries and fisheries until their numbers return.

5. Coffee and Cocoa will continue to be in demand as long as mankind is still populating the earth; to increase yields; learn to speak in faith over your agricultural endeavors in addition to improving composting and irrigation methods.

6. Farmers all over the world should divide their lands into eight sections to ensure they let one section rest completely every seventh year according to God's counsel. (Rotate such that each section is ensured of full rest for one out of every seven years). I recommend the eight sections such that one section can be left for the "poor among you" to glean.

7. Patagonia region; legalize beaver trapping (ones that cause instantaneous death) and fur products to solve the wetlands problem destroying forests and the natural ecosystem that existed before the beaver was brought in there.

Q. Central African nations

1. Unite under our Lord Jesus Christ to prevent genocides. God will show you what to do. Acts 2:17-18, Jn 14:15-26, Jn 16:13 certain insects can be eaten, even made tasty by spices. LOOK TO GOD AND HIS WORDS IN THE HOLY BIBLE, learn from Him, He will provide.

2. Your nations should unite to deal with malaria. Until bio-nano tech creates injectable, nano-bot cells that target parasitic infections, deal with high mosquito populations with bat and sparrow hotels; and in high concentrations of malaria by entrapping the bloodsuckers by taking some of the byproducts of meat processing facilities and use to incinerate them by solar concentrators heating the flight path of the mosquitoes coming to partake. (lure and funnel populations that are naturally incinerated by solar lenses)

3. Build waste recycling centers to handle the dumping contracts you have with other nations and turn it into profits by salvaging the materials for resell for manufacturing.

4. Expand your agriculture; especially coffee and chocolate.

5. Retail your precious metals and gems directly instead of wholesaling to existing distributors. Form unions for the harvesters and miners to be given living wages.

6. Mandate white water septic systems and stop polluting your rivers and lakes with human sewage.

7. Capitalize as a nation on your unique species of wildlife and fauna. Don't let a few benefit from these natural resources; by uniting as a people

and demanding rights for all citizens such as education, healthcare, mandatory minimum wages, etc. etc.

8. Document/ film the bipedal dinosaur still living in your dense jungle regions and don't let evolutionists talk you into lying to the rest of the world about its existence. (This goes for all extremely rare species worldwide; such as Sasquatch; Oki; Nessi; Yeti; and all the species currently classified as crypto zoological.) (On a side note; don't kill "Big foot" or treat that species as an animal; they have families and talk with each other and are otherwise more civil in some respects than modern man and no, they are NOT the "missing link".) For my part, I hope certain species remain hidden from modern man that has a propensity to experiment on anyone or anything they are just too willfully ignorant to understand just as it is.

R. Mediterranean Region

1. The sea is being overrun by invader vegetation; continue to find species that eat these foreign invaders, hopefully turn this into a positive occurrence by harvesting the species fed by the invaders or creating edibles from the invading vegetation itself.

2. Find out which species are in decline and immediately employ fishermen and citizens in numerous hatcheries and fisheries with a mandate to release a certain percentage of all species into the wild to rebuild dwindling populations.

3. All island nations really need to concentrate on expanding their resources to include desalination units; sea farms (vegetation), hatcheries and fisheries. Eventually, even superstructures will be limited by land space; so, it is necessary to develop underground and oceanic residential living models. Island nations also need to mandate composting and build tiered farming structures. Island nations are the litmus paper to the health of the world. If an island nation can't support its population; it is an indicator that it is possible to reach critical mass regarding numbers of persons inhabiting the earth and a warning to us all. Remember trade relations are not guaranteed; learn to be as self-sufficient as possible.

4. You are near the north African equatorial regions and would make sense to help fund the construction of the solar generators for a perpetual use agreement in reduction of energy costs. Much can be done in your own nations; but I am speaking to smaller nations without as much land mass and sun exposure. Perhaps even profit-sharing agreements depending on the amount of initial and ongoing contributions or maintenance of the solar generators.

5. All nations that embrace the Gospel of JESUS CHRIST are embracing God's Blessings; so, make the Holy Bible available to all citizens. Encourage citizens that hold to different religions or worldviews to debate verbally; never violently. If one is confident, they hold the Truth in their way of life they should be able to peaceably defend their rationale. In free discourse lies are

conquered by truth and truth is real freedom! Jn 8:32-36, Jn 14:6-9

III. Things the public is willfully kept in ignorance of by governments:

A. https://www.blastthetrumpet.org/PublicLetters/AAAUpdatedPublicAlertsMattersofLifeandDeath/Updates053016/Current%20Technologies.pdf - governments around the world have been researching technologies that they don't let the public know about sometimes for a matter of decades to indefinitely. So, you don't necessarily recognize them when they are in use.

B. These are some of those Technologies (I have been amazed how many people just assume someone telling them something they are in complete ignorance of is "crazy" and will even argue about something they know nothing about; rather than acknowledge their own ignorance and learn something new; so much so, they embrace and even fortify being willfully ignorant rather than knowledgeable. I could probably list 100 or more advancements that exist today and have even been publicly televised and yet still find people who would rather assume I'm lying, hoaxing, crazy or anything but telling them factual truth; like the hospital homicide attempts I personally survived).

    1. Holographs and VR gear already exist; DOD members can confirm. The VR headgear are decades behind the Department of Defense.

    2. X-ray glasses that look like a standard pair of sunglasses exist; in addition to multi-goggles that possess available light, infrared red and x-ray technologies on demand.

    3. Smart clothing like the movie Predator demonstrated are nearly perfected.

4. New weapons technologies that are "slow and silent kill" methods allow governments to target citizens and make them appear to die of natural causes when in fact they were targeted with intensified RF energy weapons; some weapons are actually capable of targeting isolated (12' or less radius) locations on earth from satellites! These are used on dissidents or high priority targets that the government doesn't want to turn into a martyr by outright assassinations as in the former days. (There are many methods governments utilize to assassinate targets these days that challenge these criminals in places they don't belong). Food and beverage poisoning is a favorite method and very easy to accomplish upon targets that enjoy dining out. Agents get hired under false identities or even bribe existing employees to turn the other way or flash a badge; distract and poison the target's food and beverages. If you dine out regularly and know you are a high priority target beware of food and beverage poisoning. The agent hired under the false identity just disappears under a new government issued identity after their target is assassinated in this manner. Once a target is under government surveillance; you are being scrutinized for weaknesses in how to murder you successfully or frame you for wrongful arrest and imprisonment. As such, spies pose as new girlfriends, boyfriends as the case may be and gain entrance to your private quarters for information gathering and/or framing. Governments worldwide regularly murder; assassinate those who present the

greatest challenge to their continued criminal practices. Very few governments are devoid of criminal corruption of some kind sadly and at worst many protect murderers and mass murderers as these corrupt politicians get ultra-wealthy from their criminal alliances with corrupt businesses and even such organizations that participate in human slave trafficking. If your government is not empowering citizens to defend themselves from murderers and not arrested violent terrorist organizations, the people need to make weapons that they can and hold their governments responsible for such negligence.

5. Force field technologies are emerging.

6. Sonic weapons designed for warfare are being utilized on civilians by police powers as well.

7. Laser weapons ground to space and in flight, even handheld cutting devices presently exist.

8. Plasma technologies are in process as interplanetary drives; incinerators, drillers, and weapons.

9. Nanotechnology has increased so as to make the RFID implants to be remotely powered to become transceiver devices. (Ability to listen to private conversations/ moments)

10. Chips the size of a grain of coarse ground pepper can be remotely activated to send data, digital images and can be sealed from water damage and painted even into toilets; yes, some government agents can actually spy even on your bowel movements! (Some of the voyeur feeds online have corrupt government ties)

11. Digital cameras have become so small they can ride on the abdomens of beetles and other insects and used to spy in this manner as well.

12. Digital cameras can even look like power indicators on TVs, smoke detectors, etc. and in home security systems can be used to spy on the inhabitants.

13. I encourage MIT to cease and desist with neural implant technologies as the government wants to use these implants to make programmable assassins and soldiers that receive directives via the implants much like cyborgs.

14. I encourage anti-gravitational technologies. There are technologies that could wipe mankind off the earth faster than exploding all the nuclear weapons to date at once. Not all knowledge is good knowledge; if you are an inventor, make certain you don't manifest technologies that maniacs in power would use for great evil and destruction. (Like atomic fission; scientists should have known it would be used destructively)

15. Perpetual motion machines and centripetal propulsion should be looked into in further detail.

16. One of the significant factors keeping the world from advancing sanely into the 21st century are too many existing wealthy persons clinging to the old ways that have made them wealthy and fearing change for the better. The public needs to insist on these innovations because the existing wealthy are so comfortable in general that they would rather watch the world drown in pollution and mass millions die off than embrace the needed innovations to prevent those tragedies! In other words, the masses need to get angry

enough and realize you are fighting for your lives and that of your children!

17. Genetic splicing and mutation. When the Nazis were assimilated into our government; horrible things came along with them. Like the desire to breed a super race. Human DNA has been spliced with animal and even sea life such that mutations exist in secret locations of these hybrid species. (Don't believe anyone who says this isn't possible; they are LYING) Genetically modified foods and animals are well documented and made public; and the distasteful clones and genetic mutations imagined by "science fiction" have occurred as well and are kept from public knowledge; so, these insane "scientists" aren't justly and swiftly executed for their abominable and tortuous practices. In addition, eugenic fascism in our government has also caused sterilization and abortion upon the poor masses; while secretly funding "breeders"; government agents (identified as genetic desirables) instructed to procreate with certain members of society for money. to develop "Manchurian candidates" controlled persons who do the bidding of their handlers.

18. New body armors superior to even Kevlar and the "dragon scale" varieties and individual flight devices have come into existence.

19. Transformer autos that can fly exist.

20. Individual jet craft that fly just like "jet ski" water craft exist.

21. Individual submarine craft exist.

22. Plasma drillers exist and so underground cities should begin to be made public; not just secretive government organizations.

23. Almost any technology you've seen in the movies exists except for such notable exceptions such as the "beam me up Scotty" transporters, interplanetary; intergalactic spacecraft of our origin, food replicators, but much more "science fiction" technologies exist presently than the public is made aware of. I am not for robot technologies as presently exist in the area of warfare. Our greatest advancements in robot technologies all deal with death and destruction. If robotic development was restricted to constructive uses it would be fine but the day robots are used against us; as we have been using them against other people and nations; will be the day you'll understand my point of view.

24. No nation should ever get so confident in its technological terrors or innovations that their respective politicians think to subjugate other nations; or God will humble you quickly by giving foreign powers an advancement that puts yours to shame and gives you "a taste of your own medicine".

C. Population management

    1. Policies of death and sterilization

        a) Death rate is increased by willfully creating economic recessions and depressions

        b) Abortion clinics exist in poor demographics and encouraged in public education settings (poor masses targeted)

c) Most harmful additives and preservatives exist in the cheapest food products and government handouts

d) Pharmaceutical medications contain harmful chemicals intentionally. (Drugs are designed not to cure or make well the patient but rather to make the patient have to take them indefinitely; and even more "medications" until they die (prematurely))

e) Environmental regulations are lifted; water supplies polluted upon the poor and unsuspecting masses

f) Sterilization is offered regularly to mothers with C sections (convinced of needing such); the mentally ill and all such citizens the government deems undesirable

g) Fluoride is championed though highly toxic for use upon the ignorant masses

h) Military recruiting centers exist primarily in the poorest demographics (next to the Planned Slaughterhood Clinics)

i) Ads target poor demographics for pharmaceutical experimentation (FDA approval processes)

j) FDA approves additives, preservatives, drugs known to cause serious injuries and death and leaves such substances on the market for distribution to any and all citizens ignorant enough to take them

k) Citizens are being murdered/euthanized without government prosecution by mass murdering doctors and nurses in local hospitals across the nation, and government mental institutions, even prisoners are being experimented on causing premature deaths.

l) Prisoners are under the constant threat of death regardless of their offense in the event of certain natural disasters, enemy invasions or anytime the overall security is threatened due to some catastrophe.

m) Designated battalions are being trained to suppress rioters or civilian unrest in addition to increased police powers.

n) Law enforcement using lethal measures are constantly justified publicly even when there was no legitimate reason for the shooting/murder.

o) Lower ranking soldiers are victims of bio, chemical and radioactive warfare and experimentation (the poor are expendable to the eugenic fascists in the Pentagon and other government agencies)
www.beyondtreason.com

p) Wars are incited not just for political reasons but to reduce global populations (why there are so many "civilian casualties" and "collateral damage". And why no significant effort is made to deal with the tens of millions of land mines still buried globally; and the lasting effects of agent orange, depleted uranium war heads, etc.)

q) New terms are being created as diseases, mental illnesses, and political enemies to target citizens at will for incarceration and "treatments" that

lead to permanent injuries and even death
(the most recent psychotropics carry
"lethal" side effects)
r) Lending policies put the largest usury on
the poor as "stress related illnesses" has
become well documented
s) The poor work in the most
environmentally harmful positions
and can't afford legal remedies against the
armies of attorneys the wealthy corporate
entities purchase to insulate themselves
and these criminal ways
t) The poor are suckered into hazardous
environmental cleanups while the wealthy;
if they show up at all, have superior
hazmat gear to all the slave laborers
u) The wealthy have ways of avoiding
drafts or anything they don't want to
participate in; while the poor are on the
"front lines" (The family gets a flag or
some trinket; while the wealthy eugenic
fascists get multimillion/billion-dollar
contracts and revenue in perpetuation of
the military/industrial/political complex)
v) The wealthy get preferential treatment
and extraordinary healthcare measures;
while the poor are kicked out of hospitals
to die on the streets
w) The wealthy get quality "at home care"
if they become disabled; but even
Medicare and Medicaid are of little to no
assistance to persons so poor they can't
afford even the copays! If you're truly
poor, the message the greedy USA culture

clearly sends is DIE! DIE! You're worthless and an unwanted burden to all the rest of us! Medicare and Medicaid are being improved to help the poor, but there are still elderly and disabled people dying homeless and hungry in our nation
x) Mountain blasting for coal and sludge is allowed to decimate ecologies (typically around communities too poor to fight the major money interests); shale fracturing is allowed to destroy aquifers; toxins are allowed to fill the air we breathe; the wealthy have water purification and revitalization processes; and even air purification systems in their residences and "work" places. Organic foods, and quality beverages are the most expensive commodities because policies of death are upon the poor; while the wealthy are given every assistance and encouraged to procreate. Our society is designed by the wealthy to favor the wealthy and cause the poor (genetically undesirable) to die as quickly as many be possible and still maintain "plausible deniability".
Even genetic desirables are paid "breeders" in our eugenic fascist nation.
y) Disabled veterans are left to die in the streets; too poor to obtain any adequate legal representation for just compensation from the eugenic fascists responsible for their disability
z) Certain "inoculations" cause "accidental" deaths of infants in

regions the government knows has a high concentration of Christians (because they have a reputation of "forgiving" without filing wrongful death and malpractice suits)

aa) Cures for cancer and other ailments have existed for decades for the wealthy; but the poor are systematically told they have a limited time to live by "doctors" when they're diagnosed and in desperation people are suckered into thinking chemicals and radiation that makes their hair fall out is actually going to help them (statistics show it helps them; that is, all the quicker to the grave). Antidotes are readily available for the wealthy elite for biochemical warfare; but the masses can be exterminated at will and during epidemics there are always "shortages" of anything that could save the masses from dying.

bb) Slow responses during natural disasters are intentional but just enough to still maintain plausible deniability that the elite wanted more of the poor masses to die off.

cc) Mass murdering doctors and nurses are set free to murder even more of the naively trusting poor masses; but you can bet if a poor citizen intentionally killed as many of them as they were nationally exposed of by CNN; that poor citizen would have fried in the chair. (Over a million hospital caused deaths occur every year with no investigations and no media attention; more Americans have died at the hands of doctors and nurses in hospitals across the nation than all the wars our country has been in combined)!

dd) Public schools now have sexual education in which abortion is likened to just another means of birth control and the homosexual lifestyle is actively promoted. (eugenicists know the statistical facts that homosexuals have less longevity and serve to reduce the birth rate; furthermore; brainwashing the poor masses with reasons to disdain marriage and pregnancies, having less babies in general are a successful means at reducing birth rates among the poor slave masses)

ee) If you could access the US treasury records you would find out that the most outspoken activists in such things as "abortion rights" (leadership in government subsidized Planned Parenthood (Planned Slaughterhood) have direct political ties) are government agents inciting the brainwashed masses to such a degree they insanely demand their right to murder their own progeny! (Just like the "theory of evolution", population management by brainwashing children in these manners in our public schools is all intended by our eugenic fascist leaders who look at the masses as a plague on earth and completely expendable)

Creationists and Christians are systematically forced to be silent or resign from colleges and public education forums; all as intended.

ff) sterilization effected by numerous toxins in use, like glyphosate, a chemical used in GMOs farming procedure by the herbicide "Roundup"

2. Price setting

a) To decrease populations oil is raised and coincide with publicly staged crises in order to drive prices of all goods and services out of the reach of the poorest members of society (suicide rate goes up and stress related illnesses)

b) Commodities aren't subsidized at former levels raising the price of basic staples so citizens starve. farmers are told not to plant crops, so as not to have over abundance just to raise prices

c) The public is lied to by government-controlled propaganda claiming shortages of water, food, crops, energy, virtually anything to raise stress levels and costs of goods and services even when there is plenty

d) Government friendly monopolies aren't really "regulated" but rather allowed to set unjustified prices upon the public masses simply by bribing law makers and government "regulators"

e) Having babies is expensive and ever increased the more governments want to discourage population growth; and associated costs of raising a child is repeatedly increased and spread through government controlled major media "news broadcasts"

3. Enslavement of the poor masses

a) The poor regularly end up in prison for even minor offenses while the wealthy committing even worse offenses buy their freedom regularly

b) The poor imprisoned are not procreating so sentences of many years are given out for even minor offenses to the poor

c) The poor cannot afford legal representation to help form labor unions so minimum wage stays ever lower with relation to the real cost of living

d) The cost of living goes up while government-controlled media tells the public who can't afford to purchase the same groceries for themselves as they did last year that the cost of living has gone down (lies to the public while quality of life of the poor masses is in rapid decline)

e) The poor regularly have their rights and lives abused by the wealthy insurance companies, corporations, doctors and nurses and even the government agencies and have no legal recourse or any recourse at the abuse and maltreatment as attorneys now almost entirely work for the wealthy and almost none exist taking pro-bono cases or payment based on prevailing.

f) The wealthy exercise political power upon even local governments while poor citizens trying to report crimes are mocked by public servants too lazy and too ignorant to competently perform their jobs. (A wealthy victim of crime gets not only civil remedies but assistance from law enforcement authorities; while the poor is shuffled out the door with an excuse or two that often makes them feel as if they've been victimized not only by criminals but by the apathetic authorities)

D. Secret Organizations

1. Federal Reserve

a) Members and operations not conspicuous

b) Authority to operate not clearly stated

c) Procedures for minting currency not publicly stated

d) Lending to the US government not constitutionally authorized

e) Existence not constitutionally authorized

f) Paper currency not backed with any substance of internationally agreed real value (When they showed a vault the gold stored in Fort Knox it was only a tiny amount of our national economy)

g) bottom line - the World Bank issues Credits to us and nations all over the world through our Central Banks. So Private Bankers mint the money for national economy and is why all nation that belong under the system of the World Bank are IN DEBT to those private bankers. It's why we

*pay INCOME TAX to pay off the INTEREST
the bankers charge our nations. It's all a
system set up the wealthy to extract
tribute from the poor in the form of taxes.
Free nations like ours was founded to be,
had the opportunity to fund our national
budgets with our own currency, but when
the bankers took over the Central Bank of
our Nation was formed together with the
IRS to pay the bankers off who took control
of our nation without a fight, by the
treasonous stroke of the pen of president
Wilson. And thereafter we were not a
nation of free people any longer but ones
that were enslaved and oppressed.*

2. Government programs such as MK-Ultra
I and II, Orion, School of the Americas
3. Satanism and other occult practices by
members of our government; including Molech
worshipping in the Bohemian Grove
4. Skull and Bones men
5. Masons
6. Rosicrucians
7. Bildeburger Group
8. Illuminati
9. IMF
10. WTO
11. Trilateral Commission
12. Public figures of the President, House and
Senate, operate in the light only during planned
televised broadcasts but the government lifers in
the CIA, FBI, Pentagon, NSA, and the many other
organizations run the USA in the dark;

in addition to the popular political figures that put on scientifically planned speeches and shows for the public. (Campaigns, State of the Union addresses all tell the public completely fabricated stories as the politicians put on orchestrated acts that have nothing to do with actual operations which now is politicians with corrupt corporate ties and global political ambitions to rule the world; these multimillionaires and multibillionaires increase their personal wealth by knowing which corporations are going to make profits based on the bribed political ties and many have ownership interests in the same. Bribes and kickbacks are regular practice (contributions, lobbyists) and even "fines" or payoffs to avoid them, disappear into private bank accounts doing nothing for the public; while the show goes on through government-controlled propaganda and clever orations causing the masses to focus on anything but the real operations of what has basically become organized crime! (Not all but far too many are so corrupt that this standard of practice has become expected in free items of anything from pens and paper to vacations, etc. of luxurious living; while the masses are lied to continuously by the psychologically savvy speech writers.) Even FDA approval processes are just a matter of money or someone give me some other plausible rationale of how substances with LETHAL side effects get approved for human ingestion and other substances causing chronic ailments and death to millions remain on the market. (You might argue that FDA members are given fictional data by the food and drug industries; but when statistics of body counts rise with proven links to additives, preservatives and highly toxic "medications" (poisons) are in such numbers as to alarm even the most ignorant among us; then explain how these persons neglect to remove such substances from the market.) You and I know that the pervasive corruption present today; torturing and murdering the poor masses is the direct result of personal GREED in the unholy marriage (plutarchy) between big business and politicians currently.

13. Many of these secret organizations have pledges that are outside and apart from oaths to our Constitution, nation and interest of the citizens of United States in general. Some even have luciferian pledges of allegiance at the highest levels. Some of the persons in these organizations are involved in creating a New World Constitution and New World Order; which supersedes the US Constitution and, in my opinion, could easily be construed as treasonous!

14. Christ and His Followers operated in the Light and shone before the whole world; beware of any "secret" knowledge or organization for whatsoever makes manifest is of the Light (Eph 5:13); but the hidden things in darkness the wise will expose rather than participate in.

See "Population Management" doesn't have to be a bad thing where oppressors are just making your lives so miserable, it can be a glorious thing when you have a nation full of people who KNOW THE LIVING GOD! He will give your leaders good visions for jobs, for a good quality of life for all, and for fulfilling your life purpose under the freedoms He affords the Saved.

Christians need to cease having the attitude that God said the antichrist would come; so, let's just sit back and let the devil and his unholy horde do whatever they want. We are to resist the devil, we are to offer aid to persecuted Christians and if we can to the oppressed poor of this world. We are to combat the evils of this world with GOOD.

Sadly many modern "Christians" are so apathetic and complacent to this threat to their welfare and lives; that they are practically lining up to be branded as a slave to the anti-christian "New World Order" and remaining so in love with this present world and the things of this world; that they might even accept the RFID bio-chip implants (mark of the beast) rather than suffer any hardship resisting these megalo-maniacs; intending to enslave everyone on earth.

The false doctrine of the "pre-tribulation rapture" is to blame for why Christians are not taking more aggressive actions to make certain EVERYONE KNOWS THE LORD, they are all just thinking God will remove them from the world before such ungodliness results in persecution to them. Understand that the Wrath of God is poured out upon His Return, and it appears that also is when He gathers those of the faithful to Himself.

I imagine that the ungodly will be making life so hellish on earth that the godly will be FERVENTLY PRAYING for GOD's Return in Glory! I call the true Christians today to unite, expose the plans and works of the anti-christ, and foil their plans by bringing as many souls as possible into the knowledge of Truth; our LORD AND SAVIOR, JESUS CHRIST; and then making sure all such souls understand the counsel of GOD as contained in the Holy Bible. I wish a Holy Fire of Zeal would come upon all who Know and Love the One True GOD and cause us to shine so brightly by His Grace that the entire world is enlightened by our Lord Jesus Christ and that everyone who receives Him becomes a Present and Everlasting Friend!

Apathy, Laziness, Cowardice are not traits becoming of the Gospel of JESUS CHRIST. Salvation is NOT a spectator sport! PARTICIPATE and do in the journey of your incarnation what you would be remembered for in Eternity!!!!!!!!

I want this book to end on a good note, that NO MATTER HOW MANY PEOPLE MAY WANT YOU DEAD, no matter what the ungodly plan to do, no matter what persecution ensues, our Lord Jesus Christ is GREATER. So, fulfill your Divine Purpose! Go and Make Disciples of all nations; PREACH TO EVERYONE; REJECT NO ONE! JESUS CHRIST! JESUS CHRIST! MAKE SURE YOU AND YOUR LOVED ONES TRUST HIM! Ask the Good Lord to Save and Keep You and Your Loved Ones Now and Forever. Grow into maturity by His Grace through prayer and studying His Words in the Holy Bible and applying His Commandments to your lives.

He told us to FOLLOW HIM! We come to Him by repenting of our dead works and by getting baptized in His

Name. We become His Disciples by continuing to follow Him, resisting the devil as He did! By His Holy Spirit working within us and by His Words; we send the devil fleeing any time he tries to tempt us. We set not unclean things before our eyes, we meditate daily on His Words and apply them to our lives in righteous conduct, we humbly obey our Lord always and respect the Divine Institution of Holy Matrimony between one man and one woman united in this life as one. We discipline these bodies in which we dwell as He did by fasting, praying, and filling our souls with His Words of Eternal Life in the Holy Bible. We continue following our Lord, by preaching His Gospel to the people of this world, making disciples of the nations. O Lord! Let your Kingdom Come! We continue following our Lord, whether received or rejected just as He was, and if necessary, we even follow Him in His betrayal and death; knowing that He has overcome all evil in this world and that we will rise again by His Grace and Power!

Shout with me now, our God is the Lord Jesus Christ (Yahoshuah Ha Mashiach), who came in the flesh, suffered, died and rose again the third day just as the scriptures record; who Redeemed us with His Own Holy Blood! He is the One True God, who Forgives us, who Saves us, who Empowers us, who Transforms us, and who Perfects us! GOD AND GOD ALONE! Savior and Perfector, the Author and Finisher of our Faith! Hallelujah!!!!!!!! Amen.